D0810473

Ron Kardashian is a godly man on a kingdom mission. His approach to total wellness in spirit, soul, and body is both timely and timeless, artfully combining the natural with the supernatural. I have trained with Ron and can attest to the fact that his instruction and encouragement help you progress from average to a peak performer. I know and trust Ron as a minister, fitness trainer, friend, and, most importantly, a man after God's heart.

If you want to get in shape God's way, this is your guide!

—JORDAN RUBIN
NEW YORK TIMES BEST-SELLING AUTHOR OF THE MAKER'S DIET

I have just read Ron Kardashian's new book *Getting in Shape God's Way*— and it is an excellent book I would recommend to any person who is ready to make serious physical and mental changes in his or her life. I was engrossed from the first word of chapter one. I believe this book will be the answer for people who are crying out for principles and methods to lose weight and to get in shape.

—RICK RENNER
PASTOR AND FOUNDER, GOOD NEWS ASSOCIATION OF
CHURCHES AND MINISTRIES

One of the things I admire most about Ron Kardashian is his passion and longing to help people succeed in every area of their lives—spirit, soul, and body. He has encouraged men who have come from broken homes, convincing them that they can stop the cycle of the fatherless generation and become the husband and/or father God has destined them to be. He has a genuine compassion and quest to help motivate and teach people, some of whom have been as much as 100 pounds overweight, to get fit physically, mentally, and spiritually—and to learn to love themselves in the process. Ron's most beautiful quality is the value he places on the role of being a husband and a father—he keeps this as his top priority and calls his family "the greatest gifts that God has ever given him." He has a quote he says to us, which is so special to me: "Every day is a holiday in the Kardashian house." *Getting in Shape God's Way* is the greatest investment you can make into yourself—and your family.

—TIA KARDASHIAN
WIFE OF RON KARDASHIAN

Spirit, soul, and body—this dynamic book by Ron Kardashian is a wake-up call to people everywhere to truly get in shape—God's way! Armed with Ron's clear and concise fitness instruction and solid biblical principles, this is *the book* to make the lifelong transformation toward better health and fitness in the life of every reader.

—**Dr. Phillip G. Goudeaux**
Pastor, Calvary Christian Center
Sacramento, CA

The best shape I have ever been in my entire adult life was when Ron was my trainer. I have known Ron for over ten years, and know him to be a very diligent person who knows his craft. There is no doubt that anyone who reads this book and applies the principles will experience tremendous results in life, both spiritually and physically. I see nothing but a bright future for Ron and his ministry.

—**Dick Bernal**
Senior Pastor, Jubilee Christian Center
San José, California

This is the key for all exercise programs. God has empowered Ron Kardashian with the wisdom and knowledge to unlock the door to a healthier you! As a certified strength and conditioning specialist, I have used the principles that Ron Kardashian has written in this book for almost fifteen years, and they work for anyone! Get the book…get God…get strong…get healthy!

—**André C. Morrow, MA**
Certified Strength and Conditioning Specialist
City of San José

Ron Kardashian's enthusiasm for helping and empowering people to be all they were created to be is encouraging and refreshing. His own dramatic story of overcoming destructive behavior reminds us that God is all-powerful. As a result of his personal overcoming faith and commitment to excellence, Ron has crafted a unique way for individuals to transform their lives—body, mind, and spirit. I recommend *Getting in Shape God's Way* to anyone wanting to improve their life!

—**Paula White**
Life Coach, Bible Teacher, and Motivational Speaker

# Getting
## in Shape
# GOD'S
# WAY

# RON KARDASHIAN

SILOAM
A STRANG COMPANY

Most STRANG COMMUNICATIONS BOOK GROUP products are available at special quantity discounts for bulk purchase for sales promotions, premiums, fundraising, and educational needs. For details, write Strang Communications Book Group, 600 Rinehart Road, Lake Mary, Florida 32746, or telephone (407) 333-0600.

GETTING IN SHAPE GOD's WAY by Ron Kardashian
Published by Siloam
A Strang Company
600 Rinehart Road
Lake Mary, Florida 32746
www.strangbookgroup.com

Unless otherwise noted, all Scripture quotations are from the New American Standard Bible. Copyright © 1960, 1962, 1963, 1968, 1971, 1972, 1973, 1975, 1977 by the Lockman Foundation. Used by permission. (www.Lockman.org)

Scripture quotations marked AMP are from the Amplified Bible. Old Testament copyright © 1965, 1987 by the Zondervan Corporation. The Amplified New Testament copyright © 1954, 1958, 1987 by the Lockman Foundation. Used by permission.

Scripture quotations marked KJV are from the King James Version of the Bible.

Scripture quotations marked NIV are from the Holy Bible, New International Version. Copyright © 1973, 1978, 1984, International Bible Society. Used by permission.

Scripture quotations marked NKJV are from the New King James Version of the Bible. Copyright © 1979, 1980, 1982 by Thomas Nelson, Inc., publishers. Used by permission.

Scripture quotations marked NLT are from the Holy Bible, New Living Translation, copyright © 1996, 2004. Used by permission of Tyndale House Publishers, Inc., Wheaton, IL 60189. All rights reserved.

Scripture quotations marked THE MESSAGE are from *The Message: The Bible in Contemporary English*, copyright © 1993, 1994, 1995, 1996, 2000, 2001, 2002. Used by permission of NavPress Publishing Group.

Design Director: Bill Johnson
Cover design by Karen Grindley

Library of Congress Cataloging-in-Publication Data:

Kardashian, Ron.
  Getting in shape God's way / Ron Kardashian. -- 1st ed.
      p. cm.
  ISBN 978-1-59979-362-7
  1. Physical fitness--Religious aspects--Christianity. 2.
Health--Religious aspects--Christianity. 3. Spirituality. I. Title.
  BV4598.K37 2009
  248.4--dc22

                          2008040068

09 10 11 12 13 — 9 8 7 6 5 4 3 2
Printed in the United States of America

The Getting in Shape God's Way program is intended for healthy adults, age eighteen and older. This book contains the opinions and ideas of its author. It is solely for informational and educational purposes and is not intended to replace the advice of trained medical professionals. The nature of your body's health condition is complex and unique. Therefore, you should consult a health professional before you begin any new exercise, nutrition, or supplementation program or if you have questions about your health. Neither the author nor the publisher shall be liable or responsible for any loss or damage allegedly arising from any information or suggestion in this book.

The statements about products or food in this book have not been evaluated by the Food and Drug Administration. These products are not intended to diagnose, treat, cure, or prevent any disease. Be sure to check with your doctor before starting any diet or fitness program.

The names and other identifiable details of individuals featured in this book have been changed to protect their privacy. Their success stories, as well as the author's story, represent extraordinary examples of what can be accomplished through well-balanced system of exercise and nutrition. There are no "typical" results. As individuals differ, their results will differ, even when using the same program. The author and publisher disclaim any liability arising directly or indirectly from the use of this book.

The recipes in this book are to be followed exactly as written. The publisher is not responsible for your specific health or allergy needs that may require medical supervision. The publisher is not responsible for any adverse reactions to the recipes contained in this book.

While the author has made every effort to provide accurate telephone numbers and Internet addresses at the time of publication, neither the publisher nor the author assumes any responsibility for errors or for changes that occur after publication.

*This book is dedicated to you, the reader. May my blood, sweat, tears, trials, and triumphs experienced bring you to the place of total freedom—in your spirit, your soul, and your physical body. Go for your dreams! Never give up! And you will see them come to pass!*

# CONTENTS

# Part 5

## Working It Out—Living Your Dreams!
### *Fitness Plan*

# ACKNOWLEDGMENTS

### To my God, Adonai!

Thank You, my Lord, for allowing me to be the conduit through which You emanate Your truths. What an honor it is to be Your servant and son! You have my full service—body, soul, and spirit—for eternity!

### To my girls, Tia and Sophia

My beautiful wife, Tia Kardashian: You are the very essence of my life and the reason for the breath in my lungs. You are a gift from God alone. Living with me through the tedious times of writing, you have shown me more of the love of God than any other person in the world. This book would have not been possible without your diligent sacrifice of time and your patience and prayers during my late-night hours of writing and preparing sermons. The price you have paid is more precious than gold itself. Every dream and vision I have involves spending my life with you. You have a place in my heart that no one will ever be able to enter! You are the wind beneath my wings. Thank you for encouraging me to fly!

And my little angel, Sophia: You are my living gift. I will forever endeavor to be a father who will never fail you—*never*! A portion of the proceeds of this book will go toward a life of health and development for you, your children, and your grandchildren! You are a living heritage of a future generation that will carry the torch of God's voice of health throughout the world. I believe in you and will always be yours. You and Mommy are beautifully, fearfully, and wonderfully made! I love you both!

To my wonderful mother and father! You never gave up on me in spite of the many times I wanted to give up on you and myself. Mom, you are the protector God used to shield a little boy from the wiles of hell! May all mothers allow the life you spent on your knees in prayer to prove to them the unspeakable power of a mother's prayers for her children. Dad, you were my motivator! Never did you smother my dreams; you encouraged me to go for the stars. This I know, that at the very least I am destined to touch the moon because of you!

To Gina, my passionate sister: Your passion to help the hurting youth of this world, derived in part from my youthful delinquency that you witnessed, will help to create a revolution in the hearts of other young people. Always remember to go for your dreams!

To my pastor, client, and patient advisor, Dick Bernal, and your wonderful wife, Carla: Tia and I would have never met had it not been for your obedience to start Jubilee. Carla, your prayers for my wife and me have been a shield to us. How do we repay that eternal gift? In your patience during my growing pains, both of you have spoken great wisdom into our lives. Thank you for standing in integrity, preaching the uncompromised Word of God, and walking in love! Your faithful diligence in the ministry is worthy of honor and praise!

To my friend, Anthony Arnold: I would also like to thank you. They say you can count the number of your true friends on one hand. You have shared the foxhole of intercession with me and, at times, *for* me. Your encouragement over the years, often with your face full of tears, has sent surges of God's presence down my spine, inspiring me to live to give back to mankind.

To Paul Gerlach: I never thought I would need a marriage coach! But thank God you were there when I did! Your artful passion for covenant relationships and their priority in life, which you teach that each of God's generals must have, has motivated me to polish the writings of this book. Thank you for your wisdom in coaching my life passion—to be a godly husband!

To Pastors Phil and Brenda Goudeaux: Thank you for your commitment to fathering. How the heartbeat of God is that of a father! You wrapped your arms around my family and me in an hour my soul thirsted. This is true sacrifice and the very bond of a man who understands covenant founded on agape!

To Pastor Benny Hinn: My service to you personally and your willingness to give me a "chance" has engraved the passion of evangelism in my heart that burns hot! Your life and ministry have touched the *core* of my being. You may never know the impact you have made in this young man's life!

To the Keifel family—Kimmy; Don and Carol Scifres; the Jenkins—our producers; the Coughran family; and André and Momi: I am honored for your belief in us from the beginning. Your love and kingly anointing have truly blessed this assignment. You are an asset to me personally, to this ministry, and to the kingdom of God. After all, Kingdom Conditioning did start in your garage—thank you!

To all the mentors, counselors, advisors, nuns, priests, bishops, teachers, elders, prophets, clients, the leaders of the Word of Faith Movement, the National Strength and Conditioning Association, and partners who helped birth me into my destiny: You know who you are. One of you spoke that God was working to *turn me into my vision.* This book is the product of my being shaped into the vision of getting in shape God's way. You have helped me prevail through my trials, adversities, attacks, opposition, and, yes, victories, triumphs, and conquests.

To my publisher: This book would never be possible without my publisher, who has believed in me. Mr. Stephen Strang, you are a true man of faith, esteeming and believing in the power of the written Word. Debbie Marrie, your attentive and sensitive discernment to see through my flaws and hear the heartbeat of God like a drum within the depths of my soul are helping me to become the writer I could have only dreamed of becoming. Thank you for your obedience to promote the writings of the kingdom. Finally, to my writer, Ms. Carol Noe. The last shall be first! You are a miracle of God and a gifted writer who heard His voice to assist me in this work. You were the hand of God pulling me out when I felt like I was drowning. Thank you.

# INTRODUCTION

WHY DO SO MANY sincere, well-meaning, even God-fearing people fail time after time in their heroic efforts to lose weight, to get their body into shape, and to live a healthy lifestyle? What is the underlying cause for the epidemic of obesity that is raging in our nation?

## NATIONAL HEALTH CRISIS

The self-imposed suffering caused by obesity alone is affecting the quality of life of thousands of children, youth, and adults, especially in our nation. It is shortening the lives of many and literally killing others in the prime of life. In spite of the hundreds of "guaranteed not to fail" diet plans, exercise gurus, miracle drugs, and extreme surgeries, the epidemic of obesity in our nation continues to rage, unchecked, with devastating potential for the present and future generations.

How can educated, affluent people beat this growing national malady of poor health when every aspect of the media oozes its seductive power over the taste buds of all ages? Our culture has embraced a cuisine of exotic drinks, caloric entrees, and decadent desserts as a symbol of success, happiness, romance, and just celebrating life. Is it possible to reverse this downward spiral of deteriorating health caused by overindulgence and distorted appetites?

## PERSONAL TRIUMPH

As a sickly child and a troubled youth, I experienced the miseries of poor health, including clouded reasoning and poor judgment as a result of violating sound principles established by our Creator for the human body, mind, and spirit. As a youth, inspired by a friend, I cried out to God and had a supernatural encounter with Him. My life-changing experience set me on a journey toward health and wholeness, which ultimately revealed my personal destiny—my reason for being. Empowered by this spiritual dynamic to pursue fitness and destiny, I began to cultivate a personal relationship with Christ through Bible study, prayer, and fellowship with other believers. Resolving my own health crisis helped me to realize other dreams and goals for my life.

Personally, I became fed up with gimmicks and scams promoted by all forms of the media promising to make me a perfectly fit person. I was desperate enough to realize that I did not need a "quick-fix" remedy for my unhealthy state. I needed a complete lifestyle transformation. As I searched for the answers I needed, God gave me four simple keys, which I call neglected secrets, to making everything else—proper nutrition, exercise, and other health principles—really work. These neglected secrets empowered me to gain and maintain fitness and health on the level of a professionally certified fitness trainer and coach. I now recommend to my clients that they embrace these keys and begin getting in shape God's way.

Now, in spite of the poor medical and psychological prognosis over my life since childhood, I have "beat the odds" and am reaping the fantastic results of learning to live in victory over the addictions and destructive behavior that had threatened my life. Certified by the National Strength and Conditioning Association (NSCA) as a professional trainer and life coach, I have given more than eleven thousand hours of instruction to clients in the past decade. It is wonderful to see lives changed as they embrace the simple keys of getting in shape God's way.

# FOUR KEYS TO A HEALTHY LIFESTYLE

The four keys I discovered that led me into the secret of living a healthy lifestyle are:

## REVELATION—FITNESS BELIEFS

As you open the pages of this book, be prepared to embrace the truths of divine *revelation—fitness beliefs*—that determine the outcome between trying and failing or doing and succeeding—for life. For example, you will learn to believe these truths:

- You were born to win in life!
- You were created to be healthy and happy.
- You were created to live a life filled with purpose.
- You were created to fulfill the dreams of your heart.

## DECLARATION—FITNESS WORDS

Through the power of linguistics training, you will learn how to win over every obstacle to your health by *declaration* of the real truths you are learning. Declaring the truth regarding who you are and who you can become as a healthy person—spirit, soul, and body—will empower you to develop new patterns of *fitness speaking*. By releasing the transforming power of declaring the truth, you will begin to defeat the lies that have kept you from enjoying health and fulfilling personal destiny.

## APPLICATION—FITNESS FUNCTION

You will no longer have to rely on a "gritting your teeth" discipline to try to "maintain" exercise for a while. *Application* of the life-changing principles you are learning will be motivated by the transformation of your personal belief system. It will allow you to embrace practical health principles, which will empower you to *fitness function*—for a lifetime.

## MANIFESTATION—FITNESS LIFESTYLE

The *manifestation* of health, happiness, personal destiny, and success in every area of your life will result from embracing the first three keys to getting in shape God's way. The joy of this glorious manifestation will release you into the reality of a healthy lifestyle as the "temple of God" (1 Cor. 3:16), which allows Him to fulfill His purposes in you and through you. You owe it to yourself to explore these profound yet simple truths that will enable you to enjoy the manifestation of a *fitness lifestyle*.

## MY PASSION FOR YOUR SUCCESS

There is a reason why people begin again and again to try to improve their health and yet continually fail to succeed in that good intention. After I graduated from Bible college, God began giving me opportunity to share the keys to my success with many churches and other organizations. I am anxious to share with you, dear reader, as well, the insights I have experienced and the marvelous health I enjoy as a result of overcoming the destructive cycles that kept me for years from enjoying life as our Creator intended.

My passion is to touch the lives of as many people as I can in order to share these simple biblical principles—divine keys that empowered me to leave behind a destructive lifestyle and to achieve a high level of physical prowess as a professional trainer. I have learned to experience deep compassion for others with health issues, to fulfill my personal destiny, and to enjoy the happiness and satisfaction of healthy relationships with family and friends.

This is first of all a "why-to" and then a "how-to" handbook to lasting success in living an abundantly healthy lifestyle. During the next forty days you can experience a complete change in your spiritual, mental, and physical well-being through embracing the four keys outlined here. Of course, you should know that the basic principles of these health secrets are not mine or a doctor's or even a professor's. These practical guidelines for a healthy lifestyle are based in the truth of the divine Handbook, the Bible, one of the oldest manuscripts in existence, which has proved its effectiveness in the lives of billions of people.

Whether or not you presently believe that God exists, you can dare to put your hope and faith in the time-tested principles that have empowered people through the ages to succeed in life. It is time for you, dear reader, to give yourself a chance to succeed as you read this book. I encourage you to make a personal commitment to success by signing the following agreement.

## PERSONAL COMMITMENT

I agree to read this entire book, completing it in a timely manner for greatest comprehension. I understand that the words on these pages are more than information; they explain the divine reality of who I am and who God is, with the object in view to help me achieve lasting health and wholeness—God's way.

If possible, as I learn to practice the divine principles outlined in this book, I will include a partner who can walk through this journey to health and longevity with me. We can enter into accountability with each other and together receive the benefits of the four life-changing keys in this book.

By virtue of signing my name below, I declare my agreement with Ron Kardashian, whose help I accept as my personal trainer and life coach. I hereby choose to forget all previous experiences in which I failed to become the "perfect" person with the "perfect body." I submit myself to the life-changing process of getting in shape God's way. (I understand I may need to reread this book to be able to embrace its principles more effectively.) I declare that I will achieve my goals for health—spirit, soul, and body—with God's help!

_____

Your Name

_____

Ron Kardashian, Your Personal Trainer

*Congratulations!* You are about to begin an exciting journey that has transformed the spiritual, mental, and physical health of many. It is a journey that is empowering me to fulfill my destiny! I pray the same fantastic experience will be yours as we take this journey together—*getting in shape God's way.*

PART 1

**KEY #1: REVELATION—IT MUST BE REAL!**
*FITNESS BELIEFS*

# ONE

# RESCUING A MOST DESPERATE VICTIM—ME!

**M**Y PASSION IN LIFE is to see you succeed in becoming the healthy, happy, and productive person God created you to be. I have realized that, though I was not conscious of it, I was born with this passion; it is the way God made me to fulfill destiny. And my own life experiences have served as "teachers" to fuel this deep desire in me to see you well and whole. This revelation did not come to me easily or all at once. Painfully, through years of my own personal health struggles as a child and as a youth, I began to pursue answers to my desperation. The keys to getting in shape God's way were learned in the crucible of personal suffering—mine. That is why I can attest to their effectiveness in transforming a life that was bent on self-destructive behavior into a life that is purposeful, happy, and, most of all, healthy.

Since I have become a professional trainer, I have spent thousands of hours with clients over the past decade, sharing the four keys to health that changed my life. Witnessing their success and seeing their lives transformed have been very satisfying to me. They have increased my passion to share with as many people as possible these divine secrets for living a healthy lifestyle.

As I candidly share with you my personal struggles in my journey toward health, it is only for the purpose of gaining your confidence in the validity of the principles we will explore, principles that inspired and empowered me to achieve a level of health beyond my dreams. My first client to prove to me that getting in shape God's way works was *me*!

## Unusual and Difficult Beginnings

My mother told me that another child was conceived some time after I was born. For some reason, he or she never developed beyond that early stage. I was very young when I learned about my sibling's fate, and it affected me deeply, even as a child. I wondered what my brother or sister would have been like. More than that, I wondered why I was born and he or she wasn't. If there was a God, why did He choose to let me live and not my brother or sister? These were big questions for a little guy.

I was born jaundiced, which was a precursor to future health problems. My parents contend that as a young child, I was intensely curious, active, and accident-prone. Mischief was never far away from Ron. Their constant vigilance helped me survive to the second grade, when I contracted chicken pox and scarlet fever at the same time. Doctors cited me as one of the worst cases they had seen. Pox sores covered my body inside and out. High fever, hovering around 105 degrees, caused me to hallucinate. It looked as if I had leprosy because of the condition of my boil-covered skin.

One night, as my parents attempted to reduce the fever, they decided to put me into a cold bath. Because of the sores on the bottom of my feet, I could not walk. And the boils under my armpits and all over my body made it painful to be touched. So my dad wrapped a cold sheet around me and pulled me into the bathroom, to avoid causing me more pain. I can remember the helpless, distraught look on my dad's face as he tried to help his son who was covered with boils, like Job in the Bible, all over his body.

Because of the high fever and hallucinations, the doctor told my mother there was a possibility of brain damage. He warned that it could result in a vegetative state for life. A devout Catholic, my mother told me later that when she heard the doctor's warning, she literally gave me to God. She told Him she could not stand to watch me suffer like that anymore and placed me entirely in His hands. It was her faith and trust in God that carried us all through that night and many more to come. At length, I recovered from that severe illness, though my health was impaired as a result.

## FROM HEALTH TO CHRONIC ILLNESS

The following year marked the significant change in my life from living like a normal, healthy boy to becoming a sickly child. Common ailments became chronic experiences for me. I got tonsillitis at least once or twice a year. There was almost an annual bout with pneumonia. I never escaped the colds and flu viruses that occurred every year. And allergy tests showed I was allergic to dairy products, dust, pollen, dog and cat dander, down feathers, and certain fibers. Sometimes wearing normal clothing caused a violent allergic reaction.

Because of my chronic illnesses, I was held back one year in elementary school. In general, school became a terrible experience for me. Teachers observed that I could not sit still and that I had little attention span. After staying awake all night watching movies, in preparation for a brain examination, doctors determined that I suffered from ADD (attention deficit disorder). Those were the early years of detecting this malady. Today, the diagnosis would have been ADHD (attention deficit hyperactivity disorder). This explained why I could not sit still in class.

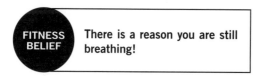

FITNESS BELIEF — There is a reason you are still breathing!

Following this diagnosis, doctors prescribed several drugs, which helped me concentrate better in school. I improved from a struggling C and D student to an A and B student. However, the medication did not eliminate all my difficulty in focusing attention as needed for studying.

Part of my difficulty began to stem from the internal beliefs that were being formed in me because of my poor health. For the first time I heard, "He'll never amount to anything." I was to hear those words from teachers and other authority figures many times during the years that followed. Along with the discouragement of the ADHD diagnosis, chronic sickness, side effects from medications, struggling in school, and never feeling normal like other kids my age, I began to overeat as a source of comfort for my psychological pain. By the age of ten, I was obese. Being overweight only increased my problems, physically and socially. I became the "fat kid" who was teased and rejected by the other kids.

Fear began to torment me in several different forms. I developed a fear of dying as well as a fear of loving other people. I remember thinking at times that it would have been better for me to perish in my mother's womb, instead of my brother. As I reached my youth, this faulty reasoning sometimes reached the intensity of suicidal thoughts.

## How Do We Get Outa' Here?

I cannot proceed with my story without giving honor and expressing my gratitude to my parents for their loving concern and continual attempts to help me overcome the difficulties of my childhood and youth. My mother was relentless in her pursuit to help me gain my health—inwardly as well as physically. She took me to counselors, therapists, and children's experts as well as many medical doctors. And my father was always supportive and encouraging to me. No matter what I was going through, I could really count on the both of them.

I remember, in my mother's desperate search for answers to all my problems, how she took care of me during all those days of missing school because of sickness. As a devout Catholic, she often went to church to make prayers on my behalf. Our priest was like an uncle to me, and the church was a great support to us, helping us through those difficult years.

Early in life, I learned the great importance our Catholic church attributed to prayer! Without the prayers of my parents and our church, I don't think I would have made it. I was caught in a vicious cycle that was rooted in my history of chronic illness and my own insecurities and fears. These destructive forces were aggravated by a lack of understanding of the importance of good nutrition and exercise to health. Added to that was my genetic sensitivity to certain foods, which was the icing on the cake. Our ancestry was Italian and Armenian, which generally cultivated a more healthy diet. However, our family ate a typical American junk food and processed food diet. My genes were programmed for a different diet that would promote health; the typical American diet was not it!

During my childhood and youth, few health professionals were talking about nutrition or exercise as a major factor in preventing, controlling, and curing sickness and disease. Those who were talking and writing books about it were generally not endorsed by the mainstream medical community. Of course, that was where my parents took me for help.

> **FITNESS BELIEF** **God is faithful, even when we are not!**

Like the proverbial snowball rolling downhill, my school troubles continued to grow bigger and more out of control. I became terrified of failing—again. My family tried to help by establishing a regimen of positive thinking. I would try to think positively, my expectations would rise, and then when I failed, it was even more demoralizing. I looked at every failure as more proof that I was inferior as a human being. I decided that of the two babies in my mother's womb, God had obviously chosen the wrong boy to come into this world.

But my parents loved me just the same—and kept looking for answers. They hung in there with me, but my continual illness took an increasing toll on our family life. I have one younger sister who loved me very much. It was hard for her to watch me suffer. She had to suffer many disappointments because of me as well. Christmas vacations and other holiday trips would be planned and canceled at the last minute because of a bout with an ear infection (I couldn't fly) or congestion from the dust in the air, which made road travel impossible. When one family member is chronically ill, the other family members suffer in many ways also.

My parents experienced other pressures besides my illness, and eventually, their marriage began to unravel. Though I wasn't their only problem, I know that, especially during my teenage years when I was completely out of control and high on drugs most of the time, my life contributed to their personal crisis. They probably would have divorced even if I had been healthy and responsible as a son, but those troubled years raising me didn't help their personal plight.

> **FITNESS BELIEF**
> Whatever life brings us, whatever laughter and sorrow we experience, we are not alone on this planet.

## PLAYING WITH DEATH

As a young person who was already struggling with deep insecurities because of my chronic illness, obesity, and learning disability, my social life in school was a nightmare. I didn't want to be there. All I could think about was what other kids thought about me, which did not help my ability to concentrate on my studies. Inside, I could still relate to that active, inquisitive little boy I had been. But my body was overweight and sickly. I longed to be able to be athletic and healthy, but my health problems hindered my passion to be "first string."

In junior high school, I started to hang out with some wild kids, who, like me, were troubled kids. My little gang was eventually kicked out of the entire junior high school district after we were caught in possession of pipe bombs. Long before the threat of terrorism, it was a fad for kids in California to blow up things in parks and back in the woods. But after some kids got hurt, the police cracked down on this kind of activity. Thus, we were expelled from school when we were caught.

By my freshman year in high school, I felt that all the doctors and specialists I had seen had failed me. I was still sick and overweight. I decided to try to find my own solutions. I knew one thing that would alter my life, if only temporarily: *drugs*. Along with abusing drugs, I added alcohol to my regimen. I decided the only way I could lose weight was this artificial means of abusing drugs. It worked. Yet, while I was smaller physically, the empty hole inside of my psyche was getting bigger and bigger.

Losing weight made me feel a little better about myself, but I still gravitated toward friends who were troubled kids. We all experimented with just about everything that we thought would make us feel happy. I worked odd jobs from the time I was thirteen, which gave me money to buy alcohol and illegal drugs. During those teen years, I became the life of the party. Enjoying my new physique, I felt released from the shame of obesity and learned to cover up the real misery inside by making people laugh. I loved the partying crowd who were my friends, getting high and drinking to prove we were happy. However, it nearly cost me my life on several occasions.

One night I had been drinking heavily at a party. A friend decided that he would drive us home in the brand-new, four-by-four truck his parents had just bought him. Six of us jumped into the back of my friend's truck, and off we went. After the other boys had been dropped off, I got into the passenger's side of the truck. When we were two blocks from my house, my friend decided to do something daring. He recklessly flipped the truck four times in the air and it landed on the passenger side—where I was sitting without my seatbelt fastened. Though I did not have one broken bone, my skin looked like someone had taken scissors to it.

We stumbled to my house. The front door was locked, so we went around to the back. It was three o'clock in the morning. As I looked through the sliding glass doors, I saw my mother on her knees praying. Forgetting about my raw scrapes, I stared at her in utter horror of what she would say about me getting home at this hour.

My mother looked up to see her son standing outside, alive but bleeding and bruised. She was weeping as she opened the sliding glass door. She embraced me and told me she had been praying for me and was so glad God had brought me home alive.

I don't want to give the impression that my mother was a pushover. She wasn't! But on this particular occasion she was more frightened than angry. As for me, I was simply relieved that she wasn't yelling at me. I felt no remorse over causing her pain. This frightening episode and others like it were not enough to motivate me to change the way I was living.

I was eventually kicked out of my Catholic high school for drinking alcohol and doing drugs. Each time I was expelled from school, I was not alone. I was part of a group who were expelled together. Not only was I looking for trouble in those days, but I was also looking for friends and companionship, which I had found. Unfortunately, I chose the wrong crowd again and again. Now I understand that if I had chosen different kinds of friends, I might have found a way to avoid all the heartache I caused my family and myself. Some of the psychologists my parents took me to shared these concepts with me, but I wasn't listening. I wanted what I wanted, no matter what pain it cost me or those who loved me.

Through high school and afterward I tried every kind of drug I could get my hands on. I was a regular customer at some of the worst night-clubs in the area. I was a sophomore in high school when I became very thin by using drugs, especially marijuana and methamphetamines, and not eating. In my mind, I lived in this fantasy that I was now the person I had always wanted to be. I was promiscuous with women even after I stared AIDS in the face one night. I no longer cared about anybody or anything except gratifying my own desires for pleasure. I did not think about my family or my friends. I just did what I wanted to do without any consideration for the danger I was putting myself in physically. I was bent on taking from the world I was living in and not thinking about giving anything back to it.

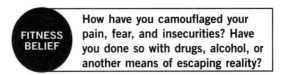

**FITNESS BELIEF** How have you camouflaged your pain, fear, and insecurities? Have you done so with drugs, alcohol, or another means of escaping reality?

## DAWN OF DIVINE REVELATION

After high school, I moved out of my parents' home and got an apartment. I would live independently for several months, until I ran out of money. Then I would go back to my parents' house. During one of the times I was living at home, I was working with some of my "friends" at a department store. One night we were going out drinking at a nightclub. As we approached it, I saw a very attractive woman standing there. She was preaching at the top of her lungs, talking about "the power of Jesus Christ." My first thought was, "Oh, great. Those crazy, Bible-thumping Christians are right in front of the club! And what is a woman doing preaching?"

As I came closer, I realized that one of the girls who were in the crowd was a former girlfriend of mine. We used to run with the same wild partying crowd. Later that night after I arrived home, I couldn't get this girl out of my mind. I was really curious to know what she was doing in that crowd of crazy Christians. Finally, not able to shake thoughts of her, I called her.

She told me about her recent encounter with God and how she had entered into a personal relationship with Him through Jesus Christ. She said that after she had been "born again," she had finally experienced peace inside. In all my years attending my Catholic church I didn't remember hearing about being "born again" or having a personal relationship with God through Jesus Christ. If I did hear it, it was never *real* to me. I was intrigued. What was she talking about? She told me to go to my room and light a candle if I had to, which was a part of my Catholic tradition of prayer. She told me to call out to Jesus to help me.

That night in my room I lit a candle and began to call out to Jesus. I desperately wanted this personal relationship with God that had given my friend such peace. If Jesus was the reason for that, I wanted Jesus. I said, "If You're really there, and deep inside I believe You are, then I need You to accept me like I am—sick, drinking, smoking, sleeping around, and all the other bad stuff I'm doing. Please forgive me, Jesus!"

That simple prayer brought startling, perhaps unbelievable, results. Please believe me when I tell you that a supernatural Presence entered my room, touching me with a tangible power that I felt in my body. Suddenly, I felt the candle go out, and the glass that was holding it cracked. It would be months later before I would understand that awesome presence of God that had come to me that night. Jesus had heard the desperate cry of my heart, and, like my friend, I had been born again! The presence of God had come to make me alive inside by the power of His Spirit. Though there were many more changes to come, they were all made possible because of the presence of Jesus in my life, who had come to forgive me and make me whole—spirit, soul, and body.

Some changes were apparent immediately. From that night forward, I knew in a profound way that I was God's child. He loved me—in spite of my sins, faults, weaknesses, problems, and all—as His very own son. I also saw Jesus differently from my "religious" training. I understood that He had died a terrible death for me and made it possible for me to feel His peace and love in that aching hole inside. He really had saved me from the pain and "death" I had suffered. And I began cultivating a wonderful relationship with Him. For the first time as an adult, I had a new desire to live right.

Though I had very little understanding of my encounter with God, from that night on my life was never the same—on the *inside*. However, the *outside* had a long way to go to catch up.

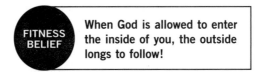

**FITNESS BELIEF** — When God is allowed to enter the inside of you, the outside longs to follow!

## WRESTLING WITH MY "SELF"

I now understand that when I cried out to Jesus, He came to me and made my spirit alive to Him. That is what Jesus called being "born" of the Spirit (John 3:5). Inside I was transformed and felt a new peace with God at the very core of my being. However, mentally, emotionally, and physically, I was still living in confusion. It was odd to be calm deep inside and still experience turmoil in my mind and emotions. I started going to my Catholic church more frequently. Similar to feeling the need for more workouts in a gym, I felt like I needed more church—attending church once a week was not cutting it. So I went every day for several months. I was the youngest person in those Catholic masses at 6:00 a.m. But I was being dramatically touched by the presence of God.

Getting in shape God's way requires knowledge of God. There is a verse in the Bible that says, "My people are destroyed for lack of knowledge" (Hosea 4:6). I could relate to that, and I still didn't have much! All I knew was that, since my supernatural encounter with the power of God, the information I had learned about Jesus seemed to have dropped twelve inches from my head to my heart—He had become *real* to me. And I was enjoying a relationship with Him because of a heart revelation and not just head knowledge!

*Realization* is the desired outcome of *revelation* (which we will discuss in detail in Part 4, Manifestation). The word *real* in realization describes the essence of *revelation*. Your vision and mission gain strength in you as you meditate on what is *real*. And realization results in manifestation. When you realize your vision—make it real—it is brought into concrete existence. That means it is manifest, readily perceived or evident to the senses, especially to sight.

It would take some time, several years in fact, before I could realize the vision for my life. There would be a process of revelation involved before my mind, emotions, and physical body could respond to my heart reality. Then I could live in the peace and clarity in my soul and body that I enjoyed from that moment in my spirit. After all, I had spent years living in an ungodly environment. I continued to hang out with a bad crowd, who were all I had known as friends, and lived more or less the same lifestyle as before my dramatic encounter with God.

My struggle continued with obesity, but most of the time I looked good. I started doing some modeling, and it wasn't long before I was in demand as a model. To the fat kid of my past, it was an incredible ego builder. I considered the world of modeling glamorous and exciting. I really thought I had everything I had ever wanted: money, success, admiration, and any woman I wanted.

I continued working at that department store and going out to the nightclubs with some of my friends. Then several of us were arrested and charged with six felonies. The department store fired me, of course, and while I awaited the trial I got a job with a millionaire entrepreneur. He saw something in me that I didn't, which was the potential to do something meaningful with my life. He began to encourage me to figure out what I really wanted to do and pursue it. He assured me that even if I did prison time, my job would be waiting when I got out.

The kindness of my new boss inspired me to take his advice. I began to consider what I really wanted my life to be. The first thing I realized was that my whole life had been consumed with becoming physically well and fit. I had learned, even through my failures, how to take care of my body and to conquer its appetites.

I also realized that in my personal relationships, I had always been an encourager. Even when I was at my worst, if my friends were discouraged or in trouble, I was there, telling them they would be OK, that they could get through it. The irony was, much of the time I was in worse shape than they were! But that ability to encourage others was part of my DNA that God had placed inside me. No matter how messed up I was, that gift of God functioned to encourage others in their difficult times.

As I considered what I wanted my life to look like, I began to see it. The defining of my dream for life began to unfold around two themes. Helping others to achieve their desire for physical fitness and encouraging them to reach their goals had become the motivating desires of my life. With that understanding, I launched the beginning of my career as a fitness professional. To that end, I began my studies to become certified as a personal trainer.

**FITNESS BELIEF** Has anyone ever reached out to help you, comfort you, inspire you, or teach you? Recognize in that kindness the hand of God.

## MOVING TOWARD HONESTY

When my court case came to trial, I was convicted of one felony charge and sentenced to several years in prison. However, the actual sentence I served was only three months at a work farm. During those months, separated from friends and family, I turned my attention to my relationship with God. I began reading my Bible avidly again to help me maintain my sanity. Soon, I invited others to join in a Bible study with me. As I studied the Word and shared it with others, I entered into greater peace in my relationship with God, in sharp contrast to the conflictive relationships I had with other troubled people.

However, when I was released from the work farm, I returned to my old pattern of life. I returned to work for the millionaire, did some modeling, and continued to hang out with old friends. Before long, God once again lost ground on my priority list.

I spent three more years on a downward spiral of partying and involvement in destructive, promiscuous relationships. In my heart, I knew I was searching for a woman with whom I could safely share my heart and life. But the Hollywood-style culture I was running in distorted that search, turning it into a long line of one-night stands that left me completely dissatisfied.

Then a time of reckoning came to me that allowed the light of revelation to shine more brightly in my heart. Through several painful confrontations, I reached the bottom of the destructive pit I had been wallowing in for years. My sister, who had always loved me no matter what, refused to have anything to do with me. Then, my mother came to see me. She and my father were divorced by now, but they continued to show their concern for their wayward son. Mother gave me an ultimatum. She said I could come home to live with her if I promised to get a decent job and clean up my act.

At that time, I was working in the glamorous world of modeling, living with a female stripper with whom I was trying to be in love, and was completely strung out on drugs much of the time. I was still fighting my physical illnesses—and was absolutely miserable. I began to realize that having a good physique, being a model, earning good money, and living promiscuously did not equate to happiness, success, or health. It occurred to me that no one would desire to be the kind of person I had become.

Drugs could not fix me. The doctors could not fix me. The psychologists could not fix me. I began to realize that Someone was patiently waiting for me to ask for His help. It seemed like God's grace was sparing my life until I reached the end of my arrogant way of thinking that I knew it all. It was then that He could prove to me that I knew nothing at all. I actually found this understanding to be quite amusing. I knew I had the choice to go with God, but I was convinced that His way was like pie in the sky—certainly not *real*.

However, I was becoming more and more aware that God was grieved with the path my life was taking. Intuitively, I felt He had a totally different purpose for my life. During these years, I would watch television ministers for hours in the evenings. My aching heart and mind gratefully soaked in their faith-filled words about a loving Jesus who was a healer and restorer of people's lives. Slowly, faith for a better life rose up in my heart. Was it really possible for me to be healed of my chronic sicknesses and freed from my addictions? In spite of my doubts, a hope stirred deep within my heart that perhaps there was a way for me to become healthy without using drugs to conquer my obesity or trying to starve myself to death to maintain my modeling physique.

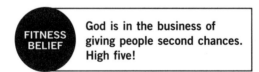

**FITNESS BELIEF**

**God is in the business of giving people second chances. High five!**

After moving in with my mother, I returned to attending our Catholic church. As God revealed His love to me, I would sit and weep and cry out for His help. I continued to watch the television ministers and began to understand more clearly the importance of reading and studying the Bible. I discovered that God was speaking to me through the Bible. The words on the pages of His Book began clearing my mind and bringing real hope and joy to my heart—emotions I had not experienced since I was a small child.

Faith was growing in my heart and giving me a "knowing" inside that as I continued to place my life into God's hands, everything was going to be all right. I gained the courage to trust Him with every part of my life. The wisdom of His Word was giving me divine revelation about what I should do and what I should not do. God's wisdom ignited my faith. It was as if the words of the Bible were clapping a high five in my heart that shot me right out of my miserable darkness and hopeless existence into an ever-brightening light. The results of this revelation were to lead me into a much more productive lifestyle.

I aggressively pursued my education in the field of fitness training, studying anatomy, kinesiology (study of the human body's movement), and human performance. I was amazed that I was able to grasp the material and do well because of my scholastic history and the negative effects that doing drugs had on my mind. At the age of twenty-four, I first became certified through 24 Hour Nautilus. Knowing that I needed more knowledge and training, I continued my pursuit as a trainer for the professional athletic field, resulting in my certification with National Strength and Conditioning Association (NSCA).

My personal health was impacted in a positive way by my studies, changing my thinking regarding my chronic illnesses, allergies, and obesity. I began to realize that it was absolutely necessary to exercise and train my body to improve my health. I understood that I needed to read educational materials, as well as the Word of God, to exercise my mind. And I was beginning to understand that prayer was essential to exercise my spirit. Revelation was dawning in my heart and mind, leading me to understand that we are truly complex beings, as the Scriptures teach—spirit, soul, and body.

As I attended church, I was making friends there who could share my struggles and rejoice with me in my victories. They were there for me to encourage me to live a better life instead of a destructive lifestyle. They helped me to admit my own problems and to deal honestly with my faults.

I felt better about myself because I was experiencing the unconditional love of God for me.

Gradually, my thinking became clearer as I studied the Bible and shared with others what I was learning. Slowly but surely, every area of my troubled life began to respond to the laws of health released into my life through personal revelation of the love of God. I understood for the first time that the Bible says our body is a temple of God and that His Spirit longs to live inside of us (1 Cor. 6:19). With that understanding, I began to think differently about what I ate, drank, and to what I subjected my body.

My personal motivation for desiring to be healthy no longer centered on my own pleasure and success. Instead, I began respecting my body as the creation of God for His indwelling presence. He created me to be used— not abused. New desires were born in me to please God and honor Him by eating right, exercising correctly, and living a wholesome lifestyle. As I gained my health, I would be able to fulfill the destiny He had created me to accomplish. I did not want to die before the tasks He had assigned for me were completed simply because I abused the body He gave to me. This revelation became the cornerstone for my lifestyle changes and helped me to maintain them.

As these concepts strengthened in me, my faith in God grew and His wisdom began to take root in my mind and heart. I was able to stop drinking and smoking. Eventually I was completely delivered from taking Dexedrine and ADHD medications altogether. My weight stabilized and my body became stronger and healthier than I thought possible. During this time, I completed my studies and graduated from Bible college. I also became recognized in the field of professional trainers as my clients enjoyed the same kind of success I had experienced in my life.

I have shared my painful story with you for one purpose: to encourage you to open your heart and mind to the keys to success that worked for me and have worked for thousands of my clients.

As we explore the four keys God showed me to getting in shape God's way, I hope you will take a similar journey to what I have taken to experience *real* success that will last a lifetime. Learning to receive divine *revelation,* unlocking the power of *declaration* of the truth, and choosing to follow personal *application* of health principles will result for you, as it did for me, in the powerful *manifestation* of a healthy lifestyle—spirit, soul, and body.

## You Can Do It!

My story is a continuing one, of course. But as I write it here, I am still amazed and humbly grateful that I chose getting in shape God's way over many other paths I could have chosen. Before you continue to discover the keys to health in the next chapters, I encourage you to think about what you have just read and answer the following questions.

## TAKE ACTION

To help you apply the truths you have just read, try to answer the following questions before continuing to the next chapter. Your story is important to your pursuit of your health and fitness goals.

1.  In what ways could you relate to my story?

    _____

    _____

2.  Briefly tell your testimony.

    _____

    _____

3.  What do you hope to gain from reading *Getting in Shape God's Way*?

    _____

    _____

# TWO

# YOU BECOME WHAT YOU BELIEVE—LET'S GET REAL!

THE ONLY WAY I can explain the dramatic and lasting change I have experienced in my health and lifestyle is that when I began to cooperate with that eternal life inside me—the *revelation* of God's love for me—He began to change me from the inside out. The moment I cried out to Jesus to help me in my desperation, He answered that prayer and came into my life. He gave me His peace and a deep sense of being loved unconditionally. I began to experience a *knowing* in the core of my being, even without having a lot of understanding about God's love.

I still struggled for several years with my health issues and destructive lifestyle after that divine encounter. But the reality of God's presence in my life was continually at work to change my belief system, my thinking, and my motivation.

The goal of divine revelation is to bring us to a *realization* of the truth that allows it to be *manifest* in our lives. I have extracted the word *real* from realization to express the difference between mere intellectual knowledge or assent and the reality of divine revelation. God eventually brought me into a healthy lifestyle and began to fulfill His destiny for my life. He was quietly, yet powerfully transforming all I had perceived as *real* by increasing my realization of the truth of divine revelation.

As I studied His Word and listened to ministers preach about Christ, the truth was having a powerful, life-changing effect. I started to become what I was beginning to believe—about God and, just as importantly, about myself. Somehow, the "dis-information" about myself that had held me in its terrible grip since my childhood was losing its hold on my mind and emotions. Truth was conquering the lies, and I began to experience the peace and joy that were the manifestation of the life of God within me. This newfound reality motivated me to seek God even more. And I began to see His wonderful promises become a reality in my life.

As we explore the meaning of *revelation*—the first key to getting in shape God's way—let me say that I did not have a degree in theology when I first received divine revelation that changed my life. If this concept is new to you, please remember that receiving divine revelation is as simple as calling out to God for help. That's all I did when my friend encouraged me to pray to God. It is all anyone can do. The Scriptures are filled with wonderful promises for anyone who will ask God for help:

> Call upon Me in the day of trouble; I will deliver you, and you shall glorify Me.
>
> —PSALM 50:15, NKJV

A decision to ask for God's help is a decision that promises you a life of peace, joy, and a healthy lifestyle. God promises that when you seek Him, He will bring you out of darkness into His marvelous light (1 Pet. 2:9) and usher you into His kingdom, which is "not eating and drinking, but righteousness and peace and joy in the Holy Spirit" (Rom. 14:17, NKJV). As you make the decision to ask God for help, in your own words and way, you can trust Him to begin to change your perceived reality and to give you His marvelous promise of abundant life. Jesus said:

> The thief does not come except to steal, and to kill, and to destroy. I have come that they may have life, and that they may have it more abundantly.
>
> —JOHN 10:10, NKJV

After receiving Christ as my Savior, my cooperation with God, in practical, everyday terms, meant gradually learning to live by God's instructions in the Bible and doing what I sensed His Spirit inside me wanted me to do.

As I cultivated a relationship with God and other believers, His divine life began flowing from my spirit into my mind, emotions, and body. His power was transforming me and setting me free from my addictions, illnesses, and faulty thinking. Life became a steady succession of what I can only call *miracles* of the revelation of God's love and power.

An understanding of the reality of God's love and care for me exploded inside me. I vowed to serve Him for the rest of my life by helping other people become free to be *real*—from the inside out. I wanted people to experience the same freedom from sin, sickness, and mental and emotional illness I was experiencing. I wanted them to feel the joy of knowing they are loved unconditionally by the God and Creator of the universe.

In time, because of God's divine intervention in my life, I established a thriving business as a personal fitness trainer. The compassion of God for hurting people has grown immensely in my life. There are times when I literally ache for those who are suffering as I did—feeling trapped and helpless in their struggles with obesity, anorexia, bulimia, BDD (body dysmorphic disorder), and other serious disorders.

I have served clients with every kind of illness, from allergies to addictions, depression, self-destructive behaviors, or simply lonely emptiness. It is amazing how many lonely people there are who are otherwise symbols of what the world calls success. My clients have ranged from the most prominent people, whose names would be easily recognized, to those who are simply solitary individuals, struggling to survive each day. My passion is to see each of them, and you, be set free spiritually, mentally, and physically by God, who loves every person unconditionally.

 **FITNESS BELIEF** Men build from textbooks and information; God builds from revelation.

## WHAT YOU BELIEVE IS WHAT YOU BECOME

If you believe you are worthless, ugly, inferior, or any number of other negative personal image "realities," you will continually act out those roles because of your self-perception. The source of this "virtual reality" inside of you may be parents, teachers, peers, or your own ideas of yourself, gained, perhaps, from comparing yourself to others. Those beliefs that form your own self-image are powerful forces that will drive you to become what you believe. You may try to cover up the belief system you are carrying inside, compensating with acceptable outward behavior. Yet, those powerful (though irrational) beliefs will ultimately govern your life, your decisions, and your emotional and mental health. They will also ultimately affect your physical health in devastating ways.

When we face physical struggles or difficulties in any area of life, there is a compelling drive within us to *understand*. Somehow, if we can just make sense of the problem with our minds, it seems almost as helpful as having a solution for it. The word *understand* is a two-part word, which can be separated into "under" and "stand." It can be construed to mean to "stand under" the facts or information we are receiving, which indicates an acceptance of their validity.

For example, if you receive information or instruction from your medical doctor, you may say to him, "I understand." That means you are "standing under" his words, which will direct you on a path to getting well. Similarly, getting in shape God's way will help you to "stand under" the truth of God's Word. Through divine revelation, you will begin to believe and receive the truth about who you really are. You will experience, deep inside, the love God has for you. As you apply His principles to your life, He will empower you to fulfill your destiny—your purpose for living. Remember, your future will be determined by what you perceive as real.

### Reality TV—a healthy trend?

Observing the most popular television programming in today's society, it is easy to realize that there are more and more shows called *reality* TV. The ratings for reality TV programs are skyrocketing. Each has different themes and different goals, but the thing they have in common is dealing with real people in real-life situations. There are problems to solve and real rewards for solving them. There is even a reality program dealing with the issue of obesity. We witness the agony and ecstasy of individuals in their struggle to lose weight as part of a team competing for the prize of being the biggest losers.

The *Leave It to Beaver* program, so popular in the 1950s, is not relevant to the issues that kids and teens face today. Beaver was not diagnosed with ADHD, and Wally was never anorexic or chronically depressed. Today's reality TV programs deal with many issues that people in our affluent culture must face in their personal lives.

I believe the underlying attraction to this type of entertainment is that human beings want to interact with real issues of life that matter to real people. On a daily basis we are facing issues, perceived as real according to our belief system. So, we can relate to the rewards and consequences of real people who confront real issues on reality TV.

I believe this trend of seeking reality, even in entertainment, is a good thing. It means that people are looking for real answers to life situations, as I was in my most desperate moments as a troubled youth. They are wanting what is real—at least what they perceive to be real. In my darkest moments, I needed to know the reality of God's promise for a healthy life:

> Trust in the LORD with all your heart, and do not lean on your own understanding. In all your ways acknowledge Him, and He will make your paths straight.... Fear the LORD and turn away from evil. It will be healing to your body, and refreshment to your bones.
>
> —PROVERBS 3:5–8

Getting in shape God's way is a journey toward what is real. God's Word promises that those who seek to know God will enjoy health and find "straight paths" for their lives. Many of us have been deceived into consuming substitutes for the real when looking for health and happiness. Instead of receiving revelation of how God intended our lives to be lived, we have been doing the wrong thing for so long that when the right thing is presented to us—the *real*—it seems wrong to us. We rely on the information that we receive through our minds and our senses instead of the revelation of truth that can come only to our spirit by the Holy Spirit.

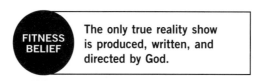

**FITNESS BELIEF**

The only true reality show is produced, written, and directed by God.

## Information Explosion

Over the last thousand years, the bodily functions of the human race have not changed. They had lungs then; we have lungs now. They had quadriceps; we have quadriceps. They had stomachs; we have stomachs. However, a significant difference between humanity then and now is the volume of information we now have about the function of the human body, which our ancestors did not have. Health experts have become wealthy by offering promises of a new breakthrough product, machine, or program that guarantees a better quality of life. There is so much "health" information out there that it boggles our minds.

We live our lives in the fast track. We race down an information interstate, filled with the latest computer technology, iPods, Palm Pilots, digital TV, and other gadgets being produced for consumers—all designed to deliver more information than we can possibly comprehend. Unfortunately, information alone cannot improve the function of your body. If it could, the health of this generation would be phenomenally better than that of our ancestors. The opposite is actually true.

According to medical statistics, our national health is degenerating at an alarming pace. Our twenty-four-hour "reality" news shows interview doctors and other health professionals who explain the latest disease or disorder. They recite the growing statistics for epidemics of various kinds that affect infants, children, youth, and adults.

In spite of the information explosion all around us, we are suffering from more ills and taking more medications than any generation before us. We seem to understand less about how to fill the basic needs of every human being for meaningful love, inner peace, and healthy relationships. As a result, our physical health is degenerating as well.

I do not intend to negate exploration and relational advancement in our information-based culture. However, God is so simple and the power of His truth so revelatory that we can miss it by having our minds cluttered with the latest information "bite." In the midst of an information-progressive world, God and the integrity of His Word never change.

## PETER'S *AHA!* MOMENT

The principles of God have worked for the last two thousand years, and they still work today. Through the centuries, millions of lives have been transformed by His love and truth. Yet, today so many people are still searching for answers to freedom from their fears and other destructive forces; they do not see the freedom God offers them—even as it is articulated in these pages.

Jesus raised the question of information to His disciples on more than one occasion as He was touring various regions, feeding hungry people, ministering hope, raising the dead, and healing people everywhere. His disciples and friends watched this miracle worker in complete amazement. One day He looked at His disciples and asked them a simple question: "Who do people say that the Son of Man is?" (Matt. 16:13).

The disciples began to respond with the information they had heard from other people:

> Some say John the Baptist; and others, Elijah; but still others, Jeremiah, or one of the prophets.
> 
> —MATTHEW 16:14

It appears that even the disciples who walked with Jesus were not sure who He was. Jesus asked them frankly to tell Him: "But who do you say that I am?" (v. 15). Only one disciple dared to respond. Simon Peter declared:

> Thou art the Christ, the Son of the living God.
> —MATTHEW 16:16, KJV

Jesus was thrilled with Peter's response. He said, in essence, "Wow! You are blessed, Peter, because no human being could have revealed that to you. They don't have that kind of information; that truth came to you by revelation. Only My Father in heaven could make that truth real in your heart." Peter had just had an *aha!* moment! Divine revelation had transcended the information sphere of his mind, filling his heart with the revelation of Jesus's true identity as the Son of the living God.

The church of Jesus Christ is built upon the foundation of the revelation that Jesus is the Messiah and Savior of mankind—a truth only God can reveal to your heart. When you receive this truth and surrender to the lordship of Christ, He promises that the gates of hell will not be able to destroy His church, of which you are a part. As you learn to live your life based on God's revealed truth, you will defeat any evil thing that attacks you or tries to keep you from obtaining all God has for you.

When you allow Jesus to be the Lord of your entire life, your Personal Trainer, you enter a relationship with God that is forever real and powerful. It is your relationship with Him that will give you the supernatural strength, courage, and wisdom to get in shape and stay in shape! Everyone else may have an understanding of who God is, but you must personally answer the question Jesus asked His disciples: "But who do you say that I am?"

It is imperative that you stop living your life based on information that comes from human sources. While information serves many good purposes, it is no substitute for the revelation you need to change your belief system that has a negative impact on your life and health.

**FITNESS BELIEF**
Information says Jesus was a great man; revelation says Jesus is the Son of the living God.

### Forming your self-perception

It is a simple fact that you make all your decisions, big and small, based upon what you truly and deeply believe—even unconsciously. Your worldview and values are formed by beliefs that have become your inner perception of reality. If you are living under a negative self-image, that virtual reality will have a negative impact on every area of your life. It will determine the friends you hang out with, your goals, and even how you care for your body. Where do these powerful beliefs come from? What formed your perception of yourself, your sense of reality? So many people and sources! So much information!

Psychologists believe that your early self-perception was formed by experiences with your parents, your brothers and sisters, and other family members. Later, there was the influence of your teachers in school, your coaches, other instructors, and your peers. Perhaps you went to church or synagogue or a mosque and were impacted by a religious leader. Your friends have had a profound effect on you too. Other forces that formed your virtual reality include what you watched on television or in the movies and what you read in books and magazines.

All these people and experiences have had their part in molding your self-image—what you believe about yourself, how you view life, what you value in life, and what your goals for happiness are. They have even taught you what to believe about God. Although some people like to think of themselves as "an independent spirit," that is simply a misnomer. What you believe to be real is a direct result of what other people and the world around you have taught you and demonstrated for you.

However, the above criteria that formed your belief system may not have been based on *truth*. That is why I referred earlier to your inner beliefs as "virtual reality." It is up to you to decide whether or not they are real, based on valid criteria, apart from the opinions, prejudices, and philosophies of other people or personal experiences in your life.

What will impact the health prognosis of this generation—the next generation— in a positive way? More information? Will the fact that you can name the latest disorder that affects you define your existence? Will more information about ailments and the drugs used to treat them improve your self-perception, your health, and your happiness? Information alone cannot change your self-perception, your inner belief system. You must look for empowerment from another source to effect lasting change in your faulty belief system. It's time to pursue the reality of divine *revelation*!

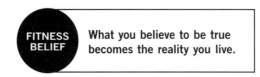

FITNESS BELIEF    What you believe to be true becomes the reality you live.

## INFORMATION VS. REVELATION

The difference between information and revelation needs to be clearly defined. This understanding came to me gradually after my first encounter with God and His divine revelation. It helped me to leave behind my destructive lifestyle and set me free to be the person God made me to be. I hope you can avoid some of the pitfalls I suffered by gaining understanding of the power of revelation and the limitations of information on which we base most of our decisions.

### Limitations to information

Much of the information we are receiving in our culture can be helpful to improving our lives in many ways. Medical science is discovering ways to diagnose and treat killer diseases, which can help to save lives. Space exploration can discover new insight into our planet, which can help us develop and preserve it. The list could go on and on regarding the benefits the information explosion could have on our lives.

However, from experience we understand that information is always subject to change. For example, the American Medical Association changes its view on many issues from year to year, based on new information that is available. What was true twenty years ago is no longer valid today. For years we were told that to be healthy we needed to be thin and lean. More recently medical experts are saying that it is healthier to be ten to twenty pounds heavier.

Changes in information can have a devastating effect on your sense of well-being. For example, if you are obsessed with your weight problem and base your self-worth on whether you are gaining or losing, the daily information the scale gives you can continually cause your self-esteem to spiral downward. First, it may even motivate you to pursue the latest diet fad, start drinking lots of water, and get more exercise. Then, in a few weeks or months, the scale gives you the information you need to see your self-worth soar to an all-time high—until Thanksgiving pie and Christmas candy do their demoralizing work—again! By January, you are hating the changing information of the scale one more time and the negative impact it is having on your self-esteem.

Caught in a vicious cycle, you only feel good about yourself when the scale gives you the information you desire. Gradually, you lose the will-power it takes to keep the right information coming. And even when you are at your ideal weight, you are not happy. Why? Because you are basing your self-worth on a criteria of weight loss, and that information is always changing. Your faulty sense of self-worth governs your sense of well-being.

In order to break this destructive cycle, you need to receive revelation of the truth of God's love for you, no matter what the scale says. That truth will empower you to love yourself, whether gaining or losing. Even though the information regarding your weight may be accurate, it does little to empower you to break the vicious cycle of self-loathing that governs your decisions about eating, exercising, and indulging in destructive lifestyle habits.

Receiving revelation of God's criteria of your self-worth will enable you to make healthy decisions for every area of your life. Consider this biblical description of how God feels about you:

> And you were dead in your trespasses and sins....Among them we too all formerly lived in the lusts of our flesh, indulging the desires of the flesh and of the mind....But God, being rich in mercy, because of His great love with which He loved us...made us alive together with Christ (by grace you have been saved), and raised us up with Him.
>
> —EPHESIANS 2:1, 3–6

## HOW TO BREAK THE DESTRUCTIVE "SCALE GAME"

Dear Reader,

If the above scenario describes your daily struggle with obesity, please make the following commitment to accept God's truth about your great worth, which you will learn in these pages, and choose to break the vicious cycle you are suffering.

I want you to weigh yourself one more time, right now, and write your weight in this blank (in pencil)_____. Notice the period at the end of the blank; please don't put a comma where I put a period. I want you to break this destructive "scale game."

Make a commitment to yourself (and to God) that you will not weigh again until you have completed this forty-day program. I am confident you will be glad you kept your commitment.

There is a limit to what information can do for you, even in a positive sense. Information does not carry within it an inherent power to enable you to change. For example, *understanding* that you are obese, knowing the apparent causes of obesity and even various cures for it, does not automatically empower you to lose weight. Information in itself is powerless to *change* your situation simply by virtue of your knowing the facts. Information alone cannot make it happen for you.

Another downside to information is its distorted form we call "dis-information." Unscrupulous politicians, world leaders, salesmen, and others use words (information) to spin a message that can incite, discourage, and deceive millions of people. In short, information can become dangerous when used to selfish advantage. It is difficult to sort out the real from the spin, the truth from simply inaccurate information. And even if we can, it is still a fact that even if information is currently accurate, it is powerless in itself to effect change.

Before I cried out to God in my desperation for help, I had received lots of good information regarding my health issues. The doctors and therapists with whom I consulted all meant well; there was no intention to do me harm. The problem was the limitation of their information. Even though well-intentioned people wanted me to succeed, they did not know the destructive belief system that was governing my behavior. They were not aware of the root cause of my cycle of self-destruction, which was affecting my physical health.

Only One could know my inner thoughts and fears—the Creator who made me. The psalmist declared this wonderful divine truth:

> O LORD, Thou hast searched me and known me. Thou dost know when I sit down and when I rise up.... Thou dost scrutinize my path and my lying down, and art intimately acquainted with all my ways. Even before there is a word on my tongue, behold, O LORD, Thou dost know it all.... Such knowledge is too wonderful for me.
> —PSALM 139:1–4, 6

This precious psalm of love reveals the loving care our Creator God takes of His own. When I first cried out for His help, He began to show me that I could not base my success in life on all the facts and information the world offered me. There was a greater force that would empower me to be free from my addictions and inner turmoil and allow me to live my dreams—a divine revelation of the love of God and the liberating power of His truth.

## DEFINING REVELATION

Revelation is the first key to getting in shape God's way. In the introduction I highlighted this key to health and related it to *fitness beliefs*. Now, I want to give you the academic definition of *revelation* in order to help you receive this powerful, life-changing force. Noah Webster, in his 1828 dictionary, defined revelation as:

> 1. The act of disclosing or discovering to others what was before unknown to them; appropriately, the disclosure or communication of truth to me by God Himself, or by his authorized agents, the prophets and apostles.
>
> How that by revelation he made known to me the mystery, as I wrote before in few words. Eph. 3. 2 Cor. 12.
>
> 2. That which is revealed; appropriately, the sacred truths which God has communicated to man for his instruction and direction. The revelations of God are contained in the Old and New Testament.[1]

Even the current versions of Webster's dictionary define revelation first of all as "an act of revealing or communicating divine truth; something that is revealed by God to humans."[2]

Divine truth…revealed mysteries…the source of revelation is God. *Divine revelation* simply means "the truth God reveals." That is why revelation has far greater power than *information* with all its limitations. As we consider the principles for getting in shape God's way, we must begin with the first key, which is *revelation* of God's love for us and His desire that we be healthy and happy.

God wants to reveal His love to your heart and mind and change your faulty inner belief system so that you can be restored to health and happiness. In that sense, the Bible becomes a how-to manual to teach you to live successfully—in every area of life. Its principles for life are as relevant to mankind today as they were thousands of years ago. God's promises for success and fulfillment of your destiny are as sure today as they were then. Until you receive divine revelation from God, you will not be empowered to believe the truth about God, about yourself, or about the real meaning of life.

It makes sense that the manufacturer who "creates" an automobile will understand best the purpose, optimum function, and value of that automobile. He will also know how to fix it if it breaks down. You would not take your car to a piano tuner for advice and instruction if it needed repair. That analogy is true as well for the "broken" human predicament. When you realize you need repair, you must learn to consult the One who made you. Again, the psalmist understood this reality when he wrote:

> Serve the LORD with gladness; come before Him with joyful singing. Know that the LORD Himself is God; it is He who has made us, and not we ourselves; we are His people and the sheep of His pasture.
>
> —PSALM 100:2–3

God knows the purpose for which He created you as a unique individual. He understands how you are supposed to function. And, most importantly, He places a higher value on you than anyone else. He can reveal your true identity and help you to walk in divine revelation that will empower you to greater success than you have ever dreamed. He only asks that you come to Him and give your heart to serve Him "with gladness."

## SPIRIT, SOUL, AND BODY

Revelation, then, is truth that is revealed—on a very deep level of knowing. You become aware of what is real. While information comes from an outside source, God reveals truth to you on a spiritual level inside your being. It becomes so real to you that you have no doubt about it. You know that what you believe is an absolute, everlasting reality—as eternally true as two plus two equals four. God's truth is the only absolute reality that exists in the universe—and beyond.

### Receiving divine revelation

Because receiving divine revelation is the first step toward living a healthy lifestyle, we need to understand how we receive it. Where does that absolute knowing reside in our human personality? How does it empower us to change?

According to Scripture, God created mankind in His own image (Gen. 1:26). Scripture also teaches that God is a Spirit (John 4:24). Therefore, we understand that mankind is a tripartite being—spirit, soul, and body—which is also clearly taught in Scripture. The apostle Paul supports our ability to train all three components of our being in 1 Thessalonians 5:23–24 by explaining that we are three-dimensional beings.

> May God himself, the God who makes everything holy and whole, make you holy and whole, put you together—spirit, soul, and body—and keep you fit for the coming of our Master, Jesus Christ. The One who called you is completely dependable. If he said it, he'll do it!
> —THE MESSAGE, EMPHASIS ADDED

Let me explain how this works. The scientific world defines us as three-part beings: muscular, skeletal, and neurological, moving in three planes of function: the sagittal, frontal, and transverse. The Getting in Shape God's Way exercise program teaches you to exercise your body in strength, flexibility, and cardiovascular exercises in all three of these scientific planes.

There are parallels for these three dimensions in the spiritual world; they are the spirit, soul, and body. In the first three photos on this page, my body is in three planes: raising my hands, which represents the spirit; extending my hands to the side, which represents the soul; and lowering my hands, which represents the body. They are three different dimensions but, as the fourth photo shows, they are one and the same.

Your soul is comprised of your mind, your human will, and your emotions. If your body is suffering because you never exercise it, feed it well, or even discipline it, it tells your soul (mind, will, and emotions) how to think. So your soul says, "OK, I'll go with that. I will feel and do what you say."

But when your spirit is rejuvenated with God's Holy Spirit, it is now able to call the shots in your soul. When your natural spirit (the essence of your being) gets touched by the Holy Spirit, your soul realizes its decision-making process has been redirected by another dimension. That higher dimension is a supernatural one, sometimes called the spiritual dimension.

That's why it is just as important to train your spiritual side as it is to train your body. You exercise and feed your spirit through prayer, reading God's written Word, and listening to His preached Word. (See Romans 10:17.) The words of the apostle Paul confirm this process:

43

> But I say, walk and live [habitually] in the [Holy] Spirit [responsive to and controlled and guided by the Spirit]; then you will certainly not gratify the cravings and desires of the flesh (of human nature without God). For the desires of the flesh are opposed to the [Holy] Spirit, and the [desires of the] Spirit are opposed to the flesh (godless human nature); for these are antagonistic to each other [continually withstanding and in conflict with each other], so that you are not free but are prevented from doing what you desire to do.
>
> —GALATIANS 5:16–17, AMP

When your soul is not trained by God's Spirit, it begins to suffer from a form of fatigue, much as your body would from not exercising or disciplining it. When you allow the Holy Spirit to take up residency within you, your soul now can listen to the Spirit instead of listening to your body. Your soul responds to the side of your being that is stronger. Be it the spiritual side of you, or the fleshly, carnal side of you that is opposing what God's Word says. If your spirit is stronger than your body, you're in a good place. But if your body is always calling the shots, you may find yourself making the wrong decisions.

While entire books are written on the nature of man, for our purposes we can only briefly define it in order to clarify how we receive divine revelation. We receive divine revelation from God, who is Spirit, into our spirit, which is that deep inner "knowing." In our first encounter with divine revelation, when we accept Christ as Savior and are born again, the Holy Spirit makes our spirit come alive to God, as Jesus taught:

> Jesus said, "You're not listening. Let me say it again. Unless a person submits to this original creation—the 'wind-hovering-over-the-water' creation, the invisible moving the visible, a baptism into a new life—it's not possible to enter God's kingdom. When you look at a baby, it's just that: a body you can look at and touch. But the person who takes shape within is formed by

something you can't see and touch—the Spirit—and becomes a living spirit.

"So don't be so surprised when I tell you that you have to be 'born from above'—out of this world, so to speak. You know well enough how the wind blows this way and that. You hear it rustling through the trees, but you have no idea where it comes from or where it's headed next. That's the way it is with everyone 'born from above' by the wind of God, the Spirit of God."

—JOHN 3:5–8, THE MESSAGE

### A mystery

The wonder of becoming alive in our spirit to the Spirit of God is a marvelous, divine mystery. It is the beginning of an awesome journey into reality and truth. Jesus declared of Himself: "I am the way, the truth, and the life" (John 14:6, KJV). We cannot know truth—about ourselves, about life, or about God—apart from receiving divine revelation into our spirit. For that reason, the "virtual reality" or our inner belief system is not complete without knowing God, the Creator and Savior of mankind.

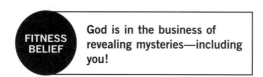

FITNESS BELIEF

**God is in the business of revealing mysteries—including you!**

We need to be changed from the inside out so that the truth of God regarding who we are and our great worth and purpose can govern our lives. In that way, the lies that have bound us to unhealthy lifestyles will be dispelled, and God's truth will empower us to enjoy the freedom of health in every area of our lives.

The scriptures also refer to our spirit as our "inner man" (Eph. 3:16). Once I understood that I was a spirit being who had a soul, which includes my mind, emotions, and volition or will, and that I lived in a physical body, many of my questions were answered.

God had come to me and revealed His love in my spirit; in that moment I had been born again—made alive to God. But until His truth could be revealed to my mind more fully, I would struggle with the same hang-ups I had before being born again. Until my mind and emotions began to be filled with God's fitness beliefs, His principles of health could not govern my body and bring me to health.

Perhaps you are reading this and can honestly say that you have received this divine revelation into your spirit; you have accepted Christ as your Savior and have been born again, made alive to Him. Yet, you struggle with a poor self-image, destructive health patterns, and other behaviors that are still affecting your quality of life. It was the same for me. Even after my powerful encounter with God, which resulted in some obvious changes in my life, I still needed more revelation of God's love and His ways to become free from a long-standing destructive belief system that still governed my lifestyle.

As your personal trainer, I want to share candidly with you the divine principles from God's Word that have transformed my faulty belief system into God's fitness beliefs. As you continually ask God for divine encounters, the information you receive, even from the Scriptures, will drop twelve inches—from your head to your heart. It will become revelation— real—to your spirit, and you will experience dramatic change through divine revelation.

## Your *Aha!* Moment

Scientists often talk about those rare moments of discovery when all the pieces of the puzzle fit together. Suddenly, the question is answered; the concept is crystal clear. *Of course! That is the way this thing works!* They describe this as the *eureka!* phenomenon or the *aha!* experience. An acrostic for *aha!* has this significant meaning:

- Attention
- Hope
- Action

First, your *attention* is drawn to something you never saw before, which gives you *hope* that there is a solution to your problem, and so you try it—you take *action*. When it works, it is like a miracle. In essence, the *aha!* experience for one who is seeking God is the moment you "see" something only God could reveal to you. It is that deep, inner knowing of a truth that God makes real to you. Suddenly you have *insight*.

*Insight* is a compound word consisting of "in" and "sight." It refers to inner vision of the very core and depth of a person, a situation, or a truth. According to Webster's, it is the "power or act of seeing into a situation; the act or result of apprehending the inner nature of things."[3] If we have insight, we have a clear and deep perception and understanding of what we are observing. Insight always says, "*Aha!* The lights just went on in my heart and my head! I see it! I understand now!"

When I was born again, I had an *aha!* experience that affected me deeply and eventually changed dramatically the quality and direction of my life. From that moment, I knew without a doubt that I was God's child and that I would live with Him always. When I died physically I was going to heaven, and until then, I knew I was of great value to God and had an eternal purpose to fulfill.

When I finally surrendered myself fully to studying the Bible and began to live according to God's principles, I began to receive more and more insight, truth, and revelation from God about who I was and what I was created to be and to do. His reality became my reality—and it brought me joy and satisfaction beyond my wildest dreams!

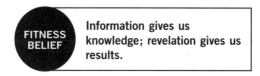

**FITNESS BELIEF**

Information gives us knowledge; revelation gives us results.

## THE BIBLE: A REALITY MANUAL

After my salvation experience, as I continued to listen to ministers and teachers on television, the truth I received made it become clear to me that all the questions I had about life would be answered in the Bible. Who I was, why I was here, and what I was supposed to do with my life were concepts to be found somewhere in that Book. As I began to read and study this "Reality Manual" for myself, it completely changed my life. I began to see myself through God's loving eyes. His opinion of me was often entirely different from mine and everyone else's!

## YOUR *AHA!* MOMENT

As you pursue the first key to getting in shape God's way—revelation—I encourage you to:

- Ask God to make Himself real to you.
- Ask Him to help you lose weight, gain weight, or otherwise gain your health.
- Thank Him immediately for what He is going to do for you.
- Before you eat, ask Him if what you are eating is contributing to your fitness goal.

Then pray this simple prayer:

*God, I need Your help. I need You to shine light on the dark areas of my life where I am clouded and cannot see. Forgive me for the way I have treated my body and my mind. Cleanse me of all my sins and failures. Thank You, God! You are a forgiving God. I have tried so many diets and health programs. I have tried to be the person of my dreams. I am upset with the way I look and feel. I need You to help me. Give me wisdom about my body, my metabolism, and my wrong habits. Help me to start Your program and finish it. Please give me the revelation I need to maintain a healthy lifestyle for the rest of my life. I want this plan to be the last fitness program I ever begin. In Jesus's name I pray, amen.*

**FITNESS BELIEF** You can do anything you set your mind to do—anything!

If you sincerely prayed the prayer above, the first thing God will make real to you is how great is His love for you. When I cried out to Him for help, He didn't see a fat boy, a skinny boy, a smart boy, or a stupid boy. He saw a person for whom Jesus died to save, a messed-up son who was calling out to his heavenly Father.

God loves you as you are—strengths, weaknesses, worries, bumps, flaws, and all! He loves you whether you had a good day or a bad day, whether or not you looked good or felt good about yourself today. Because the nature of God is love, He actually *likes* you! He wants to hang out with you 24-7!

Seeing yourself through God's eyes will have a tremendous effect on your physical health concerns. You can relax inside and begin to like yourself for who you are. Why shouldn't you? The Creator of the universe likes you! As this divine revelation fills your heart, suddenly you will possess an inner strength and supernatural inspiration to be the best you could ever be.

After my *aha!* experience with God, I was filled with real hope that I could become that extraordinary human being whom I longed to be. That hope is still being fulfilled, one day at a time. The results to date are fantastic, and I am expecting greater fulfillment of personal destiny as I continue to walk with God.

As you learn to think of yourself as a complex being—spirit, soul, and body—who is wondrously formed by your Creator to walk in God's divine revelation, you can begin to make your own the four keys to getting in shape God's way:

## GETTING IN SHAPE GOD'S WAY

**KEY #1: REVELATION**—*fitness beliefs*—invade your spirit with the real.

**KEY #2: DECLARATION**—*fitness words*—influence your soul (mind, volition, and emotions).

**KEY #3: APPLICATION**—*fitness function*—infuses health activity for your whole person.

**KEY #4: MANIFESTATION**—*fitness lifestyle*—increases your quality of life: spirit, soul, and body.

Without embracing and implementing these four keys into your life, no fitness or health regimen can succeed in helping you live a healthy lifestyle. The principles for living a healthy lifestyle that we will discuss are biblically based. That means they are timeless in their effectiveness, universal in their application, and utterly practical for every life situation. Everyone who chooses to submit to the truth of these universal principles, which the Creator set in motion, can know only success, satisfaction, and happiness in living the ultimate quality of life as God intended it to be lived.

A mere intellectual assent to this information is not the same as receiving the truth of it as revelation from the heart of God. We discussed the limitation of information, which is powerless to effect change. We must cry out to God to give us His divine revelation and embrace His truth in our hearts, which will empower us to change.

The principles of God have worked for thousands of years, and they still work today. Because I am continually embracing the truth of God's Word, I am learning to live a lifestyle of health and wholeness that is increasingly manifest in my spirit, soul, and body. No longer do I find myself living on a roller coaster, going from failure that dims the light of hope to a season of renewed enthusiasm that ends once again in a downswing of depression.

Whether you are starting from the point of choosing to receive Christ and be born again or have walked with God for many years, you can leave behind the cycle of failure caused by a faulty belief system and begin to enjoy life and health in spirit, soul, and body. When you begin to live your life based on God's revealed truth, you will learn to overcome every obstacle that has been keeping you from becoming the person God wants you to become. As Jesus becomes Lord of your entire life—your Personal Trainer for life—your relationship with God becomes increasingly real and powerful. It is that relationship that will give you supernatural strength, courage, and wisdom to get in shape and stay in shape—God's way! He alone can empower you to reign in life!

Let me share with you one of the most powerful verses in the Bible regarding your empowerment to reign in life:

> Now faith is the assurance (the confirmation, the title deed) of the things [we] hope for, being the proof of things [we] do not see and the conviction of their reality [faith perceiving as real fact what is not revealed to the senses].
>
> —HEBREWS 11:1, AMP

Like the scientific approach of the *aha!* moment, your hope in this scripture is literally a *substance.* If you hope in this biblical truth, it will never disappoint you. The apostle Paul confirms that fact when he writes, "Such hope never disappoints or deludes or shames us, for God's love has been poured out in our hearts through the Holy Spirit Who has been given to us" (Rom. 5:5, AMP).

## TAKE ACTION

We have covered a lot of information in chapter 2. To help you determine if you understand the first key—revelation—try to answer the following questions. I encourage you to write your answers in the book so that after a year of following your fitness plan you can come back and read your answers. After getting in shape God's way for a year, you will be amazed at the tremendous changes that have taken place in your life—and all for the better!

1. In the past, did you believe God was interested in the health and fitness of your physical body? What do you believe now?

_____

_____

_____

2. What have you believed about yourself? After completing this chapter, how has that belief changed?

_____

_____

_____

3. What is your greatest hope with regard to getting in shape God's way?

_____

_____

_____

# THREE

# HOW TO REIGN IN LIFE—HEALTHY ROOTS

IN THE LAST CHAPTER, we discussed the interior belief system that forms your self-perception. It is important to determine whether that powerful belief system is based on truth or lies. Do you know what really rules your life? What kinds of influences, desires, fears, people, or circumstances are controlling you and determining your decisions? Have you identified the lies that have ruled your life, forming your self-image and motivating your behavior?

In this chapter, I want to introduce the analogy of a root, which will represent the deepest part of your interior belief system located in your spirit. The Bible says, "You can't find firm footing in a swamp, but life rooted in God stands firm" (Prov. 12:3, THE MESSAGE). It is important to cultivate healthy roots for your fitness beliefs.

The roots of a plant are responsible for the growth and ultimate health of the plant. They soak up nutrients and water and distribute them to all parts of the plant. The taproot of a plant is the primary root that grows vertically downward and produces smaller roots laterally. If the taproot is healthy, the smaller roots will be also. Conversely, if the taproot is rotten, its rottenness will contaminate all the roots of the plant and cause destruction of the plant itself.

Applying this analogy to your life, the roots that produce your interior belief system determine who or what *rules* your life. If lies and deception produce the taproot of your self-perception and thinking patterns, turmoil and misery will reign in your life. When your roots are firmly planted in God's truth, then the healing nutrients of that truth will be distributed from your spirit—your taproot—to your soul and body. Scripture teaches,

"If the roots of the tree are holy, the branches will be, too" (Rom. 11:16, NLT).

When God's truth begins to replace that rotten taproot of all you believe, speak, and live, you will be empowered to reign in freedom, health, and happiness in life. As you continue to receive revelation of God's love for you, He will teach you how to reign in life with Him and experience a growing relationship in His love, blessings, and favor. Your relationship with God allows His truth to become the taproot—the anchor and life-giving source—of everything you believe. To enjoy these health benefits of God's truth, there are choices you must make. The apostle Paul declared:

> Therefore do not let sin reign in your mortal body that you should obey its lusts, and do not go on presenting the members of your body to sin as instruments of unrighteousness; but present your-selves to God as those alive from the dead, and your members as instruments of righteousness to God....Having been freed from sin and enslaved to God, you derive your benefit, resulting in sanctification, and the outcome, eternal life.
> —ROMANS 6:12–13, 22

## THE POWER OF CHOICE

Your power of choice is a gift from God. He does not take it away when you choose to have a relationship with Him—He does not want robots to do His bidding! Many of the choices you have made have contributed to your misery and defeat. Choices that were made for you have also affected your current condition of life. Yet, when you make the most important choice to ask God for help, He comes to begin to undo all the harmful choices that have affected your life.

As you choose to let go of the lies and deception you have believed, you can begin to pull out that rotten taproot that has wreaked havoc through its destructive work in every area of your life. Choosing to replace that taproot with the truth of God's love for you is His way to empower you to succeed in life.

As you learn each day to choose the life God promises to give, you begin to see and understand His reality, His love, and His wonderful promises for your happiness and success. Because you choose life, the very life of God will be distributed to your soul and body. As you choose to receive His divine revelation, He will empower you to make the right choices for your total well-being. The light and wisdom of God will direct your choices and keep you on the divine pathway of revelation. In this way, you will replace the ugly taproot of lies and deception and walk in freedom and health—spirit, soul, and body. Only then will you grasp the fantastic power of your gift of choice.

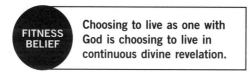

**FITNESS BELIEF**

**Choosing to live as one with God is choosing to live in continuous divine revelation.**

## CHOOSING TO TRUST

According to the Scriptures, trust is a choice. It is important that we choose to trust the right source; that choice will determine our being blessed or cursed:

> Thus says the LORD, "Cursed is the man who trusts in mankind and makes flesh his strength, and whose heart turns away from the LORD.... Blessed is the man who trusts in the LORD and whose trust is the LORD. For he will be like a tree planted by the water, that extends its roots by a stream and will not fear when the heat comes; but its leaves will be green, and it will not be anxious in a year of drought nor cease to yield fruit.
> —JEREMIAH 17:5, 7–8

When clients come to me with an eating disorder or other chronic health problem, I talk with them to get to know how they are thinking about themselves. I can usually determine what is driving them after just a few moments of conversation. When I discover what negative thing is reigning in their lives, together we can begin to get to the root of the problem. Only as we attack the real problem together can I help them apply the truth to the lie that is causing their pain.

If you were to seek out my help because you are out of shape or overweight, you must choose to get to know me in order to get into shape *my way*. Otherwise, how could you trust me? How would you be able to follow my instructions and learn my God-given secrets to success?

In order to trust me, you would need to know first that I care about you personally. You would need to be convinced that it is important to me that you succeed in becoming the person you want to be. When that truth is established, then you have to get to know my ways and methods and learn how to follow them to get the results I promise you. You cannot get in shape *my way* without knowing me, trusting me, and doing what I tell you to do.

Likewise, if you are getting in shape God's way, you must get to know God and choose to trust Him. One way you do that is to read about Him in the Bible, especially in the New Testament. That's where He reveals His love for you through Christ's ultimate sacrifice of giving His life for you. In the New Testament, the apostles who experienced this divine grace also give practical instruction on how to live in order to be happy and successful. As you learn to receive divine revelation from the Word of God, not only do you begin to trust the truth of God's love for you, but you also begin to understand yourself as well.

Jesus told His disciples, "But remember the root command: Love one another" (John 15:17, THE MESSAGE). Seeing yourself through God's loving eyes instead of your past traumas, fears, and failures empowers you to get to the root of your problems. And when you get to the root of your problems, you can begin to reign in life instead of being defeated by the lies you have believed for many years. Then you will be able to love others with the love you have received.

**FITNESS BELIEF**

To reign in life, your relationship with God must become the taproot, the anchor, of everything you believe.

## A SOLID DIAGNOSIS

My pastor, who is also one of my clients, shared with me a personal experience he had that illustrates what happens when we don't have revelation about the root cause of our problem. He said he was getting ready to go on the fishing trip of his life. Unfortunately, just before leaving on his much-anticipated trip, he developed a horrible pain and swelling in his toes. He had experienced this type of pain once before because of a gout condition, and it had been alleviated by a regimen of eating and drinking specific healing agents I had recommended. However, this time the regimen did not work.

He did not have much time before leaving on his trip, so he decided to take an antibiotic a doctor prescribed for him. It was supposed to take effect thirty-six to forty-eight hours after taking the first dose. But it did not have any effect on the pain. My pastor left on his fishing trip, still fighting the pain and swelling in his toes. He endured the four days of hiking in the mountains, limping more each day, and realizing that the pain was spreading into his leg. He hobbled over the rough terrain, enjoying his time with his friends, yet all the while suffering severe pain in his leg and foot. When he returned home he went to see a doctor. The doctor poked his toes, asking, "Does it hurt here? Here? How about here?" At first, he could not find any cause for the pain his patient was suffering.

My pastor replied, "My entire leg hurts, from up here down to my toes."

The doctor said, "Can you point to the exact place where you think the pain is coming from?"

He answered, "Right around the toe area."

The doctor finally touched the spot that was the most tender and asked, "Have you done anything to your foot in the last couple of weeks?"

"Not that I can remember. You know, a couple of weeks ago I was staying in a hotel. I got up sleepily in the night and stubbed my toe on a door. It was so painful that I asked some friends if they thought it might be broken. They all said they didn't think so. After a few days the pain went away, so I just forgot about it."

The doctor moved his hand toward the joint of my patient's toes and applied a slight pressure. His patient cried out in pain, "That's it!"

The doctor said, "You don't have gout. You injured yourself when you stubbed your toe. Here, take this and you will be fine in two days." In thirty-six hours the swelling was reduced and the foot was functioning normally again because the doctor had diagnosed the root cause of my friend's problem.

My pastor had consulted with other friends and professionals and did what he thought would cure him, to no avail. He finally consulted a doctor who could properly diagnose the root problem and then offer the cure for his painful condition. His experience illustrates the importance of going to the right source to receive the needed revelation for healing.

The pain you live with may have been intensified and prolonged because you have believed an improper diagnosis of yourself. You may even have shared your problems with friends or family. Yet, they may not be equipped to recognize the deeply rooted issues in your life. Professional therapists may actually help uncover your painful issues and identify them for you. But often they encourage you to blame others for your problems, such as parents and other people who have influenced your life. Playing the blame-the-other-person game will not give you the tools to be healed of your deep hurts, traumas, and offenses.

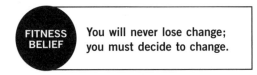

FITNESS BELIEF

You will never lose change;
you must decide to change.

## Who Owns You?

Who knows you better than anyone else? Who can get to the root of your pain, help you to pull it out, and then replace it with a healthy root? No one knows you better than God. He made you. God is the only One who can give you a solid diagnosis about the root problems in your life and then give you the cure as well. That's why Christians refer to God as "the Great Physician." He can give you the proper diagnosis, identify the root of your problem, and then heal you.

I'm not telling you not to see a doctor, a counselor, or a therapist. God can use these professional people to talk to you and point you to the diagnosis of root problems as well as the cure. However, it is important to know that no matter where you go for help, you will only move toward freedom as you choose to allow God's truth to reign in your life.

When you submit to God's control, He can expose and remove those old ugly roots of your faulty belief system and replace them with His beautiful, strong roots of love, joy, and peace. He can reveal His purposes to you regarding your happiness and destiny. As you surround yourself with people who are also allowing His truth to reign in their lives, you will be strengthened to know that you are not facing your battles alone. Find time to pray with your friends and pastors. As you do, you will learn to receive confirmation from God's Word and from the wisdom of mature believers for what you are hearing the Holy Spirit speak in your heart.

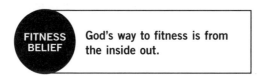

FITNESS BELIEF — God's way to fitness is from the inside out.

## The Law of Humility

God has established a law for the purpose of giving us peace, joy, and complete healing within your body, soul, and spirit. It is the law of humility. Unfortunately, human beings tend to be proud. We want people to admire us because we can "stand on our own two feet" and "pull ourselves up by our bootstraps." We don't want anyone to think there is anything wrong with us or that we need help from anyone else, especially God.

But God didn't create you to be independent of Him or other people because of pride. He created you, first of all, to be completely involved in an intimate relationship with Him and to walk with Him in a divine partnership for life. He also created you to spend quality time with other God-seeking people in church, in small groups, and in social gatherings.

I shared with you the great difference it made in my life as a new Christian to have caring and honest friends and wise, Spirit-filled mentors and pastors with whom I could share my struggles. Later, God blessed me with a wonderful, God-fearing wife as well, who is by my side encouraging me as we discover our destiny together.

There must be a balance between human relationships and your relationship with God. He instructed all believers to gather together to encourage one another. (See Hebrews 10:25.) Those relationships are important to your well-being. Yet, even in our happy home together, my wife and I understand that God is always the focal point for our lives. He made us to be in constant communion and intimacy with Him, to trust Him and seek His advice on everything.

Unfortunately, most of us have a great deal of trouble turning our lives completely over to anyone else, especially someone we cannot see with our natural eyes—like God! Even those who have been born again spiritually and are attending church regularly can have hidden areas of their lives they reserve for themselves. They are afraid of letting God into sensitive, touchy areas. They may even be unaware of deep roots of pain that are still keeping them from the happiness God desires for them.

In order to get well and find true happiness, you must be willing to humble yourself and say, "God, I need Your help. I need to know what's going on. Why am I falling into the same trap over and over again? Why can't I break out of this cycle of self-hatred, addiction, overeating, or other destructive behaviors?" When you cry out to Him, He always answers—the key is to listen. You must be willing to hear the truth about yourself. Only then can you expect to receive the freedom that God's truth always promises. Someone has suggested that for good reason you were given two ears—and one mouth.

Just as the good doctor did to my pastor, your Great Physician will begin to poke around and say, "Does it hurt here? How about here? How about what you went through as a child, the way you were treated on your job? I know that divorce hurts. I know she left you. I know he hurt you. Is the pain still there?"

You might have to say, "It hurts everywhere, Lord."

He may continue to search the root cause and say again, "What about here?"

With that last probe, you cry, "Ouch! Yes! That's it!"

You realize the pain is greater there than any other place He touched. Then, in a still small voice He says, "Take this medicine: first, My body that was broken for you so that you could be healed and whole. Then take My blood that was shed for your forgiveness. Take My Word because it is truth. 'You shall know the truth, and the truth shall make you free' (John 8:32). You have believed a lie about Me, about yourself, and about everyone else. Now I want you to live in the truth because the truth will not only make you free, but also it will keep you free."

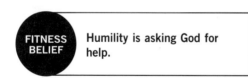

**FITNESS BELIEF**  Humility is asking God for help.

God has created you to reign in life to the degree that you are rooted and grounded in His truth and love. Without healthy roots in Him, you will not be able to know success and happiness in the fulfillment of your destiny. Remember, you are not a physical being having a spiritual experience. *You are a spiritual being having a physical experience!* So the first thing you need to settle in your heart is the reality that God must become the primary influence in your life. God's truth—divine revelation—must become the taproot of your belief system. That healthy root will keep you firmly established in God's way of truth.

By humbling yourself and submitting your life fully to God to receive His revelation—accepting what He shows you, believing what He tells you, and acting according to the reality He has revealed—you will experience instant relief, inner peace, and bodily ease. This is the amazing healing power inherent in the law of humility!

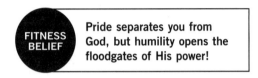

**FITNESS BELIEF**

**Pride separates you from God, but humility opens the floodgates of His power!**

## THE TAPROOT OF FEAR

I had a client, whom we will call Sue. She was extremely overweight when I met her. Although somewhat hesitant, she seemed to be serious about losing weight. She had tried everything she heard about to help her lose weight: high carbohydrates and low carbohydrates, high protein and low protein, diet pills, running, walking, and other kinds of exercise. Nothing had worked for her.

I asked Sue to tell me her medical history. When she came to the part where she had been raped one night while waiting for the subway, she said that traumatic experience was devastating to her. She said she began eating to make herself look unattractive so that it wouldn't happen again. Eventually she developed an eating disorder, and by the age of fifty she weighed almost three hundred pounds.

What was the taproot of Sue's weight problem? An undisciplined appetite? No, the root was her fear of being violated again.

An extremely thin gentleman, whom I will call Jim, came to me when he was in his midthirties. He asked me to help him gain weight and pack on some lean muscle tissue. I did a complete physical workup on him and put him on a customized diet and exercise program. All systems were go, but after months of following the prescribed regimen, there was no change.

When there are no results where there should be results, I always begin to look for a hidden root cause of the condition. I asked Jim about his medical history and his life.

Jim had been raised by his widowed aunt, with no male figure in the home; he had never felt the love of a father or a father figure. This emotional lack had a negative impact on his health. He developed the physical characteristics of his thin mother, which caused his body to appear more feminine than masculine. To compensate, he would overeat to gain weight. When he reached a good weight he would relax. As a result, food became a comfort to him, which made him keep eating until he was overweight. At that point in the cycle, he would panic and go on a crash diet to lose weight and look "handsome" again. By the time I met him, he was anorexic.

Was Jim's problem rooted in food? No, it was also rooted in the fear of rejection because of his "skinny man complex."

Both of these people had physical disorders that were rooted in the spiritual disorder of fear. The Bible teaches us how to live victoriously through faith. However, our society promotes the theology of fear. You have been trained to think and view your world through the eyes of fear. Here are some fear-based axioms regarding your appearance that you may have acquired in your life:

- If you don't lose the weight, you will die.
- You don't dare become overweight! People will think you are, lazy, stupid, and pathetic.
- You can only be accepted and successful if you are thin.
- If you are too attractive, you become a target for bad people.
- The only way anyone will ever marry you is if you look perfect.
- You will never get promoted if you don't look the part.

If you have fallen prey to these or similar harmful beliefs, you have fallen prey to a spirit of fear. In that case, here is a wonderful revelation: you do not have a weight problem; you have a *fear* problem. Since the root of your problem is fear, if you take away the fear, you will take the first step in solving your weight problem. God's Word gives you this wonderful promise:

> For God hath not given us the spirit of fear; but of power, and of love, and of a sound mind.
> —2 TIMOTHY 1:7, KJV

You can learn to declare this promise and destroy fear that has ruled your life. The way you uproot the fear is through speaking what God says about your situation, not what the situation says about you.

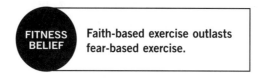

**FITNESS BELIEF** — **Faith-based exercise outlasts fear-based exercise.**

## THE UNIVERSAL PROBLEM OF FEAR

The Bible teaches that every human being is born with a fear of death and dying. Because of that deep-rooted fear, all humanity is "subject to slavery" throughout life. (See Hebrews 2:14–15.) The scriptures also teach that through Christ's death, the power of death has been conquered; it has lost its sting:

> O death, where is your victory? O death, where is your sting? The sting of death is sin, and the power of sin is the law; but thanks be to God, who gives us the victory through our Lord Jesus Christ.
> —1 CORINTHIANS 15:55–57

There are so many situations that can become the "sting" of death to you. Perhaps you are afraid of being overweight and out-of-shape; you are afraid of being sick and unhealthy. One of the most painful death stings is the fear of not being loved, accepted, and appreciated. Not feeling loved is like a living death. When you fight these fearful beliefs in your own strength, you usually end in despair. When you live in fear, you live a life that is helpless, hopeless, worthless, and friendless—a terrible world of hurt. Fear has the power to cripple, and even to kill. It is a formidable enemy.

Getting in shape God's way means you not only face your enemies, but that you also totally defeat them. With God's Spirit living in you—the same Spirit that raised Jesus from the dead—and His living, powerful promises to stand on, you are empowered to come out of the shadows of ignorance and conquer the spirit of fear that has crippled you. For that to happen, you must embrace the revelation that God loves you and wants to bless you, give you eternal life, and lead you into a life of health, wholeness, joy, and purpose.

## FAITH VS. FEAR

The ruling virtues of God's spiritual kingdom include faith, love, peace, wisdom, and truth. In contrast, Satan drives his hellish spiritual kingdom through fear, hatred, anger, ignorance, lies, sickness, disease, and painful lack. Jesus compared His kingdom to Satan's:

> The thief comes only to steal, and kill, and destroy; I came that
> they might have life, and might have it abundantly.
> —JOHN 10:10

The primary difference between God's kingdom and Satan's kingdom is that God works through faith and Satan works through fear. God promises that you can win the battle against fear by receiving His revelation: "For God hath not given us a spirit of fear; but of power, and of love, and of a sound mind" (2 Tim. 1:7, KJV).

Power. Love. A sound mind. God didn't give you a spirit of fear. He came into your life to fill your spirit with faith in His love and goodness. When you choose to place your faith in Him, you can walk confidently in His power and love. You will have a sound mind, because your thoughts will be rooted and grounded in truth. Then your entire life becomes rooted in divine revelation that will not change with the latest trends, the opinions of people, or anything hurtful that life dishes out.

The Bible also says that faith works by love (Gal. 5:6). God did not provide the awesome sacrifice of salvation through His Son so you could continue in cycles of self-destruction and self-loathing. He doesn't want you to be unhappy and unhealthy. He loves you and desires for you to pursue the dreams He has for your life—and succeed!

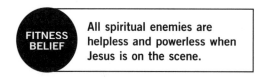

**FITNESS BELIEF** All spiritual enemies are helpless and powerless when Jesus is on the scene.

God's will was never for you to be overweight, sick, and miserable. He sent His Word to you to restore your body, soul, and spirit and give you an abundant life—here on Earth as well as in heaven (John 10:10). Abundant life includes a healthy, physically fit body and an inner peace that goes beyond your ability to reason. Abundance means more than enough and far more than you could think or imagine for your life, including your desire to get your body into shape.

## THE COURAGE TO BE HONEST

To get to the root of your fitness and weight problems, you must learn to use the sound mind God promises to give to you. That will involve getting brutally honest with yourself. Getting to the root cause of your fitness problems means exposing and renouncing the lies of the enemy that have held you in bondage to fear.

It has been my experience that many of my clients are ignorant of the cause of their fears. Unfortunately, many people remain ignorant and miserable because they refuse to be challenged in the areas of their faulty thinking and beliefs—the very areas where they need to change.

You must be willing to examine yourself and see what you are really afraid of in order to get to the root of your fitness problems as well as your overall well-being. God's Word actually tells you to examine yourself to see if you are walking in the faith: "Test yourselves to see if you are in the faith; examine yourselves!" (2 Cor. 13:5). It can't get any clearer than that! You need to examine yourself to see if you are full of faith—or full of fear. If you are full of fear, what are you afraid of? If you don't identify the fear, you cannot use the power of God's truth to defeat it. God's truth will always defeat fear and set you free!

When you think about confronting your fear problem honestly, you may complain, "But I have no idea what I'm afraid of! I don't know where to begin. All I know is that something is not right, and I keep doing what I don't want to do."

Remember, you have God's Spirit living inside you. It is His job to give you revelation about everything you need to know in life. Jesus declared that He would send the Holy Spirit and that "when He, the Spirit of truth, comes, He will guide you into all the truth" (John 16:13). If you ask Him, He will show you any root of fear that has embedded itself in your core beliefs.

Once you receive revelation of that rotten taproot of fear that holds you captive, then you must admit the truth of what you are really afraid of. With the revelation of God's truth comes a supernatural faith to defeat the lies and deception of the enemy that have tormented you with fear. As God reveals His love to you in a deeper way, you will be set free from that old fear and move into a higher quality of life. The Holy Spirit will show you what God has to say about your fear:

> There is no fear in love; but perfect love casts out fear, because
> fear involves punishment, and the one who fears is not perfected
> in love.
>
> —1 JOHN 4:18

God wants you to let Him pull out any root of fear that is holding you captive with its lies and deceit and replace it with the truth of His love and the peace of His Holy Spirit. He wants you to be free! But you have to have the courage to face your worst fears and get truly honest with Him and with yourself. You may respond, "I don't think I can do that, Ron. You don't know what I have gone through. I just can't think about all that stuff anymore."

I understand so well! This was one of the most difficult things I had to do to get well. Let me tell you how I did it. There were two things I had to do to have the courage to face the worst and most frightening parts of my life and me. First, I had to choose to trust God, believing that He would never hurt me or embarrass me; I had to believe that He would not lead me into a situation I could not get conquer successfully. Second, I needed to ask Him for the strength to face what I needed to face. I knew I couldn't do it in my own strength. I certainly wasn't smart enough! In prayer, I literally put my thoughts, emotions, and desires into His hands, surrendering to His love and power.

The moment I did this, one miracle after another began to happen inside me. It was astonishing! And guess what? That same process is still working in my life today. I didn't give God six months to "fix" me, become perfect, and never have another problem! Initially there were months of dealing with some hard issues until I finally broke free from tremendously destructive lifestyle issues. But even now, each day I wake up and surrender my life to God, talking with Him, loving my wife and family with Him, doing my work with Him. And every now and then He will point out another root of something that needs to be replaced with His presence.

Your spirit is the dwelling place of God and His love, life, and purity. But your soul—intellect, emotions, and will—is always being transformed! Every day you can grow in revelation of God and the reality of His presence in your life. As you grow in His love, you will reign in more freedom from that eternal and absolute taproot of His truth. Remember, holy root, holy branch (Rom. 11:16). Make the root right, and the fruit will be right.

## THE PRICE OF REVELATION

Have you ever wondered why you don't do what you want to do? And why you do what you don't want to do? Those unwanted behaviors come from root causes, as we have discussed. Those rotten roots came from the lies and deceptions you bought into as you were growing up. Revelation from God gives you wisdom and understanding to see the evil root and to identify the lies and deception that established it. The Bible is filled with the knowledge of God and His love for you. When you learn His ways, you are empowered by His Spirit to make choices that will enable change. Through revelation, you can learn to believe what God says about you and be transformed.

I don't want to sugarcoat the process, however. Getting to the root cause of your problem can be costly, involving a huge ordeal, especially if it includes the kind of trauma and dysfunction that Sue and Jim—and I—have experienced. Sometimes the price you pay for God's truth is sifting through painful memories and facing all your worst fears. But in order to get your body in shape, you first must get your heart and mind in shape.

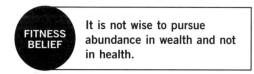

**FITNESS BELIEF** — It is not wise to pursue abundance in wealth and not in health.

One of the ways you do that is by choosing to immerse yourself in the truth of God's Word. Read it. Meditate on it. Believe it. And live it. That is how you receive revelation about who you really are and what God wants to accomplish in you and through you.

Remember my story? I began my process of "root-digging" in a completely confused mental state, just listening to television preachers. In the beginning I didn't really understand what they were saying, but every once in a while I felt something they said go deep into my heart. Their words were like seeds that grew in my heart until they exposed a painful, rotten root. Then, as I allowed the Holy Spirit to lead me through the process of exchanging the lie I had believed for His truth, healing and freedom came. I began to think differently, and my feelings changed. My desires for the rotten thing subsided, and my desire to be free was strengthened. Faith came into my heart and began to change my inner beliefs based on lies to those that were based on God's truth.

The Scripture declares that faith comes by hearing the word of Christ (Rom. 10:17). Faith comes to you by hearing the Word of God. That's why attending a Bible-believing church is important. It allows you to hear the Word of God preached with faith, which increases your faith to battle your rotten roots and destroy them effectively. In the same way that going to the gym and exercising three days a week results in physical fitness, hearing the Word of God strengthens your faith and spiritual fitness. You can't expect to get the same results by just thinking about going to the gym. You have to engage in the process. Faith will grow as a fruit in your life only as you feed it. If you choose to feed your fear, it will grow stronger. Whatever you give the right kind of nutrients to will grow stronger in your life.

Each time I listened to God's preached Word to me, each time I read His Word to me, and in the time I spent meditating about His Word to me, the truth fed my faith and filled me with hope that I could change, that I could be healed, and that I could live a purposeful, happy, healthy life. I began to learn this powerful truth of allowing faith to rule my life:

> Now faith is the assurance of things hoped for, the conviction of things not seen....By faith we understand that the worlds were prepared by the word of God, so that what is seen was not made out of things which are visible.
>
> —HEBREWS 11:1, 3

**FITNESS BELIEF**

**Become a builder of faith, friendships, and love before you become a builder of wealth and power. Your faith will sustain you, your friendships will support you, and love will never fail you!**

## IF YOU DON'T LIKE WHAT YOU ARE REAPING, CHANGE WHAT YOU ARE SOWING

Any gardener will tell you that all roots begin with a seed. One of the parables that Jesus used to explain how His Word works was the parable of the sower.

> The sower went out to sow his seed; and as he sowed, some fell beside the road; and it was trampled under foot, and the birds of the air ate it up. And other seed fell on rocky soil, and as soon as it grew up, it withered away, because it had no moisture. And other seed fell among the thorns; and the thorns grew up with it, and choked it out. And other seed fell into the good soil, and grew up, and produced a crop a hundred times as great.
>
> —LUKE 8:5–8

When His disciples asked Jesus what the parable meant, He explained the seed was the Word of God and that it fell on different kinds of hearts. Some hearts were not good soil, and the devil came and stole the words from their heart; others allowed the cares of life to choke the words out of their heart.

To continue the analogy, seeds can be planted in your heart by other sources as well. Lies, fears, and other destructive ideas can be planted in your heart by people, who are ultimately instruments of Satan. If you are really blessed, you have had people in your life who planted the truth—natural and spiritual—in your heart from the time you were born. But many have had all kinds of bad seed planted in their hearts over the years—some they had no control over, and some they invited out of ignorance.

The good news is that as a born-again believer, your eyes are open and you can choose to only allow the good seed of God's truth to be planted in your heart. It is important to recognize the false ideas and evil values the devil tries to plant in your heart—and to reject them. The moment you recognize that something is not right because it contradicts God's truth and principles, you must turn from it.

For example, in the area of health and fitness, the media bombard us with images of perfect bodies, sexual delights, and other enticements to convince us to become what they say is optimal happiness and success: *Join this club. Take these pills to melt away fat. Buy this piece of exercise equipment. Eat these nutritious fruit bars. Drink this incredible juice. Take these vitamins and minerals. Stop! Go! Run! No, what we meant was—walk!*

Some of these health regimens might be part of your answer, but they will not resolve your *root* problem. How do you see yourself? Do you see yourself through the eyes of God, who loves you unconditionally? Or do you see yourself through the eyes of every advertisement and media splash that flaunt their values before you? Is your motivation for life and happiness based on a deep longing to know who you were created to be? Or is your motivation to become the shallow, superficial image of the tabloids? Are you seeking self-gratification or truth?

These are tough questions you must begin to think about if you are going to get to the root of your health problems and achieve fitness through a healthy lifestyle. You can choose to plant and water the good seed of God's Word in your heart so that a strong, godly root will grow and drive out the rotten taproot the enemy planted. When the taproot of your self-image is immersed in God's love for you, allowing you to see yourself as He sees you, then you will reap a wonderful life! You can reign in life with His peace and joy and walk in great achievement, enjoying tremendous fulfillment.

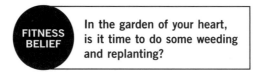

**FITNESS BELIEF** In the garden of your heart, is it time to do some weeding and replanting?

## THE DIVINE DYNAMICS OF CHANGE

Divine order is evident throughout creation. Our solar system operates in the divine order in which God created it to operate. If the planets in the solar system were out of order for one second, the earth would either burn or freeze, causing every living thing to perish.

Your physical body was also created to operate in divine order, in alignment with God and the truth of His Word. When human beings alienate themselves from God and refuse to live according to the Holy Scriptures, disease—*dis-ease*—occurs. You are only at ease spiritually, mentally, emotionally, socially, financially, and physically when your life is lined up with God and His divine wisdom through receiving revelation.

There is also a divine order to releasing the dynamics of change for your life. We have discussed the need to first submit your life to God in order to receive His divine revelation of truth. Revelation of God's truth to your heart and mind, as we have stated, is the first key to getting in shape God's way.

Then, His truth will change your thinking, freeing you from the evil root of fear and other destructive forces and empowering you to have a sound mind. Your sound mind will motivate you to make different choices. You will desire to make choices for health and life instead of hurt and death. Those choices will, in turn, transform your quality of life. When the spiritual roots you plant are God's truth, then you will make right decisions necessary to reign in life like Jesus!

This is the divine progression involved in God's divine order for health. Whatever you choose to line up with is what will determine your quality of life. If you are aligned with God's truth and life, your mind and heart will choose wisely. And your life will reflect the joy that comes from making wise choices.

It is time to begin to ask yourself some hard questions and make some difficult choices. Please remember that you are not alone in this! The Lord is right there to lead you through the inner healing process, give you new understanding that will set you free, and comfort you with His love and care.

Also, I am praying for you. I pray every day for all those who want to change their lives by getting in shape God's way. I know well what that means!

As you open your heart, allow the Holy Spirit to show you any evil roots in your life that need to be replaced with God's truth. If you need someone to help you with this, I encourage you to go to a pastor or Christian counselor whom you can trust. They will gladly help you to walk through this process.

Meditating on God's truth and allowing it to replace the rotten taproot in your heart will destroy the lies and deceptions that have held you captive to fear. Remember, God's Word is alive and powerful! You are not just reading and meditating on dead words on a page. You are planting supernatural seeds of God's love, wisdom, and strength into your heart. You are receiving His revelation—and His revelation is life giving and everlasting!

# TAKE ACTION

List all your fears you are aware of, even the smallest ones. You may have been deceived into believing that you can handle your "insignificant" worries, anxieties, cares, and intimidations on your own. But God's Word tells you to cast *every* care on Him (1 Pet. 5:7).

You may need more paper to elaborate on your fears. Take your time and be as specific and detailed as you can. Most important, listen to the Holy Spirit as you write. Let Him lead you and speak to you. Ask Him: What am I…

1. Extremely afraid of?

   _____

2. Intimidated by?

   _____

3. Worried about?

   _____

4. Anxious over?

   _____

5. Allowing to make me tense?

   _____

6. Caring too much about?

   _____

Take your list of fears, phobias, traumas, worries, anxieties, cares, and intimidations to the Word of God. Read His promises to deliver you from each of them. Again, if you need help with this, don't hesitate to go to your pastor, a counselor, or a mature Christian friend to get help. All of us need help!

75

# FOUR

## REFINING YOUR VISION—WHAT YOU SEE IS WHAT YOU GET!

LOSING WEIGHT AND GETTING in shape is almost always the No. 1 New Year's resolution. After the old year comes to an end with all the parties, delicious food, and sitting for hours watching football games and favorite holiday movies with family and friends, we are ready for a fresh beginning. But God isn't waiting for January 1. He's waiting for you to make a quality decision—at any moment—to receive His vision for your life.

Your focus may be on shedding pounds or developing muscular strength to get your body in shape; God wants to fill your spirit with His liberating truth. He doesn't just want you to lose weight physically and bulk up. He wants you to lose the wrong-thinking, bad-mouthing, making-terrible-decisions lifestyle to discover a powerful, world-impacting life of joy and productivity you cannot even imagine.

### LACK OF VISION RESULTS IN DEFEAT

Proverbs 29:18 says, "Where there is no vision, the people *perish*" (KJV, emphasis added). Another translation says, "Where there is no revelation, the people *cast off restraint*" (NIV, emphasis added). There is clearly a parallel here between a "lack of discipline" and "perishing." Relating this principle to physical fitness, we can state simply that you will not get into shape if you cannot restrain yourself from making bad decisions. And from our discussion of fitness beliefs, we can conclude that it is God's *vision* (also translated "revelation," as in the NIV) that gives you the supernatural ability to restrain yourself and become a disciplined person.

Let's say *your* New Year's "vision" is simply to get rid of twenty pounds, and that's what you set out to do. For weeks and maybe months you eat right and exercise. Finally you reach your desired weight. Without embracing the power of divine revelation and God's loving purpose for you, it is likely that you will not succeed in maintaining your fitness. Your next step will most likely be—maybe not immediately, but eventually—to cast off restraint once again and "perish." You will gain back everything you lost and likely even put on more weight than ever before. *Will*power without *God's* power is not enough to maintain fitness for life.

Conversely, if you learn to remind yourself of the vision of health and well-being God has given you, you will draw upon His life and strength dwelling in your spirit. That vision will enable you to cultivate self-discipline as a lifestyle. God will empower you to refuse to eat foods that are not good for you, take the time to exercise, and make right decisions that will lead to the fulfillment of your dreams. He will set you free from faulty beliefs, wrong thinking, and every kind of addiction, replacing them with desires for health and wholeness.

It is important to be able to articulate the vision God gives you for the abundant life and destiny He reveals to you. Refining your vision and identifying important goals that will help you toward success will also reveal things in your life that will hinder your fulfilling those goals. A simple vision statement, "writing the vision," can sum up the depth of revealed truth God has shown you about you. It is more than just a piece of paper with some clever, hopeful, or motivating words on it. Your vision statement represents your partnership with the Creator of the universe, a partnership with the goal of you becoming all you were created to be and doing all you were created to do! In this chapter I will show you how to succeed in life as you learn to refine your vision.

**FITNESS BELIEF**

"Vision looks inward and becomes a duty. Vision looks outward and become aspiration. Vision looks upward and becomes faith."[1] —Stephen Samuel Wise

## THE BASICS GIVE LIFETIME BENEFITS!

When I was a teenager, my parents introduced me to André Morrow. André, who was studying for his master's degree in sports education at the time, began teaching me the basic fundamentals of weight training. I think my parents' motive was to get me to use my boundless energy for something that was productive rather than destructive! I did not know at the time what a valuable life lesson André would teach me.

After driving for forty minutes, half asleep, I would arrive at 5:00 a.m. at André's workout room, ready for instruction. As I entered the small, rustic, equipment-filled room that looked like a playground for monkeys, I gazed at walls decorated with nothing but posters of half-naked bodybuilders. Some of them seemed to look at me with a scowl. I imagined them saying, "Look at that pathetic, overweight little boy."

As André drilled into me the basics of weight training and exercise over and over, I didn't realize that I was developing a trained eye to recognize the correct and incorrect postures of performing physical exercise. Since receiving his instruction, I have found that the basics he taught me never fail. When I see all the gadgets and equipment many people purchase to help them exercise, I am still reminded that it is in knowing the fundamentals that you will get great results every time. Repetition of the basic fundamentals is a principle you must carry with you forever in order to succeed in the area of fitness.

Basic fundamentals, faithfully and repetitiously followed, create solid foundations for successful habits—for life. This is important when your mind or body begins to fight you and say, "I don't want to exercise. I don't want to eat better." Establishing a habit of going to the gym or completing a specific exercise schedule will override your emotions or laziness when they protest. Amazing benefits result from simply establishing good habits based on the basic fundamentals of fitness. The same is true for the basic fundamentals of fitness beliefs.

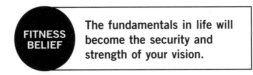

FITNESS BELIEF

The fundamentals in life will become the security and strength of your vision.

## STATING YOUR MISSION

It is time to become very practical and begin your personal how-to regimen for reaching your goals and fulfilling your dreams for life. You are going to begin by drawing a kind of map to keep you on track until you reach your destination. Without a map—a vision—you will not have a reference point to show you how to get where you are wanting to go.

It is imperative that you define your mission, stating the overall purpose that you are trying to achieve in life. Your personal mission statement will include a description of who you are, what your specific, measurable goals are for life, and a deadline for reaching them. Throughout this chapter, you will be given instructions for writing your personal mission statement as well as your vision statement. As you read on, you can be thinking about how to personalize your dreams and desires and learn to articulate them clearly so that you can make decisions based on your goals.

## VISION STATEMENT—A BASIC FUNDAMENTAL

> Give us clear vision that we may know where to stand and what to stand for because unless we stand for something, we shall fall for anything.[2]
>
> —PETER MARSHALL

We have discussed that revelation—vision—is a basic fundamental for getting healthy and fit and for maintaining health and fitness. You have learned that vision involves how you see yourself after God's revelation comes to your heart. Your vision of who you are determines your destiny, forms your future, and unlocks your passions and dreams, making them become tangible realities of a healthy lifestyle.

You could consider vision to be what is seen through the eye of faith. It is the inner view of reality that inspires your outward action. Faith sees what already exists in the spirit and brings it into the natural, physical world in which we live. That is the supernatural power of faith with a vision!

The dreams God has planted in your heart are reality to you. They exist in your spirit; they are *real*. Outwardly, they may not yet be manifest. When people look at you, they may not see the person you see on the inside of you—but God does! He has shown you who you really are and what you are to accomplish in your future. That personal vision involves a picture of a healthy and fit body as well as other life goals.

**Write it down!**

Motivational speakers and trainers often encourage their listeners to write down their vision for life. They say, "You must begin by writing a vision statement; otherwise, you will not know why you are doing what you are doing, what you are trying to accomplish, or your final destination." It was God who initiated the idea of writing a vision thousands of years before motivational speakers encouraged people to do it. The Lord told the Old Testament prophet Habakkuk:

> 'Record the vision and inscribe it on tablets, that the one who reads it may run. For the vision is yet for the appointed time; It hastens toward the goal, and it will not fail. Though it tarries, wait for it; For it will certainly come, it will not delay.'
> —HABAKKUK 2:2–3

God instructed Habakkuk to write the vision so that those who read it would know how to run toward it. He told him that even if it seemed to take a while before it came to pass, not to give up on it. In essence, he said, "Don't trip out! It will come to pass if you don't give up on it."

It is a simple fact that nothing becomes dynamic until it becomes specific. God was operating in this principle when He revealed His story in exquisite detail in the vision (revelation) we call the Bible. His written Word is the source of revelation and supernatural empowerment to equip all believers to know His will and fulfill His destiny for their lives. God reveals His reason for creating mankind and describes the nature and purpose for His creation through His written Word. And when Jesus conquered Satan's temptations in the wilderness, He declared to His enemy: "It is written" (Matt. 4:4). It is difficult to overestimate the power available to us in God's written Word.

Similarly, as you consider your God-given mission for life, you will be greatly helped by writing down specific goals and steps you must take to fulfill the destiny God has revealed for you. Writing the vision will become a fundamental basic to guide your how-to action steps and remind you what your ultimate goals are for life, making them specific in order for them to become dynamic.

For example, a fashion designer can have a vision of a garment and make wonderful sketches of how it will look. But making that sketch turn into something exciting and comfortable for you to wear will be determined by the details: choice of fabric, color of fabric, the pattern for cutting and sewing the fabric, and all the little notions that might be added, such as buttons, zippers, or other decorative items.

Consider the vision you have of yourself as the "sketch" of your destiny. It is the picture God has painted inside you, the reality of who you are and what you will accomplish. It is for you to make that sketch a true manifestation of God's destiny as you choose the "fabric" and other details that will make it a reality. Of course, unlike the fashion designer, we have a divine designer as our resource—the Holy Spirit—who will guide us even in the smallest detail.

In chapter 2 we discussed the fact that what you believe is what you become. The vision you have of who God is and who you are will determine the choices you make and thus the life you ultimately live. Your inner beliefs form your mission for life, what you *see* on the inside of you. The passion and desire that God reveals to you become the vision that you will begin to manifest in your life through the choices you make. Now, it is time to discover that God is in the details! Your understanding of those details, in the form of a written vision statement, will be a powerful tool for reaching your goals.

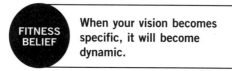

**FITNESS BELIEF**

When your vision becomes specific, it will become dynamic.

## GOD'S VISION BRINGS HIS PROVISION

After receiving the first key to getting in shape God's way—revelation—I soon realized God was asking me to open my heart and mind to receive His personal vision for me. He wanted to show me who I was, who I could become, and how He wanted me to help others.

God's purpose for imparting His revelation to you is multifaceted. He's not just giving you some beautiful ideas and concepts about His love and the power of His truth. He is birthing in your spirit a new vision of yourself and of the purpose for your life, which demands change in the way you think, the way you speak, and the way you behave.

As God makes Himself *real* to you, His purpose, beyond making you a whole person, is to empower you to convey His truths to others. That's why I asked you, as you began this book, to find someone who could walk this journey with you and to whom you could be accountable. Pouring your life into another person's life holds you accountable to your word and helps you build another life as well.

You might ask, "But what if God paints a picture of someone I don't want to be, or of something I have no desire to do?" I can assure you that will never happen! God's Word promises us that He will give us the desires of our hearts:

> Delight yourself in the LORD; and He will give you the desires of your heart. Commit your way to the LORD, trust also in Him, and He will do it.
>
> —PSALM 37:4–5

It is wonderful to trust God and His good plans for your life. He plants His desires in your heart that will lead to your happiness and the fulfillment of your destiny. In the process, you may not like everything He asks you to do. But I can tell you from experience that when you choose to have faith in Him and follow His instructions, you will always be amazed and thrilled at the results!

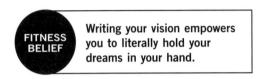

**FITNESS BELIEF**

Writing your vision empowers you to literally hold your dreams in your hand.

You will see again and again that God just wants to love you, bless you, and enable you to succeed and live a healthy life. It is comforting to know the promises of God are working for you. The writer to the Hebrews declared that Jesus is "the author and finisher" of your faith (Heb. 12:2, KJV). What a wonderful security He gives to His children. Not only does He begin a good work in you, but He also empowers you to finish it:

> For I am confident of this very thing, that He who began a good work in you will perfect it until the day of Christ Jesus.
> —PHILIPPIANS 1:6

As you learn to see how much you mean to God, you will begin to focus on His mission for your life, your family, and your career. Perhaps you would love to build an orphanage and travel the world doing humanitarian services. You may want to be the best husband and father or wife and mother you can be to your family. Others may desire to make life better for seniors in difficult life situations, discover a cure for a terrible disease, or find ways to ease the pain of today's troubled youth. Whatever your divine destiny—your mission—you need to be physically fit to fulfill it.

Once you determine your God-given mission and create your vision statement, you can be assured that His *pro*-vision will follow. Receiving revelation of your destiny is your most important goal for life. To state the obvious, the greatest enemy to your vision is blindness—not physical lack of sight, but mental and spiritual blindness.

Helen Keller suffered blindness and deafness from infancy. Yet, she later learned to lecture in several languages, and she enjoyed a distinguished career. On one occasion, she was asked this riveting question: "What could be worse then being blind?" Her answer astonished me! She replied resolutely, "Having sight without any vision."[3] Spiritual blindness is a result of ignorance of God's ways and His principles for living a life filled with vision.

God's way is always the best and the right way for you. His vision for you clothes your future with warmth in your frigid moments of fear. It brings a breeze of fresh air when the heat of the trials and frustrations of life seem unbearable. Contentment is possible only when you see the purpose for your life emanating from the heart of a loving, creative, visionary God.

In His Word, God paints a tremendous picture of who you are and the unlimited possibilities open to you. It is difficult to imagine the omnipotent power of God at work just for you. His Word reveals His character of love that desires only good for you:

> "For I know the plans that I have for you," declares the LORD, "plans for welfare and not for calamity to give you a future and a hope. Then you will call upon Me and come and pray to Me, and I will listen to you. And you will seek Me and find Me, when you search for Me with all our heart."
> —JEREMIAH 29:11–13

Your future is filled with hope as you seek to know the mission of God for your life. Your potential is based on God's unlimited resources—which means that all things are possible to you! You can trust Him to paint the most extraordinary pictures in your spirit of who you are and what your life can accomplish.

And you can trust God to be the *pro*-vision for the vision He places inside of you. When you get a glimpse of God's vision for your life, you lose all desire to do just any vision. You will not be satisfied for anything less than your God-ordained mission. And be assured that God's vision for your life includes your health. The beloved apostle John wrote, "Beloved,

I pray that in all respects you may prosper and be in good health, just as your soul prospers" (3 John 2).

Before you begin to write your personal vision statement, let's consider some of the main ideas that will help you articulate your vision of who God wants you to become.

## ALL YOU NEED IS LOVE

Every human being is searching, consciously or unconsciously, for the ultimate satisfaction of knowing they are loved. Because many have a faulty concept of what love is, they are disappointed time and again in their pursuit of satisfaction. God's mission for you is that you feel loved so that you will be able to love yourself and others. Jesus declared very clearly the greatest commandments to live by:

> "You shall love the Lord your God with all your heart, and with all your soul, and with all your mind." This is the great and foremost commandment. The second is like it, "You shall love your neighbor as yourself. On these two commandments depend the whole Law and the Prophets."
>
> —MATTHEW 22:38–40

The foundation of your mission must be love. Why? Because God is the source of your mission for life, and Scripture teaches that God is love (1 John 4:16). His very essence and character are love. Everything He says and does is motivated by love. Even His abhorrence and wrath toward evil is an expression of His pure love and goodness. Your heart aches for love because He created you to live in the spiritual environment of love. God's love dwelling in you acts as the very conduit through which God sends surges of strength to empower you to fulfill your destiny in life.

Not only will you find strength to love God as you submit your life to Him, but you will also learn to love yourself and to love your neighbor as well. Jesus taught that your neighbor is anyone who is in need. (See Luke 10:30–37.) As the love of God begins to fill your heart, mind, and soul, you will discover the joy of sharing that love with others. In that atmosphere of hope and love, you will begin to see the vision God has for your life.

The degree to which you love and respect yourself is the degree to which you will love and respect others. If you hate yourself, you will not be able to love anyone else. You must learn to think, speak, and act like God—and He thinks you are great! It will take time to cultivate this godly attitude, especially for those of us who haven't liked ourselves very much!

For a long time I saw myself as the fat kid who could do nothing right, so it took a while for me to believe what God believed about me. However, I kept reading and meditating on what He said about me through books like this and in the Bible, and one day divine revelation broke through in my mind about how special I was to Him. I felt His love for me deep inside of me. And guess what happened? The negative vision I had of myself totally changed! It was replaced by hope, peace, and confidence to move forward and achieve my dreams.

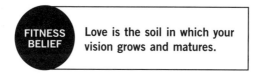

**FITNESS BELIEF** Love is the soil in which your vision grows and matures.

As you learn to walk in the love of God, the difficulties you face from time to time, whether physical, mental, or spiritual, will have less of a negative impact on you. You will understand that God has your best interest in mind. He tells you to cast all your care on Him, because He cares for you (1 Pet. 5:7). This will take practice, just like physical exercise, but you will learn to give your worries and troubles to Him and trust Him to work them out so that the weight of that problem does not overwhelm you.

Reaping a vision is the result of sowing a seed. You start by sowing a seed of truth into yourself. Consider one thing that you like about yourself. Try to choose a quality in yourself that is different from anyone you know. Understand that you are the best *you*! No one can be a better you, because there is no one else exactly like you!

As you pursue a new vision for your life, consider what it is you *love* to do. That is the starting point of learning to recognize the desires God has given you to fulfill as you learn to receive His empowerment for walking in your destiny.

Please take a moment right now to think of at least five things you like (or love) about yourself. Be specific. It can be anything from the way you clean your home or perform your job to your cute laugh, your tough handshake, or your passion for playing a sport. Give it some thought. Take a good, long look at yourself and consider who you are spiritually, mentally, emotionally, physically, socially, and financially.

Instead of looking at yourself with a critical, even condemning attitude, trying to find every weakness, flaw, fault, and error of your life, be honest and consider what you like about yourself. Then write your answers in the chart below.

FITNESS BELIEF | "A blind man's world is bound by the limits of his touch; an ignorant man's world by the limits of his knowledge; a great man's world by the limits of his vision."[4] —E. Paul Harvey

## WHAT I LIKE (LOVE) ABOUT ME

I love these things about me—these are my passion, my strengths:

_____

_____

_____

_____

_____

 **FITNESS BELIEF** **Love is the conduit God uses to empower us with His strength.**

### YOUR MISSION IS UNIQUE

There is no one like you. You are irreplaceable. And if you disappeared from the planet or never were born, there would be a big hole in the universe—a hole only you could fill. One of the most vivid demonstrations of this truth is in the timeless movie *It's a Wonderful Life*. If you haven't seen it, I encourage you to do so. An angel sent from God shows the main character, George Bailey, what the world and all the people he loves would have been like if he had never been born. In the end George is astonished at the difference his seemingly insignificant "little" life made to his family, friends, and community.

There are many things you were created to do on this earth. Yes, someone else could do these things, but they would never do them the same way you would do them. The mark they made would never be like the mark you would make. You are extremely important—and not just because you have things to do. If you never did anything, you would still be loved by

God and important to Him because you are the only you He has created! And He created you with a specific mission for your life.

I discovered the depth of this truth when our daughter, Sophia, was born. We may have many other children, but there will never be anyone like our Sophia! When I want to hug Sophia, she is the only one who will do. When I want to talk to Sophia, I don't go looking for anyone else. I want Sophia, and I love her whether or not she has made a right or wrong decision that day. Furthermore, I know Tia and I will feel the same way about any other children we have. Each one will be unique and special and will have his or her own mission in life.

This is a tiny glimpse of the way God feels about you. The effect of loving yourself as God loves you will impact you beyond your wildest dreams. Loving myself unconditionally as God loves me has given me an incredible love and compassion for others. My passion to see others succeed in realizing their dreams and becoming the person they long to be is one of the things I really love about myself. And I've noticed that others love that passion in me also!

I want you to step into the mission and reality of who you were created to be and what you were created to do *in the light of God's love for you*, understanding how He values you and honors you. When you do, you will love yourself more and have a healthy self-respect. People around you will be comfortable with you simply because you are comfortable with you. They will feel the genuine love you have for them and appreciate you. The quality of your life and your relationships will become richer and fuller as you discover and walk in the vision God reveals for your life.

*Human love* is a great motivator, faith-builder, and hope-inspirer; *God's love* brings that to the eternal, supernatural level. You cannot accomplish much of anything of real, lasting value apart from His love, and that includes getting your body in shape and staying in shape.

Your uniqueness is released when you get a revelation of God's love for you. This incredible truth establishes the reality of how loveable and valuable you are, which then pours out of your being in love and honor for other people. Your uniqueness and importance become obvious to you and to everyone around you as you share your life and vision with them.

You can see once again how revelation, in this case the revelation of your uniqueness, is key to getting in shape God's way!

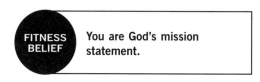

**FITNESS BELIEF** — **You are God's mission statement.**

## THE I's OF THE SPIRIT

As you prepare to write a mission and vision statements, let's consider what I call "the I's of the Spirit," which can become spiritual "eyes" to help you see yourself as God sees you. Answering the questions these five I's present will help you define and refine the personal vision God has placed inside you for life. As you consider each of them, I suggest you write your answers in preparation for formulating your vision statement.

### 1. Infusion

Infusion refers to something that permeates your life, sometimes altering it in a significant way. Whatever permeates your spirit and mind will determine decisions and behavior. It will shape your character and also your body. God's Word and His Spirit will alter your life for the good. What do you feel are some of the things that have infused you with their nature and have permeated your character? What, or who, has contributed to the essence of who you are, positively or negatively?

_____

_____

_____

### 2. Insight

Insight is simply your ability to see into yourself and honestly evaluate who you are and what makes you do what you do. In short, your insight gives you understanding of your character. Most often your character is revealed by who you are when you think no one is looking. Insight is important because it keeps you honest and helps you to avoid trouble. Using the insight you have, write the answer to "Who is the real me?"

_____

_____

_____

## 3. Influence

There are many sources of influence in your life. Does a physical substance or a spiritual revelation exert more influence over you? Where do you turn when you get hurt or just have no idea what to do? With whom do you spend your free time? What kinds of books, magazines, movies, TV programs, or other media sources do you indulge in? What influences are governing your life?

_____

_____

_____

## 4. Integrity

Integrity can be described as soundness of character. I consider integrity to be God's love in action in our lives. It is integrity that goes the extra mile, keeps promises, arrives on time, and returns what is borrowed. Even more importantly, integrity prays, believes, speaks, and acts according to the Word and the Spirit of God. Do you keep your word? Are you truthful? Do you ask forgiveness when you blow it? In what areas do you demonstrate integrity of character? In what areas to do you need to work to improve it?

_____

_____

_____

## 5. Impartation

The apostle Paul told believers that he and the apostles affectionately imparted the not only gospel of Christ to them but also their own lives. (See 1 Thessalonians 2:8.) Impartation is sharing and giving on a very deep level of interaction with your spirit and soul. Who is imparting into your life their character, habits, views, and opinions? Whom do you accept as your teacher, mentor, spiritual father and mother, brother and sister? What are you absorbing from the significant others in your life?

_____

_____

_____

As you have answered the above questions in preparation to write your mission and vision statements, review your responses. Which ones do you want to be a part of your mission for life? Which ones do you want to discard and change?

Remember, vision gives you *power*. Vision gives you the ability to pursue your dreams in a disciplined manner. For example, vision keeps you from falling off the wagon of your exercise program.

## HOW TO WRITE YOUR MISSION STATEMENT

As we have discussed, you were born for a purpose with a destiny to fulfill. As you receive revelation and insight of that purpose, you will discover the mission for your life that will satisfy you like no other. Before you write your mission and vision statements, I encourage you to pray this prayer:

> *God, please show me my mission and the vision You have for my life. Give me the strength to resist anything that will prohibit me from obtaining my health goals! I receive your strength and power over my physical body, my mind, and my spirit at this moment.*

To begin developing your mission statement, it will be helpful to compare these dynamic definitions:

- Your *mission* describes the purpose for which you exist, that for which God created you. It defines who you are and what you are about.

- Your *vision* defines where you want to be in the future, thinking optimistically, and the steps you need to take to get there.

- A *goal* can be described as the end toward which effort is directed, an aim. It is not the same as a mission or vision; it is part of fulfilling each of them.

Laurie Beth Jones, author of the best-selling book *The Path: Creating Your Mission Statement for Work and for Life,* gives three simple elements to a good *mission* statement:[5]

1. A good mission statement should be no more than a single sentence long.
2. It should be easily understood by a twelve-year-old.
3. You should be able to recite it by memory.

Beth Jones writes that the greater the mission, the more simply it should be stated. And she makes this very important point: "Forgetting your mission statement leads, inevitably, to getting tangled up in details—details that can take you completely off your path."[6]

Other personal development experts say that your mission statement should describe your best characteristics of who you are; have specific, measurable outcomes; and state a deadline. They allow for your mission statement to be as long as a paragraph, but state that it is important that your mission statement not to be too general, like stating "I want to be the best person I can be." It must reflect your unique qualities as a person with a mission and describe your goals for a specific time in the future.[7] Of course, the mission statement you are formulating is focused on the health you need to pursue in order to fulfill the destiny God has or is revealing to you.

To formulate a simple mission statement for getting in shape God's way, follow these steps:

1. List your strong desires, your passions, for life pursuits. Dream big: "If money were no object, I would…"

2. Now write a sentence or paragraph you can understand that describes your passions for life—your dreams and goals. Start like this: "My God-given mission for life is…"

3. Show it to a mentor or friend who can evaluate your mission objectively and offer input. Then make yourself accountable to this person to help you stay on track.

The following example will give you some specific direction:

Today, [date], I am beginning a program to get into shape—body, mind, and spirit—in which I will read the Word every day, work out three days a week, and eat to glorify God in my body every single day. I will learn to live a fasted life, refusing to indulge my senses with media or food that will kill me rather than give me life. In the next forty days, I will establish these new habits and determine to maintain them for the rest of my life so that I can reach my goal to become:

_____

_____

When a purpose of a thing is *not* known—destruction is inevitable.[8]

—MYLES MUNROE

## HOW TO WRITE A VISION STATEMENT

Your mission statement states your overall purpose for getting into shape. Your vision statement describes how your future will look if you achieve your mission. It includes specific goals and methods for reaching those goals, such as how much weight you want to lose and how you are going to do that. You articulate the vision of the person you will become as you determine to make all your decisions based on your mission statement—your overall purpose for life.

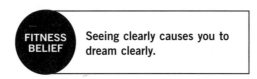

**FITNESS BELIEF** — Seeing clearly causes you to dream clearly.

As you read Part 3 of *Getting in Shape God's Way*, you will receive specific instructions for fulfilling your vision of who you want to become. The chart below gives examples of some specific goals you will want to include in your vision statement. If you have particular bad habits such as smoking, chewing, drinking, or other destructive lifestyle behaviors, you will want to include them in your list of things to eliminate in order to fulfill your mission in life.

# HEALTH AND FITNESS VISION STATEMENT

1. I want to reach and maintain my ideal weight of _____ pounds.
2. I want to lose _____ pounds.
3. I want to run a _____-mile race.
4. I want to climb a mountain.
5. I want to have enough stamina so I don't get tired playing with my kids.
6. I want to read the Bible through in one year.
7. I want to participate regularly in a good church and in Bible studies with others.
8. I want to limit TV to _____ hours a week to allow more time for reading and exercise.

## YOUR HEALTH AND FITNESS VISION BOARD

On paper or poster board with a minimum size of eight and one-half by fourteen inches, I want you be begin to cut out pictures that reflect your vision for health. Find a picture of a person whose body you like. Make sure it is similar to what yours can become when you are in shape. Cut off the head, and replace it with a picture of your head. Find photos of activities, sports, and fitness freedom you desire and place them on your fitness vision board. Add pictures of foods you need to include in your health regimen, as well as pictures of exercises and other activities. Surround yourself with visual inspiration of your health and fitness vision.

Creating a vision board enables the mind to be massaged and motivated by watching your vision come to pass. Surround yourself with visual images of your future, and they will help you become all you ever wanted to be.

In our home, my wife, Tia and I have a three-by-four-foot presentation board of our healthy lifestyle and our beautiful home we are building. We also included our kids' future and growth as well as character reminders of our manhood and womanhood. They are visual inspirations of the people we want to become—character traits we are intent on cultivating. We also show how many people we want to reach across the world and the tools we will use to reach them.

### Wall mounts

An important method to refining your vision is to envision—write it down and make it plain to see. In addition to your vision board, write your vision statement on three-by-five-inch index cards and place them on wall mounts around the house. The beauty of this kind of inspiration is that there are no limits to what you can dream. Personal development experts cite that people who take time to write down their goals achieve almost 80 percent of them.[9] Fulfilling a vision requires time, but as Scripture teaches, if we wait for them, they will surely come. You are a creator—of your personal dreams given by God!

Also, a powerful way to help you declare your vision daily is to add wall mounts to your vision board. These are simple text, designed on your computer in large poster-type lettering that you can read easily from across the room. For example, your wall mounts might read:

I am getting in shape God's way!

I love to exercise!

Today is the day of my healing!

I walk in divine health!

Make them fun to look at, and declare them aloud when you walk through the house and see them—daily.

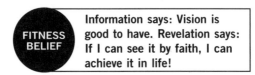

FITNESS BELIEF

Information says: Vision is good to have. Revelation says: If I can see it by faith, I can achieve it in life!

## STAYING ON TRACK

It is vital to write your mission from God in plain and simple terms, articulate it specifically as your vision, and then keep it before your eyes at all times—just to stay on track!

Without being specific about your vision for health and fitness, you can very easily be distracted from your heart's desire—your mission in life. When you don't base all your decisions on your stated mission, you can be led into projects and activities that are not really what you should be doing. They can be *good*, and your friends or co-workers or family might be really excited about them. But if all of your pursuits are not part of God's purpose for *you*, they will get you off track and keep you from fulfilling your vision. For example, you could forget what you need to be eating and how you need to be exercising to realize your mission—your overall purpose.

**Consider short- and long-term "harvests."**

Some of your vision goals will take time to "reap." Seeds will be planted now, but you will have to wait to enjoy their results. Others you can sow today and reap a harvest tomorrow; those are short-term "harvests." It will help you to stay on track if you will categorize your goals into short-term, midterm, and long-term projects, expecting to reap their results as harvests for which you have planted good seed into good soil.

*Short-term harvest*

Some goals can begin now and be accomplished immediately. For example, if your goal for exercise involves going to a gym, call or visit the gym as soon as possible to establish membership. If it involves walking, there is no time like the present to start; take a walk today. Instead of your fast-food lunch, eat a salad and soup or other healthy food. Begin to drink at least five glasses of water per day. Turn the TV off this evening and visit with a friend, read the Bible, or continue reading this book. These are instant gratification goals and will activate your vision immediately. You will begin to reap a harvest overnight for planting these short-term "seeds."

### Midterm harvest

It will take some time of diligently following your new eating plan and your exercise regimen to reap the midterm harvest of losing your first five or ten pounds. During that time, you will have to make decisions when other people invite you over for dinner and offer you coconut cream pie for dessert. You will have to plant the seed of saying, "No thank you; I am in training." Don't tell them you are on a diet; just refer to your new mission in life, and you will prick their curiosity. Then you can declare to them who you are becoming. It is these seeds that are planted in the midst of temptation to abandon your vision that will make you stronger and give you an inevitable harvest of new health habits for life. As you plant them, you will be empowered to overcome, temptation to overindulge will lose its power, and you will become more determined to fulfill your mission in life. The best harvest you will enjoy reaping is when your friends look at you and say, "Hey, are you losing weight?"

### Long-term harvest

Your long-term harvest will be reaped throughout your life as an unending supply of health and longevity, a quality of life that enables you to fulfill your mission and become the person you dreamed of becoming. Within eight to twelve months of sowing seed for short-term and midterm harvests, you will discover that you have lost the fifty pounds you had always dreamed of losing, your heart rate is strong, you have increased your breathing capacity (respiratory endurance), and walking up stairs is a joy instead of a dread. Your cholesterol has become stabilized, and your blood pressure medications are being reviewed by your physician because you are feeling young again.

If you keep your vision of a healthy and fit life and body always in front of you, you will not be led astray or get off track from what you should be accomplishing. I actually printed my vision statement and had it laminated so that I could carry it everywhere. It is something I can touch, something I can feel. I know it is real because it came from God. It helps me be more thoughtful about each opportunity that is presented to me and less likely to go off on a rabbit trail.

Life is too short for us to waste any of it, and yet we all do from time to time! Every New Year we make our resolutions to do better, and sometimes we are able to improve our lives. When God is in the picture, however, we enter a much more purposeful and powerful way of living. He keeps refining our vision as we grow spiritually until we are transformed into His image and can bring Him glory in every area of our lives. Our part is to obey the apostle Paul's instructions:

> I appeal to you therefore, brethren, and beg of you in view of [all] the mercies of God, to make a decisive dedication of your bodies [presenting all your members and faculties] as a living sacrifice, holy (devoted, consecrated) and well pleasing to God, which is your reasonable (rational, intelligent) service and spiritual worship.
>
> —ROMANS 12:1, AMP

 **FITNESS BELIEF** — It is important to always carry a picture of your healthy and well-shaped body in your mind.

## THE REALIZATION OF YOUR GOALS

The more you put into your body, the more you will get out of it. Continual effort in the small things will help you realize lasting change in the bigger things. As I have mentioned, *realization* is the desired outcome of *revelation*. Strengthening your vision requires meditating on what is *real*. Realization always begins in the heart, not the hand. This is why your core beliefs about yourself are critical to getting in shape and staying in shape.

Let me quote again the scriptural reality of this truth: as a man (or woman) thinks in his heart—so is he (Prov. 23:7). Without this first key—revelation—that can empower you and change the taproot of your belief system, you will not realize your dream and vision.

Prayer is a vital part of coming to the realization of your dreams.

Crying out to God with real concerns and asking for His help will bring His supernatural aid to you every moment of the day. When you pray for a healthy, strong body and a healthy lifestyle, you are asking according to God's will—His mission—for your life. According to His Word, He wants you to prosper and be in health as your soul prospers (3 John 2). And the apostle Paul's prayer can be yours as well: "Now may the God of peace Himself sanctify you entirely; and may your spirit and soul and body be preserved complete, without blame....Faithful is He who calls you, and He also will bring it to pass" (1 Thess. 5:23–24).

The realization will come as you pray and receive revelation and empowerment from God to apply the necessary decisions for your health. To pray and then gorge on doughnuts will nullify the effect of your prayer. The realization will follow the application of sound principles for health. You must pursue the goals in your vision statement with integrity, doing what you said you were going to do.

## Endurance Training Through Waiting

Patience is the sister to faith. If you believe in your mission and vision, patience will slap hands with faith and begin working on your behalf. As you begin to put your vision into play in faith that you will realize your dreams, you will need patience to see it manifest. For example, the day you begin to do exercises that will benefit you, there will hardly be a noticeable difference. Yet, as you continue to make the right decisions to fulfill your goals, all the while patience within you is perfecting the faith you have in the exercise and the dream you have in your heart. As you patiently endure the test of time that is required to see a difference, you are becoming a stronger person inside as well as realizing the manifestation of your health goals.

As you begin to walk in the goals written in your vision statement, here are a few things to remember:

1. Hold on! "Don't give up" must be the confession of your
   beliefs. Just for practice right now, try saying, "I refuse to give
   up!"

2. Dreams do come true.

3. You are what you believe. True faith means continuing to believe before you see. You don't need faith for what you can see. And you will see what you have faith to see.

4. Avoid despising your vision because of familiarity. Getting comfortable with your words on paper and choosing not to follow your vision is like getting lost on a road trip with the map on your lap.

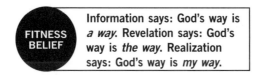

**FITNESS BELIEF** | Information says: God's way is *a way.* Revelation says: God's way is *the way.* Realization says: God's way is *my way.*

With your mission statement and vision statement in your hand, you are ready to begin functioning in the first key to getting in shape God's way: revelation! Hopefully, you will begin your short-term seed planting immediately and then be patient to reap the midterm and long-term harvest, making your decisions based on your God-given vision.

Now, you are ready to be introduced to the second key to living your dreams for a healthy future: *declaration!* The revelation of your new belief system will bring you to the realization of your health and fitness goals as you speak God's truth and begin to understand the divine power your words release into your life.

## TAKE ACTION

Now that you have written your mission and vision statement and have begun to create your vision board, you have powerful tools in your hands to pursue your goals for fitness and health. Use them, continue to add to your vision board, and create your wall mounts. Meditate on them, declare them, and fill your mind with the vision of who you are going to be—spirit, soul, and body.

# PART 2

**KEY #2: DECLARATION—IT MUST BE SPOKEN!**
*FITNESS WORDS*

# FIVE

# "LINGUISTICS" TRAINING—
# WORDS ARE POWERFUL!

**N**OW THAT YOU HAVE greater understanding of the first key to getting in shape God's way—revelation—you can begin to unlock your fitness freedom with the second key: *declaration*. Once revelation ignites in your heart, it sparks a *declaration* of the truth that has become real to you. It is simply a fact that you will say what you truly believe. Jesus declared this truth when He said, "For the mouth speaks out of that which fills the heart" (Matt. 12:34). It is equally true that what you say has the power to become the *reality* you live. God's Word teaches that the power of life or death is in the tongue (Prov. 18:21).

God is very interested in what you say and how you say it. God's Word confirms the truth that your words are so powerful they will determine your future and your health for your spirit, soul, and body. That is a very serious statement! Society in general has allowed the ropes that have held this nation together to sag by losing the integrity and value of the words we speak. Still, the principles of God cannot be violated without consequences; you will reap life or death depending on the words that come out of your mouth. This is what I refer to as the *principle of linguistics*.

## THE STUDY OF LANGUAGE

Linguistics can be defined simply as "the study of human speech including the units, nature, structure, and modification of language."[1] In many universities and colleges today, you will find a linguistics department in which you would study the place language holds in human cultures and societies. Linguistics majors study the history of words, the structure of a language, the sounds and phonetic combinations it uses, the way the words are put together to form sentences, and all the semantic nuances involved in language.

While the study of linguistics normally refers to the physical characteristics of language, I want to apply the term metaphorically to the impact spoken language has on every area of life. Every human culture has a distinct expression that articulates their worldview. Linguistics experts know that the language of a tribe or nation of people reveals not only their way of life but also their heart and soul—how they view themselves and the world around them, what they expect from this life, and their views of life after death.

God also has His own "cultural" language—His kingdom linguistics—that His children must learn to understand and speak in order to communicate with Him and cultivate relationship with Him. God's linguistic pattern, revealed in the Word of God, expresses His heart and mind through the words He speaks, the promises He makes, and the rewards or judgments He metes out for particular attitudes or actions.

I will never forget when I started hanging around "church people" after being involved in the hip-hop culture for years. I sat in church services feeling like a foreigner in a different culture. After all, the hip-hop culture has its own linguistics pattern—shop talk—that I had come to understand well. As I listened to church members around me, they seemed to be sitting on a cloud, talking a heavenly language. My heart responded to their faith-filled words with a hunger and longing to know what they meant; something deep inside me knew that what they were saying was true. But I could not understand their words; I was not familiar with their "Bible" vocabulary. This was a culture with which I was not familiar. For my heart to be satisfied with the truth they spoke, I had to become familiar with their linguistics pattern.

**Words inspire movements and change nations.**

We know that words and language allow human beings to express their thoughts and emotions, all the pains and joys we experience. Words give us insight into each other. They can also connect or disconnect us from each other. In his book *Words That Shook the World*, Richard Greene describes the powerful effect words can have:

> On a warm August afternoon in 1963, I stood in back of some 200,000 people as a young black minister began to speak. As Martin Luther King Jr. talked, I found myself pulled forward, along the length of the reflecting pool, up toward the Lincoln Memorial. Long before King reached his rhetorical climax—the "I have a dream" refrain that has long since become so familiar—the hair on the back of my neck (literally, I now think) stood up. Along with everyone in that crowd, I knew this was a Big Moment. And it was a moment etched into history by the power of the spoken word!...
>
> The appeal, however, is more than the gift of substance. Speech is the way we touch each others' deepest emotions and beliefs. A picture may be worth a thousand words, but a few hundred words, properly crafted, can move us far beyond the image. For all of the technological wizardry of computer graphics to dazzle the eye, I still believe nothing can match the power of the spoken word to move us to the core.[2]

Words are creative, powerful, and able to inspire great movements that change nations! Their power can be used for negative or for positive ends; they have power to create the reality they declare. As you learn to walk in revelation, you will learn to declare the truth about yourself and all of life. Your words can change your life positively and affect the very health and shape of your body. This is why the second key to getting in shape God's way is *declaration*. You are literally going to speak your way into a new body!

**FITNESS WORDS** — **You are what you speak!**

## THE ORIGIN OF WORDS

By now you know that Getting in Shape God's Way is a health plan based on faith in the Word of God. It is revelation of His Word that empowers you to change the rotten taproot of faulty beliefs about yourself and to dare to hope for fulfillment of your God-given dreams. So, it follows that what God's Word reveals about the power of your words is truth that, when declared in faith, can liberate you further and become a key to your ultimate success in life.

Do you realize that you are living in a world that was created by words? If you have read the first chapter of Genesis, you understand that God created everything by speaking it into existence. He said, "Let there be light" (Gen. 1:3), and light was. He said, "Let Us make man in Our image, according to Our likeness" (v. 26), and then He formed Adam and made Eve. The universe was created by God's words. The power of words out of the mouth of Almighty God has created a universe that still mystifies the greatest scientists!

Everything God does creatively becomes reality by His speaking into being what He is creating. How has God chosen to communicate with the human beings He made in His image and likeness? He communicates His love, His will, and His destiny for every human being through the same medium with which we were created—words. This supernatural phenomenon is the basis for understanding the creative power in your own words. What you are speaking is triggered by what you are thinking; what you are thinking is literally framing and creating your world you are living in today. The apostle Paul admonished all believers:

> Finally, brethren, whatever is true, whatever is honorable, whatever is right, whatever is pure, whatever is lovely, whatever is of good repute, if there is any excellence and if anything worthy of praise, let your mind dwell on these things.
>
> —PHILIPPIANS 4:8

## CHRIST, THE LIVING WORD

The Word of God is more than just words written on a page. The Bible describes Jesus as the living Word:

> In the beginning was the Word, and the Word was with God, and the Word was God. He was in the beginning with God. All things came into being by Him, and apart from Him nothing came into being that has come into being...And the Word became flesh, and dwelt among us, and we beheld His glory, glory as of the only begotten from the Father, full of grace and truth.
>
> —JOHN 1:1–3, 14

The Bible reveals that Jesus is the Word of God who came to Earth in human form. John, the beloved disciple who had touched the heart of Jesus like no other, reveals the precious truth that Jesus is the Word of God made flesh. When He lived on Earth, Jesus was literally the living Word, walking and talking with men and women like us. He was the practical, everyday, how-to-live-your-life, perfect Man Word. He demonstrated to the world as well the always-in-the-best-of-health, physically fit, and capable-of-doing-miracles Word!

The New Testament declares that Jesus is the exact representation of the nature of God and that He "upholds all things by the word of His power" (Heb. 1:3). When Jesus faced the temptation of the devil in the wilderness, He also defeated him by the power of the Word. His response to the evil one, not once but three times, was, "It is written..."

When you read and study the language of the Bible, you are learning the language of God and His design for your life—the best and most wonderful life you can live. At the same time you are getting to know Jesus—the living Word. You receive revelation of the "culture" of heaven through God's Word. As you absorb God's love, compassion, zeal for righteousness, and peace, your God-given instinct is to declare it. When you speak that revelation, you make a declaration of what you know to be eternally true and real. From the first revelation you received, that you needed a Savior, came the faith to be born again and filled with the Holy Spirit. In that moment, God gave you the supernatural desire and ability to communicate in His language—and to sit on clouds!

Leaping within me as I write these words is the wonderful revelation of just how powerful the words you speak are to create your reality. I like to say that the one underdeveloped muscle my clients have had in common is their tongue! Of all the fitness programs I have studied, I have never found one that places emphasis on the effect your words have on your health. This principle of linguistics defines the true power behind getting in shape God's way. Revelation gives you creative power when you take the next step in declaration of the truth. Take a look at God's Word to grasp this truth:

> My son, give attention to my words....Keep them in the midst of your heart. For they are life to those who find them, and health to all their whole body....Put away from you a deceitful mouth, and put devious lips far from you...and all your ways will be established.
> —Proverbs 4:20–26

> Pleasant words are as a honeycomb, sweet to the soul and healing to the bones.
> —Proverbs 16:24

The Scriptures declare that the words and promises of the Lord are pure words, like silver refined in an earthen furnace, purified seven times over (Ps. 12:6). God is making clear to all who will hear that the integrity of His Word to you is so powerful that it will literally heal your body!

## A Tongue Problem

Time and time again I have seen the same recurring problem with people who want to experience freedom in their bodies but who could not come to terms with that little "rudder" inside their mouth—their tongue. James, the brother of Jesus, lived in the same house with Jesus as they grew up. James wrote a little book of the New Testament that does not seem to get much press. In it, he emphasizes the power of the tongue. Perhaps he was reflecting on his older brother's perfection in speech when he wrote:

> For we all often stumble and fall and offend in many things. And if any one does not offend in speech [never says the wrong things], he is a fully developed character and a perfect man, able to control his whole body and to curb his entire nature.
> —JAMES 3:2, AMP

What a powerful statement. Control your mouth, and you control your whole body. In these few verses of Scripture we have discovered that our words have the power to create health and give us control over our entire life.

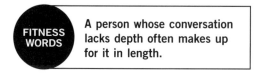

**FITNESS WORDS** A person whose conversation lacks depth often makes up for it in length.

**The answer is right under your nose.**

One of the best and worst days of my life occurred after I chose to submit to God in my family dilemma. It was the day Tia told me that she wanted us to receive marriage counseling. I was shocked at her words, but I felt relief at the same time. In my heart I knew I wasn't relating to her properly, but pride had made me cling to the deception that we had a perfect marriage. God knew I had some growing up to do, and He used Tia's confrontation to help me along in the process!

Maybe you are reading this book because someone who really loves you finally sat down with you and told you the truth, that they were concerned for your physical well-being. You may have felt shocked, embarrassed, and relieved all at once. You knew the time had come to face the reality of your situation and make some deep changes. After completing your mission and vision statements from Part 1, you may feel you have come to terms with some of the issues in your heart. Now it is time for you to come to terms with them—with your *mouth*. Declaring your mission and activating your vision for life is the next step for you to take to get in shape God's way. In order to do that, you may have to confront some of the things your mouth has been saying.

My mouth happened to be the central issue that was completely out of control in my relationship with Tia. The answer to my marital problems was right under my nose! During the first session with the counselor, I sat there thinking, "What am I doing here? How did I get to the place where this was necessary? I thought I knew it all!" Then Tia began to open up about the way I was talking to her. I discovered that my words hurt her and often frightened her. She had reached a point in our relationship that she was afraid to discuss certain problems with me because of what my reaction might be.

*Whew!* I had no idea how my words were affecting her. I was oblivious to her feelings and the impact my attitudes were having on our marriage. Then I remembered that God declares in His Word there is creative power in our words, power for death or life. I also remembered some of the things I had said to her—and to others. I realized that too many times I had spoken terrible things to someone I loved so much.

I felt like the person whom Scripture declares as "one who speaks rashly like the thrusts of a sword" (Prov. 12:18). How I longed for the second part of that proverb to become my reality: "But the tongue of the wise brings healing." The picture James paints of the unruly tongue flashed through my mind:

> And the tongue is a fire, the very world of iniquity; the tongue is set among our members as that which defiles the entire body, and sets on fire the course of our life, and is set on fire by hell.... With it we bless our Lord and Father; and with it we curse men, who have been made in the likeness of God.
>
> —James 3:6, 9

I thought of the man who is satisfied with good by the fruit of his words (Prov. 12:14) and understood that the opposite is also true. I didn't like the meal I was eating at the beginning of that first counseling session! However, when you allow God to deal with you in a brutally honest fashion, it all works to your good.

During those sessions, I discovered that I had to learn to love myself so that I could love Tia the way I wanted to love her and the way she deserves to be loved. In practical terms, that meant I had to change the way I spoke about myself and about her, as well as the way I talked to her and other people. I was merely speaking disrespectfully because I had no respect for myself. This was a hard reality that I had to learn. As I gained understanding, I began to learn to speak the truth from my heart, but kindly, in love. My self-respect and my respect for my wife grew immeasurably with the acceptance of the truth I was learning.

Similarly, it is also a hard reality to learn what is holding you back from losing weight and getting into shape. Perhaps you need to learn to respect yourself, as I did. Meditating on your vision statement and declaring it to be the reality you want to live will help you to go forward toward the freedom you desire. Respect for yourself, your health, and your regimen for improved health must be a high priority for your life, just as my marriage is for me. In both situations, our mouths have everything to do with the outcome. Whether we are considering the words we speak and how we speak them—what comes *out* of our mouths—or the food we eat—what we put *into* our mouths—the answer to our freedom is right under our nose.

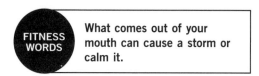

**FITNESS WORDS** — What comes out of your mouth can cause a storm or calm it.

That day in the counselor's office was the day I started on a new journey in learning to talk right, which taught me a lot about how to help my clients—and you—become people who can fulfill their dreams. Of course, my marriage is a journey for life. Learning to communicate with my wife and watching our love grow, as a result, is a daily process. It is wonderful when I succeed and painful when I fail. But it is giving me unlimited compassion for you! So I am choosing my words carefully as I write, because I want you to reach your God-given potential in every area of your life, and particularly in the area of your health and fitness.

## BIG MOUTH

God's way of optimizing your health and solving your physical, mental, or spiritual problems often utilizes two tiny muscles that can cure *big* problems (and shrink *big* bellies). The entire time I attended those marital training sessions, I couldn't help thinking that while I had learned that my mouth could be controlled to get my body and life into shape, it was my mouth that was actually making my marriage and parenthood worse. The words of my mouth had indicated to my wife that I did not love her. I really did not know the bad effect of my words at the time on her psyche. The apostle James continues his discussion of the tongue by saying, "But no one can tame the tongue; it is a restless evil and full of deadly poison. With it we bless our Lord and Father; and with it we curse men, who have been made in the likeness of God; from the same mouth come both blessing and cursing. My brethren, these things ought not to be this way" (James 3:8–10).

Though I had never wanted to admit to having a problem with this Scripture passage, I had to learn the hard way—through pain. My marriage coach looked at me one day and said bluntly, "There comes a point in either partner's life when the damage of words destroys the relationship—and it's too late." God warns us about our "big mouth" and shows us in His Word how to submit our untameable tongue to His lordship to allow the Holy Spirit to be in charge of what comes out of our mouths. The psalmist prayed, "Let the words of my mouth and the meditation of my heart be acceptable in Thy sight, O LORD, my rock and my Redeemer" (Ps. 19:14). And he determined to keep from sinning with his mouth: "I will guard my ways, that I may not sin with my tongue; I will guard my mouth as with a muzzle" (Ps. 39:1) The apostle James concludes his analogy of the tongue with these instructions:

> Does a fountain send out from the same opening both fresh and bitter water? Can a fig tree, my brethren, produce olives, or a vine produce figs? Neither can salt water produce fresh. Who among you is wise and understanding? Let him show by his good behavior his deeds in the gentleness of wisdom.
>
> —JAMES 3:11–13

True wisdom is demonstrated by those who humble themselves to the truth of this message and determine to train their tongue, speaking words of life and not death. As I grasped this transforming key of the power of my words, my marriage immediately began to turn around for good.

If your partner is obese and you find ways to call him or her "fat" or make them aware of their weight problem in a negative way, the power of your words will create a negative effect in their psyches. Not only will your relationship be impacted in a negative way, but also the hurt your words cause can discourage them and make them say, "Oh, what's the use!" or "I'll show him [or her] it doesn't matter what they say!" as they binge to find comfort in food once again. *Don't do it!* Don't say anything to a person you love that you don't want them to become. Calling a person fat, stupid, thoughtless, or other negative characteristics sets in motion negative, spiritual forces that "create" your verbal "curses."

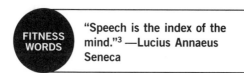

**FITNESS WORDS** — "Speech is the index of the mind."[3] —Lucius Annaeus Seneca

Even today it is a common practice in homes around the world to speak a blessing over their meal. As they say a simple "grace" over their food, thanking God for it, people are acknowledging that God gave them food to be a blessing to their bodies. As they speak blessing over their food, they incur positive benefit of the nutrition it offers to sustain their bodies in health. Unfortunately, if you are eating unhealthy food that is causing high blood pressure, diabetes, heart disease, or a terminal illness, no amount of saying "grace" will change its devastating effects on your body. The only way you can be set free from its disease-causing reactions is to *stop eating it*. Don't put it in your mouth!

You choose many times a day to bring blessing or cursing on yourself and on others by what comes out of your mouth and by what you put into your mouth. There is something to be said for the phrase "big mouth" when it comes to the power it holds over your entire life. Of course, as we have discussed, your mouth is ultimately an instrument that expresses your thoughts, which are motivated by the beliefs in your heart.

As we consider the power that declaration has to set you free, think about ways you speak that you need to change. Choose to create positive blessings and atmospheres wherever you can simply by learning to control your tongue.

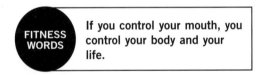

**FITNESS WORDS** If you control your mouth, you control your body and your life.

## BRAIN POWER

Even the physical brain is affected by words you speak and attitudes you express. Your brain is made up of a latticework of connections between brain cells. These connectors are called *synapses*. A synapse connects one brain cell to another and acts like a telephone wire, taking messages throughout the brain, which in turn send the messages throughout your body to evoke the appropriate response—hence the phrase "body language."[4]

Research has revealed that half of the synapses you are born with began to die off by the time you were ten years old. But never fear! There are still about 500 trillion synapses left to last the rest of your life. It is believed that the reason there are so many synapses at birth is so that the infant and young child can have a mental boost to receive input and adapt to the environment in which they are born. It is like the rocket booster that separates from the space shuttle as soon as the shuttle is safely and completely launched. It would only be more weight and baggage to carry for the rest of the voyage.[5]

It seems that these brain synapses, which communicate to all the brain cells, are activated and altered by two main stimuli: words and chemical substances. Using technological imaging devices, doctors have observed how the brain processes thoughts and various drugs.[6] A study done at the University of California at Los Angeles showed that behavior therapy produced the same kind of physical changes in the brain that drugs produced. Scientists are calling this "the talking cure." UCLA psychiatrist Dr. Lewis Baxter said that this study revealed the power words have to physically change the brain.[7]

Science is catching up with the truth revealed in the Word of God: "As he [a man] thinketh in his heart, so is he" (Prov. 23:7, KJV). And Jesus declared, "For out of the abundance of the heart the mouth speaketh" (Matt. 12:34, KJV).

## THE PURPOSE OF THE TONGUE

As you know, for our discussion I am referring to the tongue in two dimensions. First, I have described it, literally, as the physical muscle (actually sixteen muscles) in the mouth. Second, I have described it metaphorically as the instrument that helps you declare the beliefs of your heart. The physical tongue is sometimes considered in biology as the strongest muscle in your body. Depending on the specific definition of "strength" used, there are other muscles that may exhibit greater strength than the tongue. However, like the heart, the tongue is always working. Made up of groups of muscles, the tongue helps in the mixing process of foods, it binds and contorts itself to form letters, and it contains linguinal tonsils that filter out germs. Even when you are sleeping, your tongue is constantly pushing saliva down the throat.[8]

Physically, your tongue is the central organ that relates to what you put into your mouth, which will affect your overall health. Spiritually, it is also the central organ that, according to Scripture, reveals the abundance of your heart through the words that you speak. This reality gives greater understanding of the scriptures that declare life or death is inside your mouth—in the power of the tongue!

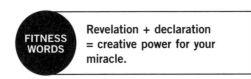

**FITNESS WORDS**

Revelation + declaration = creative power for your miracle.

I once heard a minister say, "If you don't know what your mouth is for, you shouldn't use it." This is a sobering statement, and true, because your tongue is either bringing you life or death—physically and spiritually. The mouth was designed by God to do four basic things:

1. Take food, drink, and air into the body.
2. Release creative words into the earth.
3. Communicate with others.
4. Express affection with a kiss.

As you consider these functions of the mouth, you will be able to evaluate your strengths and weaknesses in using the power of declaration to change your life and the lives of others.

## SPEAKING HEAVEN INTO EARTH

The living Word—Jesus—gives you the wisdom and strength to live life the wonderful way He ordained, when He said He came to give us life more abundantly (John 10:10). The apostle Paul wrote to believers, "You are in Christ Jesus, who became to us wisdom from God, and righteousness and sanctification, and redemption" (1 Cor. 1:30). Christ, the living Word, fills you with wisdom for life situations, imparts His righteousness to you, and empowers you to live holy, sanctified lives.

Living the good life—the God life—includes keeping your body in great shape by eating and exercising properly. Embracing the promises of God will give you the strength to persevere and to do what you need to do to become healthy and fit and to live that way. The Bible declares that strength comes from the joy of the Lord: "For the joy of the LORD is your strength" (Neh. 8:10). And Jesus said, "These things I have spoken to you, that My joy may be in you, and that your joy may be made full" (John 15:11). The words of Jesus fill your heart with joy, which gives supernatural strength and fortitude to meet whatever challenges you face. And that is the way God wants you to feel—strong, joyful, and whole!

Your joy will begin to overflow simply by reading the Bible, studying the language of God, and learning to think and talk like Him. Imagine all you could do if your heart and mind were filled with joy instead of anxiety, anger, or depression. You would have unlimited energy and strength. You would be continuously inspired and motivated to do the right thing and make the right decisions. You would love yourself, which would empower you to love others. And self-discipline would become a joy instead of a dreaded duty.

Jesus, the living Word, taught His disciples to pray so that we would have joy in our lives. It has been considered a blueprint for all prayers, and for some it has become *the* prayer. For years as a weekend Catholic I recited what we call *the Lord's Prayer*. All over the world, in Alcoholics Anonymous and other twelve-step groups, people pray this prayer together. As you read this model prayer of Jesus, as a student of the Bible, consider the power of it relating to your declaration of your mission for life:

Our Father which art in heaven, Hallowed be thy name. Thy kingdom come. Thy will be done in earth, as it is in heaven. Give us this day our daily bread. And forgive us our debts, as we forgive our debtors. And lead us not into temptation, but deliver us from evil: For thine is the kingdom, and the power, and the glory, for ever. Amen.

—MATTHEW 6:9–13, KJV

As you pray this model prayer, you are acknowledging that God is in heaven and that His name is hallowed, which simply means holy. Then you are agreeing with His will for His kingdom—heaven—which is love, joy, and peace, to come to this earth. You ask Him to provide what you need to sustain life and to help you live in love toward others and free from sin. Do you really believe the words of this prayer?

The disciples came to believe that whatever Jesus said was absolute truth, forever settled in heaven, and would certainly happen. And Jesus is telling them to ask God to make their lives to be like heaven on earth. They must have been blown away, as we are, when we consider that possibility. What would life look like if it were lived in the kingdom of God as it is in heaven?

What is heaven on earth for you regarding your physical body? If you were in heaven right now, how you would feel about yourself? Obviously, you would be in the best possible shape in your heavenly body (1 Cor. 15:42–44), and you would really like yourself, living in an atmosphere of pure love! As you read the Word, think about the words God chose to use declare His loving truth. Become a student of the linguistics of the Bible, and you will discover the character of God, His kingdom, and His promises for your health. More and more, you will be filled with joy, a supernatural joy that comes straight from God's heart to your heart. In that joy you will find the strength to get into shape inside and out—and stay in shape. Living in optimum health will become like heaven on earth for you.

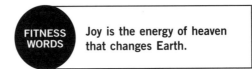

FITNESS WORDS

**Joy is the energy of heaven that changes Earth.**

## LET'S GET REAL!

So, you say, "Come on, Ron, let's get *real*. Heaven is heaven, and Earth is still full of a lot of problems and difficulties. I'm not perfect, and I have a lot to deal with here."

I hear you! But I am getting *totally real* with you. It is important to declare the answer and not just the problem. If you insist on declaring the problem and denying the power of God's Word, you will "create" your future to look like the problem. You must understand that your mouth has the God-given ability—for good or evil—to speak your future into existence. Do you want to bring the kingdom of God to the earth and experience heaven on earth, or do you want to continue living the way you have been living—in the problems of the earth? Whatever you declare is what you will have.

### Speaking death or life

According to the proverb you learned as a child, "Stick and stones may break my bones, but words will never hurt me." I am sure that you have long since discovered that proverb to be a lie. Psychology and medical science concur that words can have devastating effects on mental and even physical health. They have discovered the truth of the Word of God, which declares, "Death and life are in the power of the tongue, and those who love it will eat its fruit" (Prov. 18:21).

Incidents are recorded of people who have expressed a "death wish" and have suffered an untimely, tragic death. Anna Nicole Smith stated that she would die young like Marilyn Monroe; she even planned her burial years before she died.[9] She was thirty-nine years old when she died. I heard a minister relate the story of a young man he knew who declared continually that he would not live a day past the age of forty. He died at age thirty-nine. It is simply a fact that a spiritual law is set into motion when you declare, out of the abundance of your heart, words of life or death. Your psyche and your physical body begin to respond to the declaration of your own lips to bring it to pass.

If God were sitting with you right now, His loving eyes looking into your eyes, His hand holding yours, I think He would say something like this:

> I want you to understand the power of the words that come out of your mouth, especially if you are speaking what I am speaking in My Word. I gave creative ability to your words because this was My original intention for mankind. You are created in My image, and I created the heavens and the earth with My Word. Now I want you to change your world by speaking My words over your life—body, soul, and spirit. You bring heaven to Earth by what you declare with your mouth. I want you to get a revelation and make the declaration that in My name you have the power and authority to call heaven into your health and every area of your life.

As your coach, my prayer right now echoes what I believe God would say to you if you could hear His heart for you. I pray you will see just how *real* the power is in the words that you speak. If you grasp this truth, you will be enabled to change the way you talk, the way you live, and the fitness of your body. Over the years I have coached many clients with a variety of physical problems. As I said, the one constant in all of my clients has been their underdeveloped and untrained muscle—the tongue! Negative self-talk is the greatest enemy to their desire to experience a fit and healthy body.

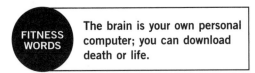

**FITNESS WORDS** — The brain is your own personal computer; you can download death or life.

## GET YOUR HEART RIGHT AND YOUR BODY WILL FOLLOW

I had a client I will call Nancy, who was raised in a good home. However, a tragic event happened to her as a child. After running away from home, she was beaten and raped. This traumatic experience affected her self-perception drastically. She ran away from home as a teenager, searching for something that would make her happy. She turned to drugs and alcohol to find happiness.

Nancy could never really believe in herself, even though others had told her she was talented, attractive, and could achieve great things in life. She could only hear that voice in her head that told her to keep killing her emotional pain with drugs and alcohol—and food. Although she wanted to be loved, her mind remained tormented and distrustful relating to men. Her way of coping was to eat anything she felt like eating, thinking that being overweight and unattractive would keep men away from her. It was her way of avoiding the problem altogether.

Nancy's mental state deteriorated to the point that she was in therapy, where she was told that she needed shock treatments. At that moment she was gripped by such fear that she cried out, "Jesus!" She could not have spoken anything more powerful, for it is in His name that we have all authority over every spiritual, mental, emotional, and physical problem. Someone asked Nancy if she could make room for God in her heart. She said yes. She asked Christ to come into her heart, and her troubled soul received His peace. Nancy describes that experience as the moment God reached down and pulled her out of hell and established her in a life that is more wonderful than she could ever have imagined. One word changed Nancy's life forever.

### No magic here

The reality in the power of declaration is not magic. There is no formula to mumble to make problems go away. I am sharing with you the power in God's Word that becomes yours as you declare it in faith. I am talking about the power of God living in you and renewing your mind to the linguistics of God's kingdom, about learning to speak the truth, and about allowing the power of the Holy Spirit to walk your talk. God literally becomes a comforter, a strengthener, and an advocate when your heart is yielded to the Holy Spirit. It is no longer the cravings of your flesh—your body and mind—that are calling the shots. You have a choice to yield your body, soul, and spirit to God and allow the power of His Word to govern your life. In that way, you can experience heaven coming to Earth as the will of God is fulfilled in your mission for life.

## SPEAKING CHANGE FROM THE INSIDE OUT

Nancy is just one of many clients who have discovered the key of declaration and experienced a miraculous cure. When she asked God to take her heart, she had no idea that the effects of shock treatment could be cured by God. She began searching the Scriptures to find out just how much God loved her. As her revelation grew, she began to *speak it out* of her mouth daily. As she began to declare what God said about her, she experienced the reality of His love for her in a greater way. As she declared the truth she was receiving in her spirit, she received the healing power of God's "shock treatments." Her mind, emotions, and body began to be healed of the trauma and pain of her past. It was a heart thing, not a head thing.

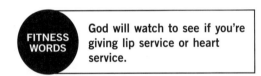

**FITNESS WORDS** God will watch to see if you're giving lip service or heart service.

What Nancy was declaring about herself created the greatest change in her life. She stopped talking about how frightened she was, how overweight she appeared, and how unloved and ugly she felt. Instead, she rejected those ideas and began to speak the truth that was *real* to her, coming into her spirit from the Word of God. As she declared that she was loved by God, she became more confident about loving others and was able to receive love from other people. Both mental health and emotional health were the wonderful result.

Nancy trusted God's Word, believing that if she changed the way she talked about herself, He would give her health and enable her to stay healthy. Furthermore, she believed she could be slim and look good without being afraid. She began to lose weight as soon as she stopped saying all the negative things she had been programmed to believe through the years. She accepted the good things God had to say about her—and He didn't say she was fat, ugly, and unlovable. When she began to declare God's truth about herself, what came out of her mouth conquered and reshaped the rest of her—so much so that today she has dropped almost one hundred pounds, she is completely sane, her blood pressure is normal, and she has become a traveling minister, giving hope to other men and women around the world who are suffering much of what she suffered. I am truly proud of her constant desire to achieve and never give up. She is an inspiration to me personally, and I can see the fruit of getting in shape God's way unfolding in her life!

## THE SOUND OF WORDS SHAPE YOUR LIFE—AND BODY

Hearing the call of a loved one is the most exhilarating sound that our ears can hear. When I hear my wife, Tia, or my young daughter, Sophia, call out to me, my heart thrills to hear their voices. I eagerly wait to hear what they have to say to me, and I hang on every word they speak. Their words are life to me. In turn, I have learned to choose my words carefully when I speak to them. I want my mouth to speak words to them that will bless them in every way imaginable.

God is the expert linguist. When He speaks to us through His Word, or when He speaks to us through the Holy Spirit inside us, His words always bring us peace and joy. That is true even if His words are bringing correction to us. So, when we speak what He has spoken to us, the words in our mouths have tremendous creative power for good. Our own souls and bodies benefit. The people around us benefit. Even the atmosphere we live in is changed for the better by the power of God's words!

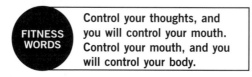

**FITNESS WORDS**

Control your thoughts, and you will control your mouth. Control your mouth, and you will control your body.

127

**Sounds affect infants.**

The sound of words, spoken in truth and love, is music to the heart and mind. Words also affect the health of the physical body and the brain. It is a scientific fact that your brain functions are affected by the sound of words and the images those words produce. In his book *Inside the Brain*, Robert Kotulak writes, "We didn't know that spoken language is such a powerful brain builder."[10] Kotulak also said that they had recently discovered that a lack of words can stunt the infant's forming brain. And it made a difference if the words were spoken with love and had meaning to the parent or caregiver. Words coming from a television or radio did not make as much impact on the infant's brain. Scientists have also discovered that the number of words an infant hears each day dramatically boosts their intelligence as well as their ability to socialize.[11]

It also appears that language is imprinted in the newly forming brain of an infant very quickly. They learn the sounds of their native language by the age of six months, and they attach meanings to the words of their language by the time they are one year old. In short, words have a tremendous impact on the human brain from the time of birth.[12]

When babies begin to talk, they speak from the reservoir of words and sounds they have heard from the moment they were born. They will declare what they have heard, and what they declare will form their lives. This is the way God designed human beings to function. But in His original plan, we were to hear only His words of blessing. Then we would have learned to speak His words of blessing about ourselves and others. Unfortunately, many of us did not grow up in the atmosphere of blessing that God designed for us to know.

**God loves to hear your voice.**

God sent His Son to redeem you from sin and all of its effects on your soul. In His loving and nurturing way, God longs for you to sit at His feet and hear the sound of His words to you. Like a little child, you may not fully understand everything He says, but the love with which He says it will soothe your soul, give strength to your body, and give you the confidence that one day you *will* understand fully. His words impart hope that no matter what you are facing, everything will work out better than you can imagine right now—including the fitness and health of your body.

You can become the healthy and fit person you have begun to envision in your heart. Just begin speaking it out! Bathe your brain in the vision of a healthy and fit body with words that describe who you really are and what you really look like. Then your brain will begin to communicate that vision to the rest of your body. God's truth will be fulfilled in your life— He designed you to work that way!

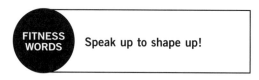

FITNESS WORDS    **Speak up to shape up!**

## IT'S A GOD THING: WORDS MATTER

Robert Kotulak asks the question: "How can a newborn with thousands of muscles, scores of organ systems, 100 billion brain cells and trillions of connections between these cells ever figure out how to get them all working together to produce consciousness, reason, memory, language, and a seemingly infinite array of adaptations to any environment in which it finds itself?"[13] I believe the answer to his question is simple: it's a God thing!

What people refer to as "natural phenomenon" is usually the design of our Creator. Science is merely catching up with what the Bible has already revealed. As Christians, we should be excited that science is discovering God's plan for the way we and the rest of His creation were designed to work. For our purposes in this book, we see that the brain was magnificently formed to process words and then direct the mouth to speak words that would transform us and our world into living a life that is heaven on earth.

The health of your mind—and your brain—depends on the words you feed it. You can feed it positive or negative words by reading, by hearing, or by speaking. Unfortunately, the world you live in says, "Skirt the truth, deny it, or lie to get what you want. Instant gratification is what will make you happy." Scripture declares, "You shall know the truth, and the truth shall make you free" (John 8:32). Freedom is not free; it requires you to make the right choices to embrace the truth and release the power of God into your life.

God has always desired for you to be bathed in words of encouragement and love. Words inspiring hope. Words giving practical instruction. Words to feed the soul and calm the body. Words of love that correct and set on the right path. Words of health, wholeness, peace, and joy. That is *God's way*.

It's a God thing—words matter! They are powerful and life changing. This truth is the essence of the principle of linguistics as we have defined it. As you learn to cooperate with this law, you will receive all the benefits of good health and shape your body into something you are proud of. Stick with it—no matter what; it will work for you!

> **FITNESS WORDS**    Small words transform BIG bodies!

# TAKE ACTION!

Write down five passionate statements you have made *in the past* about your life and your physical body—either positive or negative.

1. _____

_____

2. _____

_____

3. _____

_____

4. _____

_____

5. _____

_____

Are the above statements based on *information* you have believed or *divine revelation*—God's truth—you have received?

_____

_____

_____

The biblical principle of life and death being in the power of the tongue teaches that the words you speak can literally heal your body. If you can control your mouth, you can control your body. Write down five "life" declarations you will begin to say concerning your body and your future. Be specific about your health declarations and practice them daily. (Example: "I am losing 25 pounds; I have my appetites under control; I no longer eat _____.")

1. _____

_____

2. _____

3. _____

4. _____

5. _____

# SIX

# MOUTH FITNESS—YOUR WORDS SHAPE YOU!

I N THE LAST CHAPTER, you were introduced to the second key to getting in shape God's way—*declaration*. We described it as a biblical principle that creates your reality. One of my favorite biblical pictures of that reality states, "Pleasant words are a honeycomb, sweet to the soul and healing to the bones" (Prov. 16:24). The health of soul and body depend on what you choose to declare as your reality. In this chapter, we will continue to explore specific ways you can cultivate *mouth fitness* in order to change destructive ways of speaking and realize your health and fitness goals for a new *you*. It is a fact that your words shape you—inside and out.

Consider for a moment what it would be like if you did not have the ability to speak. How would your life be different? Realizing the purpose of your mouth is a powerful revelation in itself! Sometimes we take for granted what we have always had, without realizing its true significance until it is gone. God created us to communicate with words. When it is physically impossible for a person to communicate by speaking, they can still write their words to communicate. Whether you speak or write, words are the common medium of communication for mankind—and your words are powerful.

As we consider the power of your words, we need to focus on the impact they have on your life—and health—as you communicate your beliefs, attitudes, and personal worldview. I invite you to consider the truth of Jesus's words:

> The good man out of his good treasure brings forth what is
> good; and the evil man out of his evil treasure brings forth what

is evil. And I say to you, that every careless word that men shall speak, they shall render account for it in the day of judgment. For by your words you shall be justified, and by your words you shall be condemned.

—MATTHEW 12:35–37

| FITNESS WORDS | Your mouth was created to create. |

## EXPRESSING HONOR

As you cultivate your relationship with God, reading His Word and learning to pray and hear His voice, the Holy Spirit will bring conviction to your heart regarding evil ways of thinking that are lodged there. He will replace truth for lies, love for fear, and peace for turmoil. According the scriptures, the heart of every man without God is filled with wickedness:

The heart is more deceitful than all else and is desperately sick; who can understand it? I, the Lord, search the heart, I test the mind, even to give to each man according to his ways, according to the results of his deeds.

—JEREMIAH 17:9–10

As you allow God to cleanse your heart, you will find new joy and peace flooding your mind and body. You will learn to live in honor and delight in honoring others. The word *honor* finds its roots in the word *honest*. When one is an honorable person, he or she is honest. Honesty is vital to your personal health, as you choose to honor your body with your words. You are also, even unconsciously, honoring or dishonoring people with your words. For example, a person who swears, using the name of Jesus, is not honoring Him. Yet, some of us dishonor Jesus in more subtle ways with our words without knowing it.

We dishonor God with our words by saying things that do not agree with His Word. Often we do not even realize we are saying something that doesn't line up with what the Bible really says. If you want to honor God with your words, you must know what He says. Honor is an important element of the key of declaration because to achieve and maintain a God's way healthy body requires that you say what God says about it. If you get your mouth fit, you will get your body fit. Put another way, if you honor your body with your words, your body will begin to honor you. It will be helpful to consider the high honor God places on your body.

**Your body is a cathedral.**

God's way of helping you get into shape is to give you a revelation of the value He places on you—body, soul, and spirit. You are more than a physical human being trying to relate to spiritual truths. When you receive Christ, you become the temple of the Holy Spirit:

> Or do you not know that your body is a temple of the Holy Spirit who is in you, whom you have from God, and that you are not your own? For you have been bought with a price: therefore glorify God in your body.
> —1 CORINTHIANS 6:19–20

Allow those words to sink into your mind and spirit. *Whew!* God says that your body becomes a conduit through which He can emanate His divine power and glory. He says that it does not belong to you because He redeemed it with the price of Christ's blood, His very life. He has honored you by coming to dwell in your spirit with His truth and life, and He asks you to honor your body as His cathedral to glorify Him.

Have you visited some of the great cathedrals of the world and stood in awe of their extravagant beauty and the costly materials used to construct them? Have you wondered at the hundreds of years they have endured? They are majestic in appearance and have survived wars, opened their doors to people in need, and pointed lost souls to God. By their very appearance these towering temples remind people of God's presence, power, and love. Consider the awesome fact that God calls your physical body His personal home—His temple! The way you speak about your body and the way you treat it determines how you glorify God in it, expressing honor for yourself.

When you glorify someone, you honor them for who they are and for everything they do for you. So your body should always be honoring God. Your stomach is in your body; let it honor Him. Your brain is in your body. Your heart is in your body. It is time to put down the high-fat foods that are hardening your arteries. It is not merely a choice for health; it is a spiritual reality involved in honoring God in your body. As you choose to use self-control when you eat, you will be able to control what you speak as well. Exercising control in one area will help you to exercise control in your whole life.

It becomes a lot easier to honor yourself and your body, keeping yourself in good physical shape, when you have a revelation that your body is the "God Box" that is to demonstrate His goodness to everyone around you. With that revelation, you realize that the purpose of your body becomes much more than a means to impress or attract other people. Your body is the vessel of God, which He uses to reveal His love to the hurting world in which we live.

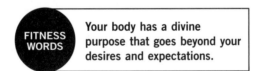

**FITNESS WORDS** — Your body has a divine purpose that goes beyond your desires and expectations.

### Their belly is their god.

Trying to separate the physical you from the spiritual you is impossible. What you do with your body and your mind affects your spirit. And when you allow your spirit to be filled with truth, it positively affects your mind and body. You can't fill your mind and heart with trash and expect your mouth to be in line with God's truth. Jesus declared that a man is defiled by what comes out of his heart, not by what goes into his mouth:

Do you not understand that everything that goes into the mouth passes into the stomach, and is eliminated? But the things that proceed out of the mouth come from the heart, and those defile the man. For out of the heart come evil thoughts, murders, adulteries, fornications, thefts, false witness, slanders. These are the things which defile the man; but to eat with unwashed hands does not defile the man.

—MATTHEW 15:17–20

When you honor God in your heart, you will speak good things with your mouth. Your mind will be renewed to think thoughts that are filled with truth, love, and peace. You will honor yourself and others because you will realize the high value God places on you and on every person. And you will have a reverent respect for your body that will motivate you to do what is needed to get in shape God's way.

Scripture talks about people whose god is their belly and who are headed for destruction:

(For many walk, of whom I have told you often, and now tell you even weeping, that they are the enemies of the cross of Christ: Whose end is destruction, whose God is their belly, and whose glory is in their shame, who mind earthly things.) For our conversation is in heaven; from whence also we look for the Saviour, the Lord Jesus Christ.

—PHILIPPIANS 3:18–20, KJV

The apostle Paul said he wept over people who were honoring their bellies as god; we would say they live to eat. It is important to note that he goes on to say that for those who follow his example, their conversation is in heaven. What a direct link to the impact of our words and the relationship of people to their appetites. Speaking of life as God ordains it delivers you from becoming obsessed with the shame of earthly things that take the place of God Himself in your life.

On another occasion, the apostle Paul made it clear the place that food holds in the grand scheme of things:

> All things are lawful for me, but not all things are profitable. All things are lawful for me, but I will not be mastered by anything. Food is for the stomach, and the stomach is for food; but God will do away with both of them. Yet the body is not for immorality, but for the Lord; and the Lord is for the body.
>
> —1 CORINTHIANS 6:12–13

To honor God in your body, you cannot allow it to be mastered or conquered by anything. You must be in control of what you speak and do regarding your body. Learning to walk in the power of this revelation will affect your declaration of your worth and the care you will take for your body. For example, not only will you think to put out your cigarette before it enters your beautiful temple, you will put it out forever. You are the beautiful temple of God. Before you gorge yourself on fast food, you will consider the trash you are about to shove into God's cathedral.

If you show honor to your body with your words, you will not abuse it. You will treat it with the same respect with which God treats you. I'm sure it hurts God's heart when He sees men, women, and children dishonoring and abusing their bodies. Whether they eat unhealthy foods, take illegal drugs (or abuse legal drugs), drink alcohol in excess, get little or no exercise, perform sexually immoral acts, or cut and physically harm themselves, He is grieved. They are dishonoring the body He created to be the home of His Spirit.

When you get the revelation that honoring God means honoring yourself, and honoring yourself means honoring your body as the house God lives in—in your thoughts, in your words, and in your actions—your life will change! Words that come out of your holy cathedral must be in character with the divine presence who lives there.

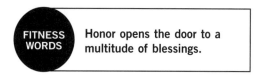

**FITNESS WORDS** Honor opens the door to a multitude of blessings.

## LISTEN TO YOURSELF

One of the interesting aspects of language is what it reveals about what people honor or do not honor. We mentioned that their words tell us what they believe about life and the afterlife, what they believe about God and their purpose on Earth, and what they expect from life in general and from each other in particular. All these things are apparent from the language they speak.

On a smaller scale, I can tell a lot about a person just by listening to them talk to other people or to me for a while. The words they use to describe themselves and others, to express their thoughts and feelings, and to describe events and situations often reveal what they honor or do not honor. I can hear what or who has had the greatest influence on them and understand something of the environment in which they grew up. Their words tell me what they honor. They also reveal whether they are honorable—honest—as well.

Jesus made this fantastic statement about words when He conquered the devil in the wilderness: "It is written, 'Man shall not live on bread alone, but on every word that proceeds out of the mouth of God'" (Matt. 4:4). Your very life depends on how you speak. Learning to speak the language of God regarding the value He places on you will bring life to you that mere food cannot.

If you want to find out who you really believe you are, listen to yourself talk. As you speak with others, "see" yourself and listen to "you." You could even record your side of phone conversations for a couple of days, wait a week or two, and then play your words back. You may be surprised and even shocked at what you hear coming out of your mouth! On the other hand, you may find that you are doing a lot better than you thought you were.

Now that you know your words have creative power, you will listen to yourself with a more enlightened and understanding view. As you hear your words, you will gain insight into what is really going on inside you. This may also be a means by which you can pinpoint the roots of destruction in your life and replace them with roots of life and truth. Changing the words you speak is not a great price to pay to transform your inside and outside into the person you've always dreamed of being!

Up until now, you may not have believed that your own words have such a great impact on your well-being. If you still doubt this fact, try this exercise. Pick up your Bible and read it aloud in front of a mirror. Choose a passage that speaks His promises for you. Listen and watch yourself, saying what God says. You will find that your faith in what you are reading will soar as you hear yourself and see yourself speaking those powerful words.

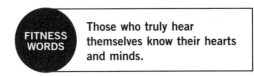

**FITNESS WORDS** Those who truly hear themselves know their hearts and minds.

## INTEGRITY

Integrity is a synonym for honesty that carries the important concept of an "unimpaired condition; soundness." It also refers to a "firm adherence to a code of moral or artistic values" and relates to a "state of being complete or undivided."[1] Integrity relates to the word *integrate* in the sense that to integrate something means to make one thing out of two. If your speech says one thing and your actions say another, you need to integrate them to cultivate integrity—soundness of character.

Have you ever known a person who constantly told you they would do something for you yet never seemed to come through? Why? No integrity. No soundness. No wholeness in their character. They have not allowed their words and actions to become integrated into one entity.

Remember, when you point the finger at someone else, there are three fingers on your hand pointing backward—to you. Working to correct your own character flaws before you work on others is essential to your credibility. It's not that you must become perfect, but you must learn to consistently do what you told yourself you would do. This impregnates you with the powerful reality: "I am a person of my word." Integrity establishes an inward strength that will bring an outward result. Others will begin to see you are who you say you are.

Applying integrity to your determination to get in shape means that you create the inner discipline to help you keep your word to get to the gym or work out at home, and eat the right kinds of foods. Integrity helps you in the larger arena of life to be a good employee, relate well to your family and friends, and so forth.

Jesus was a man of *integrity*. It was impossible for Him to lie! When He made promises and gave us His word on the matter, He was a man of His word! He is still fulfilling everything He said He would do. What He did and what He said were integrated into one reality. However, let me encourage you not to expect perfection from yourself in this important area of integrity.

I am so grateful that as I go through the process of learning to speak honor and to walk in integrity, Jesus gets my struggle. More than that, He is involved in it. He is there to help me shut my mouth when I need to shut it. And He prompts me to open it to speak the truth in love when the Holy Spirit leads me to speak. He understands when I mess up and forgives me and sets me free. Getting in shape God's way is not only thinking, speaking, and doing what He says—it is also doing it *with* Him. He's participating in my life. This entire process is supernatural and miraculous!

One's eyes are what one is; one's mouth what one becomes.[2]
—JOHN GALSWORTHY

## SPEAKING FORGIVENESS

It is commonly accepted that harboring unforgiveness, a grudge, resentment, or any kind of bitterness has a negative impact on your body, mind, and spirit. Jesus told a parable of an unjust man who had been forgiven a huge debt but who refused to forgive a fellow worker a much smaller debt. The unjust man who refused to forgive was handed over to the torturers until he paid his own huge debt in full. In that same way, when we refuse to forgive, we open our hearts and minds to torment.

This may be a good place to address the need for speaking forgiveness and learning to forgive the blunders of others as well as your own mistakes. Speak forgiveness for those you know who have wronged you. And forgive yourself this moment for letting yourself get in the shape you are in or for anything you have done to another. Place your hand on your heart and declare, "I forgive myself this moment!" According to *Strong's Exhaustive Concordance,* the Greek word for "forgive" literally means to "send forth, leave, yield up." When you "breathe out" unforgiveness toward yourself and others, you can literally breathe deeper. You will experience a new freedom from the unforgiveness that wants to pull you down.

Jesus taught His disciples to pray, "Forgive us our debts, as we also have forgiven our debtors" (Matt. 6:12). Then He made a very sobering statement: "For if you forgive men for their transgressions, your heavenly Father will also forgive you. But if you do not forgive men, then your Father will not forgive your transgressions" (vv. 14–15). Without receiving the forgiveness of our heavenly Father, we can expect only misery to be our lot in life.

One of the greatest gifts God gave you was the gift of forgiveness, which is a supernatural miracle. Receiving forgiveness from God gives you a supernatural ability to forgive others—and yourself. But like anything else in life, you must exercise that ability and develop it. The effects of this kind of exercise are phenomenal! Not only does forgiving call off the demonic tormentors and give you peace in your soul, but also your body becomes healthier too.

When you speak harshly to your kids, be quick to ask them for forgiveness. God will heal all any hurt or shame that resulted from your angry words. If you lose your temper and say something disrespectful to your boss next week, ask your boss to forgive you—and pray for a good outcome! Your initial declaration may have been dishonorable, but you made it right by doing the honorable thing, and God will honor you for it.

Asking forgiveness for saying or doing something wrong is one of the most honorable things a human being can do. Some of the sweetest words ever spoken are, "I'm sorry. Please forgive me." Those words can melt the hardest hearts and dissolve the most violent conflicts.

After asking for God's forgiveness, maybe you still need to forgive *yourself*! Perhaps you need to forgive yourself for overeating and not exercising. Maybe you need to forgive yourself for polluting your body with drugs and alcohol, or having sex outside of marriage with anyone to whom you were attracted. Maybe you need to forgive yourself for starving your body and making it sick just to look the way you think you should. Or maybe you need to forgive yourself for physically hurting your body and causing yourself physical pain.

Whatever you are feeling shame for, say to yourself, "I forgive myself for _____." Name those things you have said or done, and those words will be sweet to *your* ears. Forgiving yourself will bring healing to your heart. Knowing that God forgives you should help you to forgive yourself. When you do, you will feel the peace of mind that comes from knowing you are forgiven.

## Your Mouth and Service

In his book *The Purpose Driven Life,* Rick Warren says, "Service is the pathway to real significance. It flexes our spiritual muscles."[3] How true! Your service to God is what gives your life meaning, and part of your service to Him is to honor Him in your physical body. The Bible says in Romans 12:1 that we are to present our bodies to God as *living sacrifices.* This simply means that we are to live for Him to the fullest potential of all of our faculties.

When you begin to see the purpose of your life as service to God, your body takes on a whole new value and significance. Your body has one ultimate purpose, which is to serve the God who loves you. When you walk in the light of this revelation, you no longer see yourself as an overweight or unhealthy person needing a quick fix to look good and be admired and respected by others.

Your confidence comes from understanding that you are already impressive because the God of the universe is your spiritual Daddy! He accepts and loves you as you are, so that means you are OK. Now you simply want to be all He created you to be—even in your body. Your primary desire is to love Him and serve Him with all the gifts, talents, and abilities He has given you, and to care for our body in such a way that it honors Him.

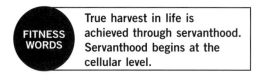

**FITNESS WORDS**

True harvest in life is achieved through servanthood. Servanthood begins at the cellular level.

## THINK BEFORE SPEAKING

Earlier I listed four main functions for the mouth, two of which are to release creative words into the earth and to communicate with others. These are similar because they both can release God's creative power; they are different because of the context in which words are released. It is important, whatever we are speaking, that we learn to think before we speak.

Releasing creative words into the earth involves making proclamations, declarations, and professions of your faith and hope according to the Word of God. As a child of God, you have the responsibility to proclaim His will in the earth. Jesus made a fantastic statement regarding the power of proclamation: "Have faith in God. Truly I say to you, whoever says to this mountain, 'Be taken up and cast in the sea,' and does not doubt in his heart, but believes that what he says is going to happen, it shall be granted him" (Mark 11:22–23).

I related the testimony of my client Nancy as an illustration of this powerful truth. She proclaimed her emotional and physical health by faith, and she received it supernaturally—and you can too! All you need to do is to trust the God who loves you and declare what you believe and desire in your heart. That is the power of releasing creative words into the earth.

Communication with others involves conversations with your family, your friends, other church members, your colleagues at work, or strangers with whom you come into contact. You might not think that your words are imparting something, releasing either good or evil, into their lives. But consider what Scripture teaches about communicating with others: "But encourage one another day after day…lest any one of you be hardened by the deceitfulness of sin" (Heb. 3:13).

When you are feeling depressed or lonely and a friend calls to tell you they have been thinking about you, that friend is communicating by releasing comfort and joy into your life. Their words lift your spirits and give you new inspiration and strength to get up and keep moving forward in your life.

On the other hand, if someone yells at you for making a mistake at work, going on and on about how incompetent and useless you are, your depression would most likely become worse. Both people are communicating, but one leaves you feeling encouraged, and the other will probably make you not want to get out of bed!

I believe I have to be even more thoughtful about the words I use in everyday, informal conversations than when I am making declarations of faith or preaching and teaching. When I am declaring what I believe, instructing my clients, or teaching other people, I just naturally pay attention to the words I use and the tone in which I deliver them. I'm usually very aware of my attitudes and moods during those times. However, when I'm just chatting with a friend or talking with Tia during the day, it is a lot easier for my mouth to release something I regret later—simply because I wasn't thinking before I spoke. In those unguarded moments, I wasn't weighing my words carefully and considering my mood and attitude at the time.

How often do we take out our frustrations and fears on friends or loved ones? Too often! This is one of the greatest battles to win in order to have mouth fitness. We usually don't do this to strangers or acquaintances at work or church because we want to have a good reputation in our communities. It is when we get with our family members and close friends that we can unload. We feel safe with them, so we let down our guard, stop thinking, and just say whatever we feel like saying. Too often, the people we hurt are the ones we love the most!

We can also take out our frustrations and fears upon ourselves. We berate ourselves. We put ourselves down. We think and say terrible things about ourselves. We eat things and drink things that are not good for us. In our times of stress, we generally abuse ourselves because we feel trapped.

At times like these if you will just stop, be quiet, and listen to God for a while, perhaps you can get off the self-destructive path you are on. Listen to your self-talk. Pray for a moment. Perhaps you need to turn to a good friend, a spouse, or someone you trust to "let down your hair" and tell them what is troubling you. You need to do that without being rude or mean to them. After all, they are there to help you sort it all out.

I believe that if people understood the simple truth of the creative power their words have, they could eliminate all kinds of abusive behavior and conflict directed toward others or toward themselves. Also, they would all be healthier because their bodies would not be undergoing continuous tension and strain from speaking words that should not be spoken about others or about themselves.

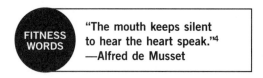

FITNESS WORDS

"The mouth keeps silent to hear the heart speak."[4]
—Alfred de Musset

## THE "LAW OF ATTRACTION"

It is so important to think before you speak and to learn to speak positive, faith-filled words. As you learn to yield more and more to the Holy Spirit, filling your mind with the Word of God, your language will begin to change. The Holy Spirit is a gentle but firm advisor who will not force His wisdom on you but who will encourage you to listen. The more you learn to listen to Him, the better your life will become. When you consider that He knows everything and you know very little in comparison, you should learn to consult with Him for every situation.

When it comes to mouth fitness, the Holy Spirit is your trainer and the Word of God is your training manual. Throughout the New Testament you can read many verses of Scripture that deal with how God wants you to communicate with others and express yourself. His Word is also very specific about the will of God that you should be declaring in this earth. Regarding your body and your health fitness, you should never lose sight of the revelation that you are God's temple, the home where He dwells. Your life reflects a small representation of His kingdom in the earth. When you keep this truth in the forefront of your mind, getting in shape and staying in shape will be much easier because you will be declaring good things about your body. Your faith will release God's supernatural, transforming power into your body. This is the essence of what I call the "law of attraction." You want to attract the blessings of God to your life that He has made available to you in His Word.

However, there is a flip side to the law of attraction as well. If you are speaking negative declarations about yourself or others, the creative power in your words will have an equally devastating effect. In the bullets below, I have listed common statements that people make, which puts the law of attraction into motion in their lives in a negative way.

- I can't do this.
- I can't seem to lose weight.
- I always fail eventually.
- I will never be able to get in shape.
- I was born this way.
- My problem is genetic.
- I always get sick this time of year.
- My mom was built like this.
- My dad was built like this.
- I'm too scared.
- No matter how hard I try, it never works
- I'm so fat.
- I have no special talents or gifts.
- I have a slow metabolism.

- My mother and father have slow metabolisms.
- My body just won't burn fat.
- I'm just not attractive.
- I have no energy.
- I hate exercise!
- I don't have any help.
- I can't afford it.
- I am a lost cause.
- It's too late for me.

If any of those statements or similar statements have come out of your mouth, from now on put them on your blacklist! All of these statements have one deadly effect: they exclude and reject the miracle-working power of words to work in your favor. When God says, "A man will be satisfied with good by the fruit of his words," in Proverbs 12:14, you can take it to the bank. His Word works. Perhaps you are reaping the fruit of the negative words you have spoken. There is only one thing to do. Change the way you speak.

Something terrible happens when you reject what God wants you to speak and choose just to just speak your mind. Instead of light and truth, you release all kinds of negativity into your life and, in this case, your body. You will have what you believe and say, according to the Scriptures. That is God's way of defining the law of linguistics and the power it has in your life.

Your words have creative power, either for the positive or for the negative. That's why you must seek the counsel of the Holy Spirit and consider what God's Word says before you open your mouth to speak.

From this day on, choose to dedicate your mouth to speaking only good things about your body. Work to get your mouth fit by speaking what God says about you. I believe you will be amazed at the difference you feel about your body and how much easier it is to become fit and stay healthy.

## WHAT YOU SAY IS WHAT YOU EAT

When your mouth fitness reaches the point where you are speaking only good things about your body, numerous changes will take place. The most astonishing change you will experience is a change of appetite. This happens particularly as you identify the foods that are not good for you and those that are, and then speak accordingly. For example, you will say, "No, I do *not* desire to eat that bag of potato chips—yuck! I want to eat a beautiful salad, with all kinds of fresh veggies, tomatoes, and a really great-tasting dressing on it."

You may be amazed to learn that as you declare these kinds of statements over your body, your taste buds will change. Your appetite will change. This happens because your brain has changed the way it thinks about food, and it is sending messages to your body that will change the way you feel about food.

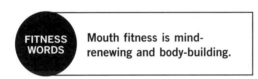

FITNESS WORDS

Mouth fitness is mind-renewing and body-building.

One morning you will wake up and no longer salivate over thoughts of doughnuts, muffins, and cinnamon rolls. You will be hungry for that healthy cereal with fresh blueberries on it or a couple of scrambled eggs with multigrain toast and a glass of fresh-squeezed orange juice. When you finish eating, you will be satisfied and excited to begin your tasks for the day.

Lunch will roll around, and you will ask yourself, "What will really give my body the boost it needs to be productive during the afternoon?" Have you noticed that your entire perspective of food has changed? Instead of looking at food as instant gratification and comfort, you are viewing food as fuel that can be enjoyed. Mouth fitness means enjoying food that is good for you!

Which type of mouth do you have for food? Do you have a sugar mouth or a vegetable mouth? Do you have a fresh-food mouth or a junk-food mouth? Do you have a broken-record mouth ("I want a candy bar! I want a candy bar! I want a candy bar!") or a mouth that asks for a variety of healthy foods throughout the day? And most importantly, do you have a mouth that honors and consults with God before you declare what you want to eat?

The principle is that when you talk about a certain food, it captures your mind. When your mind is captured, it sends signals to the rest of your body to desire that food. Therefore, if you talk about food that is good for you, your mind will be focused on what is good for you and will send signals to your body to desire it, and before you know it, you will be eating what is good for you—and enjoying it!

## HEALTHY LOVE, HEALTHY FOOD

Earlier in the book, I talked about the cycles of destruction that can ruin your life. You eat too much and don't exercise, which leads to out-of-shape body, low self-esteem, and lack of productivity, which leads to depression. Then you decide to go on a diet and get in shape. You start eating less and exercising more. You strain to control yourself until the weight comes off, and finally you are looking good. Then you feel great about yourself and are able to function better in life. After a while, however, you start slacking off on the exercise and start eating some things you shouldn't. Before you know it, you are right back where you started—again.

One of the reasons this happens could be because you love food more than anything else. In that sense, it has become your god; you have given food first place in your life. Your desire for food is what motivates you; it is your source of comfort and satisfaction. Another reason for this destructive cycle is that you love yourself when you look and feel a certain way. In that case, your body may be your god. The shape of your body determines whether or not you are happy and fulfilled.

In either of these scenarios, the sad truth is that God is not your God. That is the root problem that fuels the vicious cycle in your relationship to fitness. For that reason, you try to get in shape every way but His way, and consequently you fail again and again. Once He really becomes No. 1 in your life, everything else will begin to fall in line with what He wants instead of what you want. Or what your body wants. Or what your friends and family want.

So what does God want? God's plan for food is that it be nourishing and enjoyable. In keeping with His primary objective, which is to see you blessed in every area of your life, He created food that you would like. You were designed to enjoy it and strengthen your body by eating it. You were not designed to love it more than God or anything else in life.

When your first love is God, you will have a healthy love for everyone and everything else. Food will not run your life. Drugs and alcohol will not run your life. Television will not run your life. Other people will not run your life. Your job will not run your life. Sports or the arts will not run your life. Nothing will dominate you and drive you to destructive behaviors because God will be making the calls in your life—and He wants only good things for you and your body.

Obviously, this kind of healthy love will cause you to speak healthy, and when you speak healthy, your brain is going to tell your body to eat healthy!

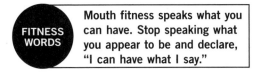

**FITNESS WORDS**

Mouth fitness speaks what you can have. Stop speaking what you appear to be and declare, "I can have what I say."

## SPEAKING IS AN ART FORM

Art has been the cornerstone that defines great cultures across the world for centuries. The geniuses of art have expressed themselves in Michelangelo's *David*, Beethoven's Ninth Symphony, Emily Dickinson's "That I Did Always Love," or Monet's *Water Lilies*, along with hundreds of others that have made an impact on our lives. While it takes genius to produce such masterpieces that transcend time in their appreciation by generations, every human being can participate in the art of speaking.

## The secret of genius

Great artists don't pick up their paintbrush; pull out a music composition notebook; get pen, ink, and notepad; or purchase a slab of marble to begin a masterpiece without previous thought or grand intention. They begin with a definite image, sound, or thought in their minds that they have pondered and considered over time. Then they methodically and carefully move through the process of bringing that idea in their imaginations to a brilliant conclusion as sculpture, music, poetry, or a colorful painting. The secret of genius is the ability to capture every detail of the imagination in the medium of art chosen to express it.

We should be no less methodical and careful—and prayerful—when it comes to the art of speaking. Christians especially, who have the revelation of the creative power of God's Word on their lips and who are aware also of the creative ability of their words, should become the best at the craft of expressing themselves in words. Whether we are declaring that our bodies are healthy and whole or telling our spouse about our day, we should express ourselves with sensitivity and excellence.

As I have mentioned, the people who have enjoyed the greatest success in getting in shape God's way are those who decided to train their mouth as they trained their body. I observed one client drop one hundred pounds easily simply by saying to herself over and over again, "I am losing weight. My metabolism is fast." She fully embraced the law of linguistics and made it a key part of her total fitness regimen. As a result, she achieved her dreams and is continuing to live those dreams.

## Perseverance

Another aspect of great art is that it takes great effort. Perseverance and self-discipline, as well as creative genius and ability, are needed to produce great works of art. If you sat down to interview a few of the celebrities who are considered some of the greatest artists of their fields, they would all tell you the same thing: "I had to stay focused and keep moving, no matter how many mistakes I made or how discouraging other people were. No matter how many times I failed, I had to keep working and training to become more and more skillful, to become the best I could be."

Michael Jordan was one of the greatest basketball players of our time. Luciano Pavarotti was one of the greatest tenors of our time. Katharine Hepburn was one of the greatest actresses of our time. But none of these people were overnight sensations. They spent years practicing and working at their respective professions to reach the level of skill and artistry they achieved.

Mouth fitness is like any other discipline worth pursuing, with this difference: mouth fitness is necessary for success in any discipline. If you approach mouth fitness the way Tiger Woods approaches golf, you will be on your way to becoming healthy, wealthy, and wise! Tiger Woods, perhaps the greatest golfer in history, has been chasing his dream since he was two years old. His focus for life has been to learn everything he could and fill his mind with the information needed to win as a golfer in any arena. He is quoted as saying, "I smile at obstacles."[5] His determination to become the best is reflected in his words, "I will do it with all my heart."[6] These kinds of statements have motivated Tiger to become the great person and golfer that he is today.

The Bible says that your words spoken in faith, when you believe what you say in your heart, is what will move the mountains in your life (Mark 11:23–24). God's Word also tells us that faith is fueled by hearing His Word (Rom. 10:17). When you declare God's Word over yourself, you are increasing your faith. This faith-filled art of speaking replaces your vicious cycle of words of destruction and failure with a divine cycle of realized dreams and joy! When you declare that your body is wonderfully made, faith rises up in your heart. And the next time you declare your body is wonderfully made, you declare it with even greater faith.

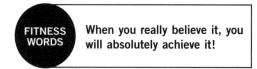

**FITNESS WORDS** — When you really believe it, you will absolutely achieve it!

## Repetition

To excel in the art of speaking also requires repetition. Great athletes and musicians are perfect examples of how repetition produces excellence. As he was growing up and all throughout his career, Michael Jordan practiced free throws for hours at a time. The story is told about a stranger who was lost on the streets of New York. He asked a man walking by, whom he did not recognize as a famous violinist, how to get to Carnegie Hall. The musician answered, "Practice, practice, practice!"

You can apply this principle to everything we want to master in life. When it comes to getting in shape God's way, you must practice speaking good things over your body, along with eating well and exercising regularly and in the correct way. The more you do it, the easier it becomes. The more you do it correctly, the more improvement you make, and your speech will become an art that will give God, you, and those around you great pleasure.

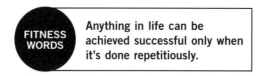

**FITNESS WORDS** — Anything in life can be achieved successful only when it's done repetitiously.

## EMBRACE THE MIRACULOUS

Years ago a pastor looked me in the eye after hearing my message and declared, "We tried that declaration stuff, and it just doesn't work."

I heard the pain in his voice and gently said, "If it didn't work for you, there has to be a reason. It has worked for many of my clients, and it has worked for me. I believe somewhere, in some way, you have misunderstood the principle. Perhaps you did not know to persevere until you could experience great results. And I am not saying this to defend my methods or me. I believe in God, who cannot lie, and these are His methods."

If I spent my time thinking about the lack of success of a few people, I could get discouraged and give up before long. My thoughts are focused on the truth of God's Word and on the people who have embraced His miraculous working in their lives to transform them beyond anything they could have dreamed.

You are going to get your mouth and body in shape God's way because He understands all your special needs, problems, preferences, and idiosyncrasies. He will give you His supernatural help, take you at a pace you can handle, and lead you in a way that will bring you success. That's what a great trainer does. As long as you give Him your best by following His instructions with your whole heart, He will supernaturally see to it that you succeed.

Always remember that although others may have failed and may tell you that what you are doing did not work for them, they are not your god. The Creator of the universe is your God. He made you, and He knows what is best for you. He knows what *you* need to get in shape, and He will get you there if you simply trust Him and follow His instructions. Sometimes this means believing God for a miracle, but He is in the business of doing miracles. Furthermore, He loves doing miracles!

Before we were married, my wife, Tia, suffered from a cyst on her ovary. The doctor told her that if he had to remove the ovaries, she would never bear children. Other women, she was told, learned to accept this condition and had adopted children instead. But the doctor was not Tia's God, so he did not have the last word on the subject. Tia prayed and did not accept the report of the doctor. She knew it was absolutely God's will for her to bear children, and she declared her faith in God.

When the doctor did the surgery to remove the cyst, it was not necessary to remove the ovaries. Tia and I are now the proud parents of our lovely Sophia. She is not only our hearts' delight, but she is also proof that God's way works! As we embrace His miracle-working power, we are able to rejoice in His goodness to us.

**Your body in 3-D**

When you look at your overweight, underweight, or out-of-shape body, it is hard to speak positive words. When you consider all the difficult situations you are dealing with in your life, it is difficult to think of something good to say. I know, because I've been there! But I promise you that if you will choose to speak the truth of God and get a vision for your "masterpiece," the mouth fitness principle will work for you. It's real.

Take a step of faith and begin to speak positive things about yourself and your body—in spite of what you see now. You will feel different. And when you get to the point where you feel like you are a stupid parrot just reciting, "Polly is healthy! Polly's body is the perfect shape! Polly is the person God created her to be!" over and over and it seems like you've hit a wall, don't stop! Keep going! Your miracle is just beyond the next few declarations! God will empower you to do everything you need to do to get into shape—God's way!

I have included a list of scriptures that will help you to establish mouth fitness as part of your healthy lifestyle. (Please see Appendix A, "Mouth Fitness Scriptures.")

**FITNESS WORDS** Declaration of greatness is the beginning of greatness.

# TAKE ACTION!

To firm up your body, you must first firm up your words. Exercise your mouth just as you would exercise your body. Following are some positive, God's way declarations you can memorize and speak over yourself every day. They will change the way you think about yourself and ultimately change the way you live. (For positive declaration scriptures to speak over yourself, please see Appendix A, "Mouth Fitness Scriptures.") Begin to declare the following daily over your life, and see the difference they begin to make in your decisions and your sense of well-being.

## POSITIVE DECLARATIONS

Lay your hands on your heart throughout the day (and especially when you work out) and declare these truths:

- My words are powerful and working for my good.
- My body is special; it is a gift of God. My body is God's property!
- I am blessed, gifted, and loved by God!
- I can get in shape God's way.
- I will get in shape God's way.
- I am getting in shape God's way.
- I command my body to function the way God intended it to.
- My metabolism is normal and just as it should be.
- My metabolism is fast.
- I lose weight easily.
- I gain lean muscle tissue easily.
- I'm getting better at this every day.
- My body is different from my parents' bodies.
- I have an awesome shape and size.
- I am an overcomer; I am going to overcome this!
- I am getting healthier every day.

157

- I have a divine motivation working within me.
- I don't have a spirit of fear or timidity.
- I have a spirit of love, power, and a sound mind.
- My body is the temple of the Holy Spirit.
- There are not two mes in this world.
- Nothing can stop me except me, and I will not stop me!
- My heart is made up, and my mind knows it.
- I will make it!

# SEVEN

# BEHAVIOR MODELS—YOUR BELIEFS MOTIVATE YOUR ACTIONS

**Y**OU HAVE PROBABLY HEARD the old cliché, "Actions speak louder than words." There is a tremendous amount of truth to that statement! In the previous two chapters we discussed the creative power of our words and explored the key of declaration that unlocks the promises God has revealed to us and makes them a reality in our lives.

Declaration can be made in a powerful way without words as well. The way you live your life—your behavior in action—demonstrates the power of declaration in many areas, including the value you place on health and fitness.

When Dan Rather, the famous newscaster, interviewed Mother Teresa, winner of the Nobel Peace prize in 1979, he asked her what she says to God when she prays.

Mother Teresa replied, "I don't say anything. I just listen."

Not to be taken aback, Dan quickly found another approach to the question: "When you are in prayer, what does God say to you?"

She replied, "He doesn't say anything. He just listens."[1]

Mother Teresa was describing the paradox of communing intimately with God on a level of "declaration" that was much more profound than any expression of words. It was also mystifying to her interviewer, who was left speechless himself for the moment.

Here was a woman who walked with God in such a powerful way that her entire life made a bold declaration of the love of God to the whole world. She was so in tune with the heart of God that prayer could be realized by sitting in His presence and feeling His heartbeat, then declaring it to the most needy by her actions motivated by the love of God. Her life declared her love for Jesus and for the people He loved. She served Him well by serving those no one else wanted to serve—the homeless, the dying, and the rejected. People who knew her personally had the feeling that they knew who she was because of what she *did*—not just what she *said*.

Because of the declaration of her loving *actions*, Mother Teresa's words had much greater influence on others. She just lived her life doing what she knew she was supposed to do, never seeking fame or fortune. Not many of us will ever achieve such great notoriety for our actions, but all of us make declarations by the way we live our lives. People observe how we live and base their assumptions of who we are and the integrity of our character by our actions.

## BELIEFS PROVIDE MOTIVATION FOR YOUR ACTIONS

It is a fact that what you believe drives not only your thoughts and your words but also your actions. Your behavior, as we have discussed, is a result of what you believe. Your beliefs motivate and control your actions as well as your words. Models of behavior reflect core beliefs that can either help you reach your fitness goals or keep you mired in destructive lifestyles. For example, if you believe you were born to be anorexic because that is the only way you can maintain the thin shape that makes you feel good about yourself, your motivation will be to live with anorexia. In that state of mind, you will not be motivated to gain weight; you are motivated to continue to binge and purge and exercise excessively to keep the weight off.

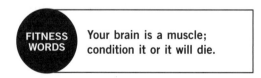

FITNESS WORDS

Your brain is a muscle; condition it or it will die.

In order to change your motivation from this destructive behavior, you need to question the validity of your belief: Is it true? Is all fat horrible?

Can you only be happy with yourself by starving yourself and harming your physical health? Will no one love you if you have a body with a normal amount of fat on it?

What does God have to say about all this? Nowhere in the Bible does He say that a human being is born to be anorexic. On the contrary, God says that He made you to be His son or daughter, uniquely created with wonderful giftings and potential. While He desires for your body to be the temple in which He dwells, He does not describe the perfect shape, height, or weight that He prefers. Instead, God places emphasis on the inner beauty of your person, not on the outward physique that will one day perish. God considers the good behavior that proceeds from integrity of character more important than a "Hollywood-type" figure.

His Word instructs women specifically in this regard:

> And let not your adornment be merely external—braiding the hair, and wearing gold jewelry, or putting on dresses; but let it be the hidden person of the heart, with the imperishable quality of a gentle and quiet spirit, which is precious in the sight of God.
>
> —1 Peter 3:3–4

The apostle Paul instructs the man of God to:

> Flee from these things, you man of God; and pursue righteousness, godliness, faith, love, perseverance and gentleness.
>
> —1 Timothy 6:11

According to Scripture, what is most precious to God? The shape of your body? The size of your waist? Your muscular legs? While your body is precious to God, His Word does not teach that a certain physique makes you more or less delightful to Him. What is most precious to Him is your inner beauty, the integrity of your character that reflects His love. That inner beauty will cause health to govern your mind and will result in a health and fitness lifestyle.

God does not consider being sickly, thin, fat, or miserable as His game plan for you! Therefore if you have believed you are born to be anorexic, fat, or unhealthy, you must change your belief by receiving the revelation of God's will for you. You must accept the truth of God's Word that you were born to be healthy and energetic. To that end, you can ask God to give you the wisdom to eat nutritious food and to exercise wisely while maintaining a proper weight for your height. That change in your motivation will change your behavior that was bent on the destruction of your health.

When your beliefs begin to agree with the truth of God's Word, they will motivate you to make good decisions regarding your health. Proper exercise becomes a normal way of life, not something to be driven to do night and day out of fear of getting fat. You will be motivated to eat healthy food. Suddenly, junk food really lives up to its name! You desire fresh, nutritious food and drink as part of your normal routine instead of harmful things you once craved.

Before long, the powerful motivation of believing the truth will reveal that your life holds possibilities you had never considered you could achieve; health and fitness become an exciting goal. You have changed your behavior by changing your beliefs and motivations. By reshaping your inner life—your motivation—you are able to change your behavior and reshape your body.

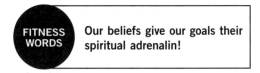

FITNESS WORDS

Our beliefs give our goals their spiritual adrenalin!

## MOTIVATION PLUS

Motives can lead to either miracles or messes. Mother Teresa was highly motivated, but so was Adolf Hitler. The motivation of the first led to unimaginable good for the world; the motivation of the second led to incalculable evil. It is important to analyze your motivation for getting in good physical shape. Are you driven to satisfy an anorexic image that is destructive? Or are you motivated to follow the godly principles of *Getting in Shape God's Way*? God teaches you the way to think about life that will keep you in shape long after you have reached your fitness goals. His love will motivate you to live well in every area of your life.

I trust that as you completed the Take Action steps in Part 1 you began to discover your true motivation for your health and fitness goals. Let me ask you a couple of questions to help you consider what you have discovered. How much is your body worth to you? Do you value yourself as a person? What you believe about the purpose of your body will determine the value you place on it. And the value you place on your body reflects the value you place on yourself as a person.

There is a lot of talk today about values. Some people place their highest value on their spouse and their children. Others value material things supremely, like houses, cars, bank accounts, and retirement benefits. Some people place high value on works of art, rare books, or antiques. Because your beliefs determine your motivation, which affects your behavior, it is important to have revelation regarding what is truly of highest value. What does God value more than anything else in the world? The answer is simple—in a word, *you*!

The Word of God clearly teaches that God set the universe in motion to have communion and relationship with His highest creation—mankind. And when Adam and Eve spoiled that purpose by disobeying the Creator, God continued to enter the world of mankind to redeem us from the law of sin and death that had robbed us of His presence in our lives. He sacrificed His son, Jesus, to pay the penalty of sin for us so that He could save us from the destructive forces of sin that cause us such misery.

More than anything else, God values people. Jesus died for us so that we could walk with Him on Earth and be with Him forever in heaven—that's what I call motivation *plus*! And when you supernaturally receive God's motivation, you will value yourself and your body the way God values you. That is the heart of *Getting in Shape God's Way*!

**Recognizing your assets**

Your body is the most valuable *tangible* asset you have in this world. As I mentioned, it houses the real person you are: your spirit and your soul. Your body is like a glove that covers the hand (your spirit and soul) to protect it. Without the body, the spirit and soul will leave this earth and will cease to accomplish anything here. To the extent your body is not in good physical shape, the spirit and soul are hindered in what they can accomplish of the divine purpose God has for you.

To value your body as God does and walk in His motivation plus, you must evaluate your beliefs about yourself in light of what God believes about you. In that way, you can identify the false beliefs in your heart, which cause you not to value yourself as God does. When you receive revelation of how God sees your body and the value He places on it as His temple, He will help you to change what you believe about yourself. You will begin to walk in greater truth and enjoy the satisfaction of God's divine motivation plus! When that happens, get ready for a big behavioral change for the better!

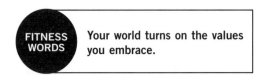

FITNESS WORDS

**Your world turns on the values you embrace.**

## YOUR MOTIVES DETERMINE YOUR METHODS

My task is to get you to believe in the highest values possible by learning to think as God thinks and dream extravagantly, because God thinks and acts big! Achieving your best body fitness and health will be determined largely by your methods. And your methods are dictated by your motives. Let me share a client's story to illustrate what I'm saying.

A client we will call Tom had a career as an actor. He had a handsome face, a debonair demeanor, and was very intelligent. Yet every time he looked in the mirror he saw a fat man. He would gaze at himself and say,

"I look so bloated and out of shape." This was a man who was over seven feet tall and weighed 205 pounds—hardly fat!

Deep within Tom's mind was a belief that he was fat, and that became his answer to not getting the best jobs or having a beautiful woman in his life. His motivation to continue working out and eating the right things was to keep his "fat" under control, get the good acting jobs, and attract a woman to his liking. Yet his behavior was a camouflage for what was really motivating Tom—his fear of being fat. He was afraid someone else would find out who he really was; he was afraid of who he might really be. So his *method* was to act like a perfect macho man who would make people think he had it all together. He could remain aloof, as a professional, and keep them from trying to get to know him on an intimate level.

When you are afraid of who you really are, you do everything you can to avoid finding out. Tom was afraid of himself. As a child, he had a learning disability and grew up in a rough neighborhood where cursing and drinking were the accepted norm—including in his family. Now, as an adult, he was afraid he was really a crazy, stupid, cursing, and fat drunk! He covered up all this fear by doing what he could to create an image of exactly the opposite of what he feared he might be.

Often, people will join a clique or club not because they really want to be there but because they just want to belong to a group that gives the appearance that everyone is OK. And their association with them makes them OK. They have someplace they can forget about their fears. Hiding behind the façade of social acceptance, they can blame anything to the contrary that might surface on others around them or excuse it by saying, "That was the way I was raised." Tom's façade was career; actors look perfect.

When Tom became a client, it was not long before his study of getting in shape God's way addressed his root problems. Tom was simply covering up his real fear issues by projecting an image of perfection. As God became real to Tom, and as he began to understand God's love for him, Tom gained the confidence to face his fears and uncover the lies he had believed about himself. When he discovered that God not only *liked* the real Tom, but that He also wanted the real Tom to be free and happy, his new beliefs changed his motivation for life, which in turn changed his modus operandi—his methods for living.

Instead of being motivated by fear to run from himself to keep up an image, God gave Tom the courage to find out who he really was. Tom began to compare the lie of what he had believed with the reality of what God said was true about him. God didn't tell him he was fat. He didn't tell him he was stupid or crazy or a sloppy drunk. God told him he was unique and special, with great gifts and abilities, and that He had a plan and purpose for him.

Before submitting to this health plan, Tom's declaration to the world around him, through his behavioral methods was, "I'm the perfect guy. I look perfect. I act perfect. You can't possibly relate to me. And by all means, do not try to find out who I really am!" After following the principles of *Getting in Shape God's Way*, Tom still looked really good. But his perspective of himself had changed. His declaration, seen through his behavior, was, "Hi. I'm me. I have problems just like you, but I like who I am because God likes who I am—and He loves me. I eat the right food, drink a lot of water, and exercise regularly because it keeps me healthy and fit to serve God. Hey, let's talk."

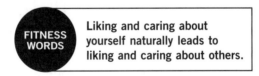

**FITNESS WORDS**

Liking and caring about yourself naturally leads to liking and caring about others.

## AVOIDING DISEASE AND DEATH

One of the healthiest pursuits—behaviors—of mankind is avoiding disease and death at all costs! Most human beings will do anything keep from dying. Since God is a God of life and not death, pursuing life is a God-kind of thing to do.

In God's Word, He declares His intended life span for people: "Then GOD said: 'I'm not going to breathe life into men and women endlessly. Eventually they're going to die; from now on they can expect a life span of

120 years'" (Gen. 6:3, THE MESSAGE). To achieve the long, healthy life God intended for you, take care of your body, honoring it as the temple of the Holy Spirit.

According to the American College of Sports Medicine (ACSM), a well-rounded training program, including aerobic and resistance training and flexibility exercises, will be of great benefit to quality of life and length of years. They encourage a lifestyle of physical activity for your entire life.[2] Adhering to these sound principles will enable you to fulfill the length of days that God has promised you. You can live in agreement with His promise and build your daily routine upon it.

A more dynamic belief would be to strive for an optimal *quality* of life. I want you to begin thinking of yourself and developing your fitness goals to become a TFP— totally fit person. This is possible! Your motivation should be to reach the ultimate goal of honoring God in your body all the days of your life. A lesser goal will cause you to see death earlier than God has ordained for you, simply by wearing out your body.

You can rely on the wonderful promises of God to help you attain to all He has ordained for you. One of my favorites is this: "But my God shall supply all your need according to his riches in glory by Christ Jesus" (Phil. 4:19, KJV). You are not alone; you can draw on the wonderful power and presence of God in your life.

You are created by God—the God of life—to achieve two major objectives: avoid disease and delay death! As the ACSM proposes, to avoid disease you must cultivate awareness. A lack of knowledge about food and exercise will militate against your objectives. In that regard, it is important to maintain yearly medical checkups. Use the doctor's findings as a guide to know more about what you need to be doing to keep your body healthy and strong. Then begin to declare God's Word into whatever area your health needs to be corrected or strengthened.

It is simply a fact that what you believe determines not only your behavior but also your quality of health. Years ago a good friend of mine was diagnosed with a terminal disease. The doctors said there was no hope; she was going to die. Her belief in God was greater than what the doctors had told her. So she began to think God's thoughts for length of days and to speak what she believed. We discussed earlier the physical effect your words have on your brain. I believe that is the reason my friend is still alive.

She painted the reality of health in her heart and mind, giving her brain a picture of herself being totally well. She believed the Word of God that declares: "Now ye are the body of Christ, and members in particular" (1 Cor. 12:27, KJV). She concluded that, as a part of Christ's body, which is not sick and dying, she could not be sick and dying. She *saw* herself completely whole and *declared* herself completely whole, her brain sent the message of being completely whole throughout her body, and her body became completely whole. She did not die; I am convinced that she lives today because she believed, spoke, and behaved as a completely whole person. As a result, she received God's supernatural miracle for her body.

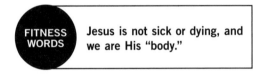

**FITNESS WORDS** Jesus is not sick or dying, and we are His "body."

## THE BASIS OF GOOD BEHAVIOR

I sat with a Hindu man and talked to him about this amazing gift of Jesus Christ to the world, and he just shook his head and said, "This sounds too good to be true." It's too good for us, yes! But God did it anyway—and the Christian's life is too good to be true.

As you consider the price Christ paid to redeem you, including your physical body, how will you behave? What will be your body's declaration to the world around you? The Bible teaches that every human being is born in sin (Rom. 3:23) and needs to be redeemed—bought back. It follows, then, that every person also needs "behavioral modification"—a change in behavior! However, God does not just tell you to stop doing bad things to your body; He gives you a basis for good behavior. He supernaturally changes you from the inside out and gives you His strength, wisdom, and ability to modify your behavior so that you can enjoy getting in shape

God's way. That involves choosing to live a healthy lifestyle all of your life.

God's redemption applies to every human being. It is not something you need because you are the exception to the rule and are so incredibly messed up. No, everyone is messed up! No matter how you were raised, how your parents treated you, or what values they gave you, it is still a fact that you need Jesus. You need to learn God's way of living.

For example, my wife and I were raised in very different lifestyles and with different values. Tia grew up with a physically and verbally abusive father. Both of her parents suffered from addictions. Her home situation was so difficult that she sought emancipation when she was fourteen. Because her parents were dealing drugs and didn't want to draw attention to themselves, they let her go without a fight. Because of her parents' lifestyle and poor example to their daughter, Tia should be a mess—unloving, angry, and bitter. Yet she is the most kind and compassionate human being I have ever met. She is so sweet, why, just being around her can give me a toothache!

When you meet Tia, you get the impression that her gentleness and loving personality came naturally to her; they didn't. They are supernatural qualities that are a result of her being born again and having Jesus change her heart and fill her with His love. The truth of God's Word began to set her free from feeling unloved, unworthy, and undesirable. Coming to know God's exceptional, unconditional love for her deep in her heart gave her the ability to love others the same way she was loved.

On the other hand, I was raised by two hardworking, loving parents who saw to it that I had everything I needed without spoiling me. They were wonderful parents. With that good upbringing, you might expect me to be the one who could just naturally love others. As you read my story earlier, you found that was not the case! I was so miserable I could barely live with myself. I was rude, foulmouthed, short with people, and selfish. In spite of my good upbringing, I too needed Jesus to change my heart so that I could learn to behave toward others and myself with honor and love.

<table>
<tr><td>FITNESS WORDS</td><td>God measures success by love.</td></tr>
</table>

## The Basis for Bad Behavior

We could conclude that since the basis for good behavior is love—God's love motivating and working in us—the basis for bad behavior, then, would be an absence of the love of God. What some people consider to be love is actually a form of self-hatred. Yet, without the love of God in their hearts, they are blinded to the self-destruction that motivates them.

Let's take binge eating, for example. Stuffing your face with anything and everything you crave at the moment would seem like indulging your love for yourself. You are giving yourself a break, allowing yourself the freedom to satisfy your physical cravings. But this is the devil's counterfeit for freedom and love; it is not satisfying. Any action that destroys something good—in this case the health of your body—is not an act of love.

When you have eaten until you cannot eat anymore, if you are honest, you feel no trace of satisfaction or fulfillment. Your body is experiencing all kinds of discomfort and even pain. Your mind is filled with tormenting thoughts of sickness and death. Your emotions are raging out of control because of the levels of sugar and fat coursing through your body. And then there is the shame and guilt. Inside you instinctively feel condemned because of what you have done to yourself.

All the binge has done is reinforce your belief that you are good for nothing and that you don't deserve any kind of real gratification. You thought tasting all this food would drive away your sadness, anger, loneliness, anxiety, and desperation. Instead, it only made things worse. The most effective way to break an emotional attachment to food is to learn to love yourself as God loves you. When you love yourself as He does, your behavior will change.

170

# EMOTIONAL EATING

If you suspect you might have an emotional attachment to food, here are some of the physical symptoms to look for:

- Weight gain (unless you are purging afterwards, in which case there may be excessive weight loss)
- Diabetes
- High blood pressure
- High cholesterol
- Chronic kidney problems or kidney failure
- Osteoarthritis
- Irregular menstruation in women
- IBS (irritable bowel syndrome)
- Uncontrolled eating when nervous or under stress

Some abnormal eating behaviors you will notice are recurring episodes of binge eating, eating much faster than normal, eating beyond being full to the point of discomfort, eating a lot when not physically hungry, and eating alone. A person who struggles with an emotional attachment to food is usually obsessive about eating, planning times to eat and binge ahead of time. These eating patterns generally exhibit symptoms of self-disgust, depression, guilt, and shame, which are felt strongly, especially after overeating.

Whatever form your "bad behavior" takes, *Getting in Shape God's Way* is the answer that can help you change, first in your inner person and then in your lifelong approach to health and fitness. Admitting you have behaved badly toward your body and asking God to help you will bring wonderful change to your heart, your mind, and, ultimately, your body. Choose to receive His forgiveness and love for you. Then forgive yourself and read His truth about His love for you. Open your heart to embrace the concept of loving yourself.

Try it! Take a chance, as thousands have done with miraculous results! Before you know it, the basis for your behavior will start to change. Your declaration to the world will no longer be, "I am completely trapped in a lifestyle that is destroying my body and keeping me from living the life I was created to live."

Instead, your declaration will be, "I am a child of God who is greatly loved, and because of that, I love myself. With God's help I have the physical strength and health to realize my dreams and do everything I was created to do."

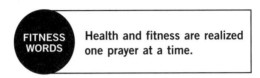

**FITNESS WORDS**   Health and fitness are realized one prayer at a time.

## THE HEALING EFFECTS OF CHANGED BEHAVIOR

I have asserted throughout the text that the most impacting belief in your life is your belief in God. We have discussed practical ways in which that taproot affects your health and fitness lifestyle. Your relationship with God also dramatically affects your ability to be healed of illness and disease, as well as their prevention.

In recent years medical science has begun to study how faith in God affects the physical condition of a person's body. Dr. Harold Koenig, founder of the Center for the Study of Religion/Spirituality at Duke University, has been involved in several studies pertaining to the effects of faith on health. Here are some interesting findings from these scientific studies:[3]

1. A study of nearly four thousand people, age sixty-five and older, found the risk of diastolic hypertension 40 percent lower among those who attended religious services at least once a week and prayed or studied the Bible daily.

2. A study of more than seventeen hundred older adults from North Carolina found that those who attended church at least once a week were only half as likely as those who did not to have elevated levels of interleukin-6, an immune system protein involved in a wide variety of age-related diseases.

3. A study of eighty-seven depressed older adults found those who recovered from depression the fastest corresponded to the extent they relied on their religious beliefs.

4. A study of 542 patients, age sixty or older, admitted to Duke University Medical Center found those who attended religious services at least weekly reduced hospital stays by more than half. Those with no religious affiliation spent an average of twenty-five days in the hospital compared to eleven days for patients affiliated with some religious denomination. Also, patients who attended religious services at least weekly were 43 percent less likely to have been hospitalized in the previous year.

5. A study was made of 116 depressed geriatric patients, who were given standard medications over twelve weeks. The recovered patients in the study reported "significantly more frequent public and private religious practices, greater positive religious coping, and less negative religious coping" than those who remained depressed.

> **FITNESS WORDS**    **Science is in the business of discovering God's truth.**

### TAKING A STAND

Some of your friends, family, and co-workers may not think that getting in shape God's way is the right thing for you to do. Their opinions may dissuade you from your decision to follow through on your goals for fitness. Your drinking and dining buddies may be angry that you won't go to the bars and restaurants with them anymore. Your family may think you have become a religious zealot and suggest that you see a counselor of their choice. It's hard enough to change, but when it seems as if everyone you know is against you, it makes it even harder to focus on your goals.

At that point, what is your declaration going to be? I recommend: nothing! Just smile and trust God; keep exercising your heart, your mind, your mouth, and your body. Continue to eat the right things as you exercise patience with those who oppose your new lifestyle. Let your God's way quality of life do the talking. Without any verbal argument for what you are doing, you will be making a declaration loud and clear—about yourself and about the power of God's love being revealed through you.

 **FITNESS WORDS**
Declare every day that your body belongs to God by eating and exercising His way.

Before we consider the practical application of how you are going to change your behavior to reach your health and fitness goals (Part 3, "Application"), let's review some of the factors we have discussed that affect your current behavior patterns.

## LET'S REVIEW THE MAIN POINTS

### Culture
The culture you have grown up in and now live in is probably not an expression of the culture of God's kingdom. His kingdom is spiritual, and as a child of God and a citizen of heaven, you keep His laws by simply abiding by His Word and following His Spirit. Unlike an earthly kingdom, God's kingdom operates on the basis of intimate relationship between Him and each one of His sons and daughters.

### Attitudes and relationships
Your attitudes and behavior have been greatly influenced by the significant relationships in your life. From now on, your relationship with God is going to become the primary influence in your life. His Spirit and His Word will guide you through life to reach your health and fitness goals. He will honor your faith and give you the great results you can only dream of at the moment.

### "E"motions
What you feel deep inside is what motivates you to make the decisions you make. Bishop T. D. Jakes, in his book *HE-Motions: Even Strong Men Struggle*, writes, "If

you want to stop the madness and stabilize your emotions, you must define who you are apart from what you may be going through."[4] I like to extract the word *motions* from emotions and describe them as "feelings that inspire movement." Your changed emotions will motivate you to move toward your health and fitness goals.

## Values

What you value and esteem highly in life determines your behavior. You have to determine how you value yourself and your body. My prayer is that as you read this book, you will value yourself and your body as highly as God does.

## Ethics, honor, and integrity

What you believe ultimately determines your ethics, what you honor, and your personal integrity or character. Ethics, honor, and integrity all deal with right and wrong behavior toward yourself and others. They include behaving legally, morally, and according to the good manners of your society. All three are cornerstones to the God's way health program.

## Authority

Throughout your life you may have believed that you were the final authority for your life. As a result, you felt the need to feel superior to other people and to control things in your life in order to be happy and successful. That faulty belief changes when Jesus becomes the authority and final word in your life. As God's son or daughter, you now walk in His authority and power.

## Rapport and discernment

When you believe in God and choose to have faith in Him for your fitness, health, and healing—inside and out—it creates a rapport between you and God based upon trust and a deep emotional attachment. His love for you becomes the reality and basis for your wise discernment: how you see yourself, other people, and the world around you.

## Persuasion

You believe what you have been persuaded to believe, which then determines your behavior. Accepting God's persuasion by the power of His Holy Spirit is the answer to your physical fitness and health problems. And I make no apologies about the fact that I have written this book to persuade you to trust God with your entire life. I do this because I know, my clients have proven, and we are all continuing to prove that getting in shape God's way is the best way.

## Dealing with the enemy

While the devil is a real enemy, tempting and deceiving us where he is able, it is our choice to yield to temptation or resist it, eat the pie or refuse it. The biggest enemy is the "old sin nature" with which we were all born—in simple terms, plain old selfishness. God will give you strength to defeat every enemy as you seek Him and ask for His help.

## Genetics

We discussed the fact that beliefs and behavior can be influenced by your acceptance of the genetics of your family: "My whole family is out of shape. It's just the way we are." By getting in shape God's way, your eyes will stay blue because you inherited your mother's blue eyes, but your weight and shape can change!

**FITNESS WORDS**

"I can do all things through Christ which strengtheneth me" (Phil. 4:13, KJV).

## TAKE ACTION!

In Part 1 you began to receive greater revelation of who God says you are and the plan and purpose He has for your life. In Part 2 you were instructed to make a declaration of God's truth about yourself and your body, not only in the words you speak but also in the entire way you conduct your life. To determine what changes you are already experiencing, I encourage you to answer the following questions based on the ten factors that we reviewed regarding their effect on your health and fitness.

1.  Describe some differences between God's culture and the culture in which you grew up.

    _____

    _____

    _____

2.  How have your attitudes toward yourself and your body changed since you decided to pursue a relationship with God?

    _____

    _____

    _____

3.  Describe any emotional changes you have gone through concerning the way you feel about yourself and your body, and list the ways your behavior has changed because of these emotional changes.

    _____

    _____

    _____

4.  What value do you place on yourself and your physical body now? How is that different from before reading these chapters?

    _____

    _____

    _____

5.  List specific behaviors that you now realize involve ethics, honor, and integrity with regard to yourself, your body, and other people.

    _____

    _____

    _____

6.  Give reasons why it is in *your* best interest that God should have final authority in your life.

    _____

    _____

    _____

7.  Given your growing rapport and trust in God, what things have you discerned about life that you may not have before reading *Getting in Shape God's Way*?

    _____

    _____

    _____

8.  In what areas do you still need to be persuaded that God's way is the best way for you to get in shape? How will you go about becoming persuaded?

    _____

    _____

    _____

9.  We discussed the fact that Jesus has defeated the devil and all your enemies. You have been given the name of Jesus to declare against them and keep them from your life. How has that truth changed the way you think, speak, and act?

    _____

    _____

    _____

10. What are your genetic concerns, and how does the truth of God's Word and the love God has for you affect your beliefs about them?

_____

_____

_____

PART 3

**KEY #3: APPLICATION—**
**IT MUST BE WORKED OUT!**
*FITNESS FUNCTION*

# EIGHT

# PROGRESSING THROUGH MOVEMENT— YOUR HEALTHY LIFESTYLE

**L**ET ME CONGRATULATE YOU on completing your assignments in the first two sections of this book, which are designed to help you begin living life in a new dimension of revelation for your destiny. As you practice declaring the truth of God regarding your life, keeping your vision and mission statements in focus, you can expect to experience wonderful success in reaching your goals for health—spirit, soul, and body.

Without embracing those keys of divine revelation and declaration of the truth, anything you try to do to change or improve your lifestyle will be ill-motivated and short-lived. As you continue to allow God to reveal His love for you and choose to think His thoughts and desires for you, your life will progressively change until you become a glorious temple for the presence of God.

As you actively embrace these keys to *Getting in Shape God's Way,* you are positioning yourself for a limitless potential of fulfilling your divine destiny and enjoying a successful future. There are still two other keys, however, that you must make a part of your life in order to attain the goals for health and abundant life that God has for you; they are the keys of *application* and *manifestation.*

## Putting Your Declarations to Work!

It is time to put your new belief system and the power of your positive declarations to work for you. To do this, you will need to unite the efforts

183

of your words and the exercise of your body into a winning combination that will help you reach your fitness goals.

Scripture teach that, "Faith, if it hath not works, is dead, being alone" (James 2:17, KJV). When the spirit is separated from the body, you get a corpse. When faith is separated from works, you get the same thing—a corpse. The law of application requires that, in order to enjoy abundant life, you need to obey the laws God has set in motion for your health.

The apostle Paul declared, "Work out your own salvation with fear and trembling. For it is God which worketh in you both to will and to do of his good pleasure" (Phil. 2:12–13, KJV). And he speaks of doing his part to subdue the appetites of his body: "But I keep under my body, and bring it into subjection: lest that by any means, when I have preached to others, I myself should be a castaway" (1 Cor. 9:27, KJV).

While it is clear from Scripture that we are not saved by our works, but by grace alone through faith (Eph. 2:8–9), it is equally clear that obedience is required to enter into the freedom and wholeness God brings to us through salvation. For example, New Testament believers were instructed firmly that, "If any would not work, neither should he eat" (2 Thess. 3:10, KJV). Laziness is condemned in Scripture, as well as gluttony and other forms of irresponsible behavior that work against godly character, health, and wholeness. The Bible is a very practical handbook to living a great life.

You may make excuses for your obesity by saying that you compensate in your Christian life by being a generous person and giving to others. You may work for the Lord in various ways, which is commendable. But God is asking you to believe in your heart that He can help you lose weight and become healthy in the same way He has helped you to be a generous person. Accepting the reality of God's revelation to your heart will lead to action—motivated by God's love, not your excuses. The results will be a wonderful manifestation of peace, hope, and health.

## A Body in Motion Stays in Motion

In this chapter we will discuss the how-tos of getting in shape God's way. In order to progress toward your healthy lifestyle and fitness goals, you need to embrace the principle of *movement*. When you understand the law of motion and how it applies to your physical well-being, you will be set free from the dread of exercise and the "couch potato" syndrome. God's intention is that freedom of movement bring exhilaration to the body, soul, and spirit.

God's law of movement is so authoritative that there is no possibility of health, wealth, or success without obeying it. God's way can sometimes be described by a four-letter word: *W-O-R-K*. It is simply a fact that health and wealth don't fall out of the sky. God's principles must be "worked out" in your life in order to experience the success He has ordained for you.

First, God's principles must be worked out in your character through spiritual discipline. The principles of receiving divine revelation and declaring the truth in every area of life must be embraced and practiced— worked out—in order for you to walk in the wonderful reality they offer.

Second, it will be impossible to get anywhere in your pursuit of health and wholeness if you speak right words but do nothing to apply them to your "temple." The apostle James condemned this attitude in Christians of his day. He wrote:

> But be ye doers of the word, and not hearers only, deceiving your own selves. For if any be a hearer of the word, and not a doer, he is like unto a man beholding his natural face in a glass: For he beholdeth himself, and goeth his way, and straightway forgetteth what manner of man he was. But whoso looketh into the perfect law of liberty, and continueth therein, he being not a forgetful hearer, but a doer of the work, this man shall be blessed in his deed.
>
> —James 1:22–25, kjv

It is important to apply this biblical principle of working out your salvation to your exercise workout—the focus of this chapter—in order to promote your physical health. When you apply faith to exercise, it immediately adds a supernatural dimension to your pursuit of a healthy lifestyle. If faith were characterized as a "muscle," it would need to be flexed and trained to stay healthy. In that same way, your natural muscles need to be trained and exercised so they can provide a long, healthy life for you. As you exercise faith to pursue a healthy lifestyle, you can be assured of achieving health—spirit, soul, and body. It is good to know that faith is a not just a gift but also a fruit (Gal. 5:22) that can grow in your life. It also holds true, that as a fruit, faith can wither and die if you do not properly nurture it.

Once you have the revelation that your body is the temple of God's presence and begin to declare who you are, embracing the key of application will thrust you into a faith-filled workout. You will become passionate about presenting your body "a living sacrifice, holy, acceptable unto God, which is your reasonable service" (Rom. 12:1, KJV).

As you begin to work out your faith through your exercise program, you will find that it is easier to keep going than to stop. God's law of movement is intended to give you the thrill of freedom that only movement of a healthy body can experience. Once a body is in motion, it stays in motion. The exhilaration, relaxation, and sense of well-being that results from exercising your temple properly will become addictive, in a very positive sense of the word. God made you to move; illness and disease result from violating the law of movement that God ordained for your body.

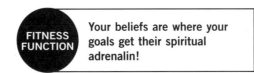

**FITNESS FUNCTION**  Your beliefs are where your goals get their spiritual adrenalin!

## FULFILLING THE LAW OF MOVEMENT

Your heart is always beating, pulsating—moving. Just the beating of your heart burns calories. Breathing burns calories. Blinking your eyes also burns calories. However, to give your organs and muscles—and even your psyche and emotions—the movement they need will require more overt movement such as walking and functional training exercises.

Life is about movement—God made you that way. Anything designed to move that is not moving becomes more and more lifeless and will eventually die. As you learn to strengthen your core muscles, stabilizing your heart rate, you will extend your life span and live a healthy life, losing excess weight and maintaining core strength to a ripe old age.

Dr. Michael Rozien, in his book *YOU: Staying Young*, discusses the process of atrophy, which involves the decrease in size or wasting away of a body part:

> Your body is too efficient to waste energy feeding limbs and organs that aren't being used. So if you aren't using it your body says you are losing it. And the nerves that help control those limbs and organs will wilt away. This mechanism of aging— disuse atrophy—is a classic example of resource allocation. If your body knows that you are using crutches instead of quadriceps then it figures, *Forget this, I'll put my energy elsewhere,* and so you let muscles atrophy when you don't use them for long periods. We need to put our bodies to work in our lives. We need to work our muscles and brains and virtually every other organ and system in our bodies to make them stronger for longer.[1]

Dr. Rozien confirms God's fundamental principle of movement that is required to keep the body healthy and functioning at its optimum potential for your entire life. Your sedentary lifestyle militates against the health of your organs—like your heart—and your limbs, which you need to be strong until the day you die. Dr. Rozien also warns against the extreme of too much exercise: "Use them too much and you suffer from wear and tear, but don't use them enough and you suffer from dis-use atrophy. The ideal, of course, is to find the middle ground where you do just the right amount to make your body parts thrive and not age."[2]

### Movement and your overall health

Movement does not only promote the health of your physical body, but it also affects your mental and emotional health as well. Woven into the intricate mystery of life is the reality that the muscles and other organs of your physical body are intricately connected to your spiritual being. Perhaps there is more to the phrase, "I have a gut feeling," than you have imagined. In his *New York Times* best-selling book *The Maker's Diet,* my friend Jordan Rubin cites scientific studies that describe your "gut" as a second brain.[3] For example, it is commonly believed that irritable bowel syndrome (IBS) is caused and affected by your emotional and mental state, especially relating to stress, anger, fear, and other negative emotions. Jordan Rubin writes:

> According to scriptures common to the Judeo-Christian tradi-tion, the "bowels," or the "belly," are described as the seat of the emotions (Song of Solomon 5:4)....Most people would say the brain determines whether you are happy or sad, but they have their facts skewed. It seems the gut is more responsible than we ever imagined for mental well-being and how we feel.[4]

Other doctors have studied the effects of colonies of bacteria in the intes-tines on obesity. They conclude that certain microbes contribute to obesity by extracting calories from food and turning them into fat. Reducing food intake and replacing sugary foods with wholesome food groups, which improve elimination from the bowels, is a great antidote to the production of harmful intestinal bacteria. Doctors also concur that death begins in the colon.[5] For that reason it is important to keep the bowels clean, eating an organic diet low in refined sugars and high in fiber. Water flushes and cleanses disease-promoting toxins and bacteria from the bowels as well.

Another helpful antidote to disease (dis-ease) is obeying the law of movement through proper exercise. Exercise—aerobic movement and breathing—is vital to promoting the elasticity and overall health of your internal organs. God's law of movement was intended to keep all the systems of your body working at their optimal level of function, beginning with your heart.

As you choose to embrace *movement*, the first fundamental of the key of application, you are ready to proceed to your personal fitness program. Approaching these simple, "moving" exercises with faith in your heart, you will begin to actually enjoy the freedom of movement God intended for you to experience. And you will have the added reward of knowing that you are increasing your quality of life—spirit, soul, and body. Your heart—both spiritual and physical—will function at its optimal capacity for living a victorious life.

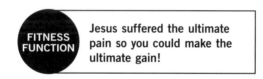

**FITNESS FUNCTION**

Jesus suffered the ultimate pain so you could make the ultimate gain!

## THE MUSCLE THAT MAKES ALL WEIGHT-LOSS PROGRAMS WORK

Your muscles, as well as your internal organs, crave movement. They need the oxygen that is a result of aerobic exercise and the stretching and strengthening that anaerobic exercise provides. Do you know how many muscles you have in your body? Most sources state more than 650.[6] Of those hundreds of muscles, the muscle that is most important to your health is your heart. It is the muscle that determines the success of all weight-loss programs.

Your physical heart muscle must receive the nutrients and exercise it needs to sustain a high quality of life. It is impossible to separate spirit, soul, and body and still maintain life; it is also impossible to neglect your physical heart without affecting your spiritual heart. There are specific requirements for your physical body to maintain health so that your spirit and soul can enjoy wholeness.

**Did you know?**

Here are some interesting facts about your heart:[7]

- Your heart is a 10-ounce muscle that contracts one hundred thousand times a day without missing a beat.
- During a lifetime, the two self-lubricating, self-regulating, high-capacity pumps in your heart beat two and one-half billion times.
- During a lifetime, your heart pumps sixty million gallons of blood without pausing to rest.

It is amazing to consider the effectiveness of your heart, this marvelous machine God created to keep you alive, without your even knowing it is working. Yet, cardiovascular disease has become the leading cause of death worldwide as a result of our civilized lifestyle. Much of this tragedy could be prevented or reversed by simply giving your heart what it needs—moderate movement, healthy nutrients (including water), and a lifestyle filled with peace of mind.

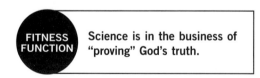

**FITNESS FUNCTION** Science is in the business of "proving" God's truth.

**Strengthening your heart**

For you to fully start moving and solving problems effectually will require a strong heart. The Greek word *kardia* gives us the medical terms *cardiology*, *cardiac*, and so on, referring to the large muscle we call the heart. When the heart muscle is worked in moderation, it gets stronger. If it is overworked, it actually becomes smaller, less able to function normally.

For those who may be driven to over-exercise, let me state this caution:

Too much of anything can hurt you. While most people fall into the category of needing to add exercise to their lives to strengthen their hearts, those who are overworking it through too much bodybuilding exercise—usually with the wrong motives—can actually damage their heart and their entire body.

The term *exercise* refers to exertion, which causes stress on the body. The right amount of stress will be very positive for the health of your body. However, God's way is about moderation in all things. He does not approve of radicalism; God is into "real-ism."

It is interesting to me that we can extract the word *ear* from the core of the word *heart*. I am impressed that God gave us two ears and one mouth. Perhaps we should consider spending more time listening—with our heart—than we do speaking with our mouth. Then we will undoubtedly declare the truth we hear and become motivated to get into shape God's way.

The heart is placed in the core of your body and protected by the skeletal system and organs that surround it. Of course, without this amazing pump circulating your blood, wherein is life, you would cease to exist. The heart stops—you stop! It follows, then, that the better your heart functions and the more efficiently your blood flows through your body, the better health you will enjoy. Exercise enhances those vital life functions of the heart and strengthens the heart itself.

*Core stabilization* is a term used to define functional fitness exercises that strengthen the core of your body, making the rest of your body more stable. In an article targeting the importance of exercising during pregnancy, the American College of Sports Medicine confirms that this core work should become a central part of your exercise regimen:

> Just as cardiovascular activity is the foundation of an overall fitness program, core and pelvic floor stability should be the foundation of a targeted strength-training program. An active core and pelvic floor functions as a corset to protect the structural integrity of the joints, primarily the pelvis and lumbar spine, before any arm or leg movement is begun.... The core

and pelvic floor should be engaged at a low level during any movements and exercise. Core stability exercises should be done prior to or in conjunction with other increases in strength and be repeated regularly.[8]

In the workout, I will show you how to get fit fast by doing simple core stabilization exercises.

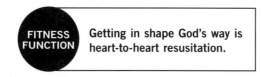

**FITNESS FUNCTION**

Getting in shape God's way is heart-to-heart resusitation.

## KNOW YOUR HEART RATE TRAINING ZONE

One of the biggest mistakes people make when they work out is that they don't exercise in a specific training zone. Your optimal training zone is a safe parameter for you to maintain so that you do not have to worry about exercising too hard. It is the desired rate at which your heart should beat, based on your body's present capacity, during your workout. Calculating your safe training zone is a *must* for optimal weight loss and cardiovascular health, as well as for assuring your safe rate of progress.

When you become comfortable with your workout, you can increase it until you are functioning within your fat-burning zone. When you have achieved a level of exertion that keeps you in your fat-burning zone for thirty minutes, you are doing very well.

Learning to calculate your training zone will help you progress to your fitness goals through the freedom of movement, safely and efficiently. There are three percentages that are important to your overall knowledge of a cardiovascular workout regimen. They are 60 percent, 75 percent, and 85 percent—which represent the low-end, middle-range, and high-end heart rate targets, respectively.

In preparation for your participation in the fitness plan, please fill in the charts below, which will help you determine your safe training and your fat-burning zones. As with any fitness program, please see your physician before starting.

| CALCULATE YOUR SAFE HEART RATE TRAINING ZONE |
|---|
| Calculate your safe training zone by completing the following equation.[9] From the number 220 subtract your age: |
| • 220 – _____ (your age) = _____ (maximal heart rate) |
| • My maximal heart rate is _____. |
| Multiply your maximal heart rate by .60 to know your low-end training zone: |
| • (Maximal heart rate) _____ x .60 = _____ (low end) |
| • My low-end training zone is _____. |
| Multiply your maximal heart rate by .85 to know your high-end training zone: |
| • (Maximal heart rate) _____ x .85 = _____ (high end) |
| • My high-end training zone is _____. |
| Say this: "My safe heart rate training zone lies between _____ (low end) and _____ (high end)." |

**Fat-burning zone**

When you exercise, you always want to try to stay between your low-end and high-end heart rate training zones, which you calculated in the chart above. Don't be afraid to push yourself a little harder each time you exercise. The body responds well in a controlled stress environment.

Maintaining a heart rate target of 75 percent of your *maximal* heart rate during your workout will allow you to burn fat continually.

## FAT-BURNING HEART RATE

Calculate your fat-burning heart rate by completing the following equation:[10]

Find your resting pulse. It is best taken in the morning before exertion or after sitting quietly for five minutes. Place two fingers on your neck to find your pulse. Count the beats for six seconds.

Multiply that number by 10 to get your resting pulse. (For example: if you counted seven beats in six seconds, 7 x 10 = 70, which would give you 70 beats per minute [bpm]).

- My resting pulse is _____.

Now subtract your resting pulse from your maximal heart rate, which you determined from the chart above, to get your heart rate range:

- _____ (maximal heart rate) - _____ (resting pulse) = _____ (heart rate range)

Now multiply that number (heart rate range) by .75 (which is your fat-burning intensity), and then add your resting pulse to get your personalized target fat-burning heart rate:

- _____ (heart rate range) x .75 (fat-burning intensity) + _____ (resting pulse) = _____ (fat-burning heart rate)

Say this: "My personalized target fat-burning heart rate is _____."

Your personalized target fat-burning heart rate is your goal for exercising at a level that will continually burn fat. You will most likely not begin your workout regimen working at that level. It is a goal, which must be achieved as you become stronger and get comfortable with your workout, keeping your exertion level between the low- and high-end numbers of your safe heart rate training zone.

I strongly recommend to every serious client that he or she invest in a heart rate monitor. Whether your goal is to strengthen your heart or to burn fat, the heart rate monitor lets you know if you are succeeding by maintaining your workout at a level that is accomplishing your goals. You can find good quality monitors in all price ranges. (Please see Appendix E for more information on purchasing a heart monitor.)

As you become more fit through training, your strengthened heart muscle is able to pump more blood with every beat. As a result of strengthening your heart, it does not have to beat as often to get the required oxygen to your muscles, which in turn decreases your resting and exercise heart rate. When your muscles utilize oxygen more efficiently, they allow you to put more effort into your workout and still maintain the same heart rate. This process will allow you to achieve your goal of working out at your fat-burning heart rate, which will increase your metabolism rate effectively.

## FUNCTIONAL INTERVAL TRAINING

Functional interval training is a specialized program that offers you the ability to combine anaerobic exercise with aerobic exercise. You get a two-for-one benefit when you use this approach to your workout. You may be aware that *anaerobic* exercise refers to strength training and *aerobic* exercise promotes heart health by requiring exertion that makes oxygen and blood flow freely.

*Functional* simply means movements in your exercise program that mimic real-life movements, such as reaching for a book on a shelf, driving a car, bending over, squatting to pick up a small child, and so on. *Interval training* refers to performing certain movements intensely for thirty seconds and then resting for at least ten seconds before continuing with another exercise movement.

Functional interval training is absolutely the best form of exercise for overall cardiovascular health and weight loss. It helps you to raise your heart rate very high and then lower it quickly. A graph of your heart rate during this type of exercise would look like a shark's tooth—spiking up and then down, over and over. This "shark tooth" graph line during interval training is actually evidence that your exercise is making your heart stronger. Making sure that you stay within your training zone, you will be safe, reduce the risk of injury, and get great results as well. (Remember to consult your primary care physician before beginning any exercise program. Make sure your physician knows what your target training zone is.)

### Resting from ten to sixty seconds

To determine the length of time you should rest between exercises, consider these two factors:

1. How do you feel?
2. Are you a beginner, or have you been working out for six months to a year?

If you are a beginner, be patient with yourself. You will get stronger in time as you exercise regularly. If you have been working out for at least six months, in order to determine the intensity of your exercise routine, take your pulse and check your heart rate monitor. If it is *below* your fat-burning zone or target rate—"Get movin'!"

Functional interval training has been proven overall to be the best type of movement for your heart, decreasing your risk for cardiovascular disease, regulating blood pressure, and aiding in the prevention of many other health disorders. Studies show that when you do functional interval training, it is so effective that ten minutes of exercise is as effective as thirty minutes of other aerobic exercise.[11]

## BEGINNER, INTERMEDIATE, AND ADVANCED WORKOUTS

The key to your success with your workout is to start slowly and avoid injury. Don't assume that you are ready for the intermediate level workout. Complete the beginner's level first and see how difficult it is for you. Then work your way up to the next level gradually as you take time to build up your strength and endurance carefully. You will be the winner in the long run.

With each phase of your workout (beginner, intermediate, and advanced), perform three sets of each. For example, go through the beginner workout three times comfortably before you consider going on to intermediate. Each time, try to shorten your overall exercise time—a sort of "beat your best time" competition, if you will. If your beginner workout took you forty minutes, try to do it the second time in thirty-five minutes. When you can do it in thirty minutes, you are ready to move on to the intermediate level.

| ACTUAL EXERCISE TIME FOR EACH LEVEL |
| --- |
| Without including the rest periods between each movement, these are the actual minutes involved in your interval exercise routine: |
| • Beginner workout: 7–8 minutes |
| • Intermediate workout: 11–12 minutes |
| • Advanced workout: 16–18 minutes |

Completing all three workout levels during one workout session will be challenging for the advanced level person, but stick with it! When you get to the intermediate and advanced sections, try to finish them in less than one hour. If you can meet the challenge of finishing in forty minutes or less, you may even beat the world record!

## FIVE THINGS BEGINNERS NEED TO KNOW

If you have never exercised or don't know much about it, please consider the following important information before you begin your workout. Even if you have been involved in training or workouts, it will be good to refresh yourself with these safety tips as well. Again, remember to see your physician before beginning any exercise program.

### 1. Learn correct form

Take time and effort to learn the correct form for your workout so that it can become a natural part of your lifestyle. It is easier to learn to do something correctly the first time than to have to unlearn what you have practiced incorrectly when you realize it is not working for you. Patient endurance is a character trait that few of us have naturally. But it can be cultivated as you choose to use the key of application in your workout sessions. Doing exercise correctly is a safety issue as well as a key to making your efforts effective in reaching your fitness goals.

## 2. Prevent injury

God puts a high priority on order and consistency. Just look at the universe, and you will understand something of the precision with which God operates. The key to preventing injury during your workout, after learning to exercise correctly, is to proceed slowly and with caution. When you are first learning the movements, I encourage you to stop whatever DVD or video you may be using and practice doing each movement correctly before continuing with the workout routine. I have worked with many people who think they are doing exercises correctly, but their lack of form is actually tearing down their fitness rather than improving it. Mastery of the art of exercise requires repetition of the fundamentals—practice, and then practice some more!

## 3. Muscle recruitment/isolation

Muscle recruitment does not mean that you are asking for volunteers to beef up your muscle mass. It is a term that refers to learning how to isolate or flex every muscle separately. For example, if I asked you to flex your calf muscle, you most likely could isolate it and do that. But if I asked you to flex your *infraspinatus*, you might ask me to repeat the question. Your infraspinatus is a muscle in your back near your underarm. It is possible to mentally locate and flex muscles you may not know that you have. These isolation techniques are vital to burning fat and increasing your lean muscle tissue in those hard-to-lose areas of the body. I encourage you to adopt the practice of recruiting your muscles—learn where they are and practice flexing and isolating them.

## 4. Cardiovascular work/breathing practice

You may be aware that it is possible to live without food for weeks. You can live without water for several days. But you can only live without oxygen for a few minutes. Learning to breathe deeply will lead to *voluntary exchange*, which means that oxygen flows into and throughout your body efficiently. You can consciously work on your breathing to improve the circulation of oxygen to every cell. Proper voluntary exchange will make you look and feel younger!

During your workout, make sure that anytime you are feeling pressure, you breathe out. For example, if you are doing a squat, when you begin to stand up, breathe out. As you are lifting up in a bicep curl, breathe out. As you reach and throw, breathe out. As you coordinate your breathing with your movement, it will create a wonderful oxygen flow—voluntary exchange—to all parts of your body.

## 5. Adaptation

It is important to understand the principle of adaptation working in your body. For example, when you stress your muscles through resistance training, the bones to which they are connected are also slightly stressed. This stress will actually improve their function and cause them to adapt to your new muscular fitness. The more resistance you apply in your workout, the better your muscles will work for you. We discussed earlier the flip side, that lack of use of muscles causes atrophy, making the body degenerate much faster.

As God's highest creation, you were designed to grow under times of stress. Exercise is a form of physical resistance that actually relieves stress. Resistance is required in order to adapt in every area of life. There are three major areas in which you will experience resistance in order to strengthen you and help you adapt in life:

1. Your spirit—the eternal part of you—resists temptation.

2. Your soul—mind, will, and emotions—resists the sins of the flesh.

3. Your body—the physical part of you—resists challenges of movement and exercise.

Exercise helps you decrease risk factors to your health, reduce muscle tension, and regulate breathing. Physical adaptation simply involves the improvement in your body's ability to function in strength and freedom because of your fitness training.

Before turning to your personal fitness guide in Part 5, please let me introduce you to the fourth key to getting in shape God's way. It will assure your success in not just beginning well, but also in maintaining your efforts to achieve your health and fitness goals—for the rest of your life. Learning to avoid failure and reach your goals through perseverance will be a vital key to your overall success.

## TAKE ACTION

1.  Make sure that you have calculated the equations in the charts in this chapter to determine your safe heart rate training zone as well as your fat-burning zone. You may want to write them on your vision and mission statements to keep them with you at all times.

2.  Refer to Appendix E to learn how you can obtain any equipment you may need for your workout.

PART 4

**KEY #4: MANIFESTATION—
IT MUST BE LIVED OUT!**
*FITNESS LIFESTYLE*

# NINE

# MAINTAINING YOUR FITNESS LIFESTYLE—DON'T QUIT!

Y OU MAY HAVE NOTICED that there is a progression in understanding the keys to getting in shape God's way. You must begin with the key #1, *revelation*, which unlocks the divine power of God's love into your life. Revelation makes it possible for you to know the truth and change your motivation and core beliefs that have contributed to your destructive mind-set and behavior patterns. Scripture teaches that God gives revelation to every believer:

> But to each one is given the manifestation of the [Holy] Spirit [the evidence, the spiritual illumination of the Spirit] for good and profit.
>
> —1 CORINTHIANS 12:7, AMP

Only through revelation can you begin to realize the wonderful person God created you to be. We pulled the word *real* out of *realization* to empha-size the new reality you can live, which comes through revelation. As a result of your new vision of what is real, you were able to write powerful vision and mission statements to help you refine your vision and reach for your dreams.

Then, you were ready to take key #2, *declaration*, in your hand and begin to unlock the power of your words to change your atmosphere and your life situation. As you learn to agree with the truth of God's Word for your life, your words begin to embrace your purpose and destiny He wants to reveal to you.

Of course, that means you must embrace the necessity of change through key #3, *application*. You will need to become a doer of God's Word, not just a hearer (James 1:22), in order to reap the wonderful harvest that you will plant through speaking and acting as the beautiful person God has made you to be.

As you embrace the first three keys to getting in shape God's way, you will begin to experience key #4, *manifestation* in your life—spirit, soul, and body. When you are manifesting the reality of keys one through three, it simply means that your healthy lifestyle is evident to all; it is easily perceived by the senses and especially by the sight. A good synonym for *manifest* is *obvious*.[1] Your progress toward a healthy lifestyle will be obvious to all who observe your life.

Manifestation involves more than simply arriving at your stated fitness goals; it involves your entire life journey. When God ordained you to become His temple, He wanted you to enjoy the journey—the process. Learning to love yourself as He loves you will require a lifetime of receiving revelation and adjusting your thinking and speaking to embrace divine truth. And at every stage in life, there will be new challenges to face to maintain your goals for health and manifest your destiny in every area of your life—spirit, soul, and body.

God's intention is that love become the greatest source of power on Earth for you to unlock your destiny. As you learn to love God, love yourself, and love others, fulfilling the greatest commandment (Matt. 22:38), your lifestyle will be transformed. When love becomes your motivation, one of your main objectives will automatically become to honor your temple. That will include manifesting to the world that your lifestyle is one that establishes fitness for your body. You will care for the health of your body, as well as your spirit and soul, as a gift of greatest worth.

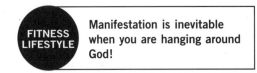

**FITNESS LIFESTYLE**

Manifestation is inevitable when you are hanging around God!

## THE BATTLE BETWEEN YOUR EARS

Your greatest battle to gain mastery and manifest a health lifestyle occurs in a six-inch area between your ears—your brain. Earlier in the book, we discussed the impact your thoughts and words have on your health. As you continue your journey toward health and fulfilling your vision for fitness, it will be helpful to keep the following *E*s in mind. They will inspire you to maintain your progress in your battle against faulty thinking, which, of course, results in faulty doing and being.

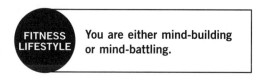

FITNESS LIFESTYLE

**You are either mind-building or mind-battling.**

### Exercise

The term *exercise* refers to any physical movement, especially with the purpose to improve some components of physical fitness. It is bodily activity that develops or maintains overall health. Exercise alone is credited with boosting the immune system and helping to prevent "diseases of affluence," such as heart disease, type 2 diabetes, and obesity. It is also a factor in improving mental health and helping to prevent depression.

Exercise is a gift to you and to the ones you love. Doing ten to fifteen minutes a day of moderate exercise increases your use of oxygen, which enhances your life expectancy. It also improves your quality of life, bathing the skin with natural beauty, reducing anxiety, and diminishing stress.

An ancient proverb says that every time you walk a step, it adds a minute to your life. Consider that the next time you ride an elevator or escalator instead of taking the stairs. A person who exercises regularly knows the true wealth of the health it provides. Do you believe you are worth reducing your risk factors for stroke, heart disease, osteoporosis, bloating, obesity, insecurity, and so on? Then you understand the true wealth of exercise health.

**Energy**

Energy is a serious asset and a sweet friend. You may relate to the term *energy* by its scary definition—calorie. But when you are taking in the right kind of calories—energy—you receive the benefit of this sweet friend, which is a satisfying quality of life. You know that it takes energy to enjoy anything in life.

Wrong kinds of calories, like those found in a tall mocha, spike your energy and then cause it to crash a few minutes later. When you choose to consume good forms of calories, you turn the days of your life into memories of a quality lifestyle and a treasury of wealth, manifested in your success in living your dreams and fulfilling your destiny.

**Equanimity**

*Equanimity* is a little used word that refers to being calm and even-tempered.[2] It is a quality that is welcome on every level of life—spirit, soul, and body. The value of this quiet demeanor cannot be measured in dollars and cents. It guards against panic attacks, depression, and a lack of peace. The apostle Paul instructed believers:

> And let the peace (soul harmony which comes) from the Christ rule (act as umpire continually) in your hearts [deciding and settling with finality all questions that arise in your minds, in that peaceful state] to which [as members of Christ's] one body you were also called [to live].
>
> —COLOSSIANS 3:15, AMP

Anyone who knows the game of baseball understands that it is futile to argue with an umpire; he has the final word. When peace becomes the umpire of our souls, nothing can disturb that "soul harmony," no matter what difficulties we face in life. Americans spend billions of dollars a year to purchase over-the-counter drugs in an effort to produce equanimity for their mind and body; they place a high premium on searching for peace of mind. They are trying to counteract the effects of life stressors such as anxiety, anger, frustration, worry, doubt, unforgiveness, lust, insecurities, and lack of confidence.

Yet, peace is absolutely free for those who seek to know the One who is called the Prince of Peace (Isa. 9:6). Instead of consuming drugs that harm the body, you can choose to become the temple of God and to follow His laws of wealth and health. As you embrace His revelation, the fruit of His Spirit fills you with love, joy, peace, patience, kindness, goodness, faithfulness, gentleness, and self-control (Gal. 5:22–23).

Consider the wealth of your health. How much are you worth? You can choose to maintain a life of equanimity in the face of global conflict as you learn to maintain these principles and allow God to empower you to manifest to all your healthy lifestyle.

| FITNESS LIFESTYLE | Putting your life in order with God causes you to focus on your self-worth rather than your net worth. |

## WHAT TO DO ABOUT FAILURE

One of the greatest obstacles to your success, which you face on a daily basis, is the fear of failure. Internally, you were designed to win. As you have applied the principles of this book so far, you are positioning yourself to win, to manifest your goals for a healthy lifestyle. An important reason for establishing your vision and mission statements and diligently applying the principles of *revelation*, *declaration*, and *application* to your life is to diminish the dread of a relapse into wrong thinking and destructive living.

### Manifestation through motion

You may be aware of Newton's law of motion, which states that a body in motion stays in motion. Of course, he is referencing the planets of the universe. But I like to apply the principle similarly to the human body. When you choose to move, you become addicted to the sheer exhilaration and joy of movement. Freedom is expressed through the ability to move without restraint, which gives you an exquisite sense of well-being. In short, when you choose to put your body in motion, it will stay in motion.

Motion is an inevitable reality of life on many levels. Your physical body was made to move, as we discussed. To avoid the tragedy of atrophy, your body requires healthy and continual movement. On a philosophical level, motion is an inevitable reality of life, working for your good or for bad. As you live your life, you are constantly in motion, moving farther from your dreams or closer to them. The difference will be determined by your choice to maintain your progress, creating a lifestyle that moves you continually toward for your fitness goals.

**Keep moving in the right direction.**

Moving toward a healthy lifestyle requires that you maintain the information you have learned and the revelation you have received about who you are and what motivates you to reach your goals. True revelation hovers over your realities, keeping you focused on the lifestyle you desire to live—for the *real* you. Information helps to guide you in the dos and don'ts that affect your health.

For example, you know that eating late at night increases weight and body fat. However, unless you relate that information to the revelation of who you are and your fitness goals, you will violate what you know and do what you *feel* like doing. In that moment of temptation to eat before bedtime, you have a choice to make. Becoming motivated entirely by the revelation of God's purpose and destiny for your life is essential to manifesting your purpose in life and maintaining your fitness lifestyle to accomplish your goals.

Moving away from late-night eating moves you toward the manifestation of your life goals and fitness lifestyle. Maintaining that decision will involve a fight in your mind against old ways of thinking and self-indulgent behavior. That is a battle you can win if you will totally embrace the four keys you are learning in this book. Revisit them, become accountable to them, and you will receive the help God is waiting to give to you. He will help you to embrace His truth—His revelation of His love for you and of

His wonderful purpose for your life. Begin to declare that truth over your desire for that late-night snack. Just say no! Insist on moving toward the freedom of health that will empower you to fulfill your God-given purpose in the earth. Ask for His help, and you will receive it:

> Call to Me and I will answer you and show you great and mighty things, fenced in and hidden, which you do not know (do not distinguish and recognize, have knowledge of and understand).
>
> —JEREMIAH 33:3, AMP

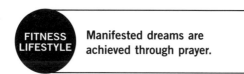

**FITNESS LIFESTYLE** Manifested dreams are achieved through prayer.

## OVERCOMING RELAPSE

You are being empowered to make choices based on the revelation you are receiving of God's love for you. You are becoming the temple of God, and His power dwells in you. Overcoming the fear of failure—and failure itself—is a choice. When you are struggling to complete the designated reps of your workout, the thought of failure may plague your mind. You may believe that you are headed for another relapse. It will be important in those moments to fight against the fear and weird feeling that the dread of failure brings. Begin to declare with your mouth, to anyone who will listen, the goals you have for your fitness lifestyle. Ask God to strengthen your resolve and help you to make the right choice in your moment of temptation to quit.

When I decided I was going to lose weight, I began telling other people. Some looked at me as if I was crazy when I declared, "I am going to lose fifty pounds and quit smoking and drinking." And I cringed inside when I said it, wondering what they would think of me if I failed. I want to share with you some of the revelation I received about how I broke the cycle of failure in my life regarding my fitness lifestyle. I know these principles will help you in the same way they helped me to overcome failure.

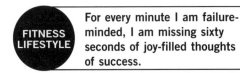

**FITNESS LIFESTYLE**

For every minute I am failure-minded, I am missing sixty seconds of joy-filled thoughts of success.

You may ask what happens if you do begin well and have a relapse into old ways of thinking and bad habits of eating. You may feel like you have failed and cannot move forward again. That is never true. Anyone who has succeeded in life has known failure in the past. It was their reaction to their failure that made the difference. To maintain your progress and reach the manifestation of your goals, you will need to have a plan to overcome any momentary relapse you experience. Remember to use the powerful key of declaration, even though you may feel like circumstances are against you.

These are my top five affirmations that I declare to help me maintain progress in my weakest moments (I suggest you make them into a wall mount):

- My body is a temple of God.
- My appetite is under control.
- I am a success.
- I am no longer a victim but a victor!
- I can do all things through Christ who gives me strength!

To overcome relapse if it occurs, it is important to understand the principle that whatever you feed lives; whatever starves is doomed to die. You can apply that to bad habits, wrong thinking, and wrong attitudes and actions. If you choose to starve them, they will die. If you choose to think positive thoughts and declare the truth of God concerning you, feeding those positive thoughts will cause you to live them. Remember, Scripture declares that as a man thinks in his heart, so is he (Prov. 23:7).

**Bottom line—if you fall, get up again!**

You need to decide that any relapse you may suffer is not forever. It is normal for a toddler to fall when he is learning to walk. But he doesn't decide that, because he keeps falling, he will just sit there and never get up. Every time he gets up again, his equilibrium gains strength of balance, and soon he is not falling at all.

If you fall, reinforce your diligence to think positive thoughts that are true, according to the revelation you are receiving in your heart. As you do, you are strengthening your taproot for life, and it will bring forth good fruit in every area of your life. Learn to focus on managing "God thoughts" through times of adversity instead of trying to manage the problems you are facing.

One of the best ways to do that is to rehearse your goals—your vision— and the steps you are taking to fulfill them. Stare at your vision board and declare that what you see is what you get! Your efforts will not be in vain. God will empower you to live the truth He is showing you so that you can be a glorious temple for His presence.

Just love yourself enough to get up again and keep truckin'. You will be the winner, and before long, falling will be just a distant memory as you begin to manifest your true identity in life.

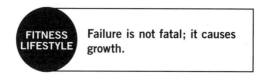

FITNESS LIFESTYLE

Failure is not fatal; it causes growth.

## SUSTAINING YOUR EFFORT

Few things are impossible to diligence and skill. Great works are performed not by strength, but perseverance.[3]

—SAMUEL JOHNSON

It is an obvious fact that maintaining the blessing of having a great physical body requires effort on your part. While it is the revelation of God's love and purpose for your life that motivates you to make a healthy lifestyle your goal, He requires that you make choices to reach those goals and sustain your healthy lifestyle.

Sustaining victory in any area of life requires our willingness to make correct choices. For example, to sustain the blessing of becoming a spiritual person of faith, you must develop a powerful prayer life. To sustain your reputation as a person of integrity, you must be careful of what you say and do and with whom you associate. And sustaining a healthy lifestyle will require effort on your part to make wise choices throughout your journey in life. It is important to be diligent in your efforts, as Scripture confirms: "The plans of the diligent lead to profit as surely as haste leads to poverty" (Prov. 21:5, NIV).

The Scriptures also promise long life and satisfaction to those who trust in the Lord and obey His commands. (See Psalm 91.) The psalmist declared the promise of God for fruitfulness and stability to those who learn to obey His law:

> How blessed is the man who does not walk in the counsel of the wicked, nor stand in the path of sinners, nor sit in the seat of scoffers! But his delight is in the law of the LORD, and in His law he meditates day and night. And he will be like a tree firmly planted by streams of water, which yields its fruit in its season, and its leaf does not wither, and in whatever he does, he prospers.
>
> —PSALM 1:1–3

The basis of sustaining the integrity for your health goals involves proper exercise and eating correctly. Making excuses for overeating or eating incorrectly and not exercising, after you have promised yourself to work toward goals of a healthy lifestyle, destroys the possibility of manifestation of your successful living. If you want to be planted firmly in life as a healthy tree, becoming fruitful for all of your life, you will need to make good use of the four keys we have discussed:

- Revelation
- Declaration
- Application
- Manifestation

## THE END IS JUST THE BEGINNING

You have come to the end of studying the keys to getting in shape God's way. But the end of this study signifies a wonderful new beginning for you to pursue your dreams and conquer every obstacle that has kept you from your destiny.

Let me encourage you to read again your vision and mission statements. You may want to revise them as you receive greater revelation of God's love for you and His purpose for your life. As you begin to use the key of application to unlock your dreams, let this text become a reference guide for you. Follow the workout faithfully and use the food guide to help you establish new eating patterns.

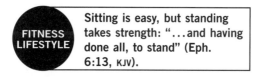

FITNESS LIFESTYLE

Sitting is easy, but standing takes strength: "...and having done all, to stand" (Eph. 6:13, KJV).

If you falter, go back and read Part 4 about maintaining your goals. If you discover another rotten root in your core belief system that needs to be extracted, read Part 1 again to establish the principle of receiving revelation of the truth and allowing it to set you free. Not only have these keys unlocked my personal destiny and transformed my life dramatically, but I have watched them transform the lives of my clients as well.

And I am excited to know they are working for you, dear reader. These keys cannot fail because they are based on God's way. And you cannot fail when you choose to continually embrace them, regardless of what circumstances you are facing. Let the prayer of commitment below empower you to make God the center of your life and allow Him to make you whole—spirit, soul, and body.

## CONCLUSION

Faith must always pass the test of endurance and discouragement. For that reason, the apostle Paul encouraged us, "And let us not lose heart and grow weary and faint in acting nobly and doing right, for in due time and at the appointed season we shall reap, if we do not loosen and relax our courage and faint" (Gal. 6:9, AMP).

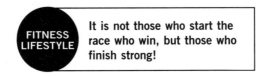

**FITNESS LIFESTYLE**

It is not those who start the race who win, but those who finish strong!

You can survive the test of discouragement! This is your sign. As crazy as it sounds, the greatest victories have only been won after the greatest fight! Anything that is worth getting is worth fighting to get. Do not expect it to come easy; you will have to fight for fitness!

Facing the transition from where you want to quit is the sign that there is a powerful breakthrough for you right around the corner. When you face discouragement, encourage yourself! Speak to yourself! Call out to God! Your endurance training includes this mental aspect that requires you to *fight*! I can promise you that the victory and destiny you were created to walk in will be a living reality filled with health and abundance—God's way!

I encourage you to pray this prayer with me, which will never fail to help you gain the victory you need:

> *Lord, help me and bless me today! I need You to strengthen me when I am weak. This is Your promise to me, and I receive it! I want to be healthy and see my dreams fulfilled—literally. Please manifest a miracle in my life. I receive Jesus in my heart and ask Him to shine the light of revelation into the areas of my heart*

*that have been blind to His love. Forgive everything I have ever thought, said, or done in error. I am sorry! I pray that the eyes of my heart will be flooded with divine light so I can fully comprehend the purpose of my existence and calling. I understand that You hope in me, and because of that I can win! Please show me that hope! And Father, let me truly come to know the love You have for me. I know You can do it. I believe You are the Great Physician. Thank You, Lord! In Jesus's name, I pray. Amen.*

After you have completed the following Take Action evaluation, you are ready to proceed to your personal workout and eating plans. Thank you for allowing me the privilege of being your personal trainer as you make the life-changing choice of getting in shape God's way.

# TAKE ACTION

Answer these questions thoughtfully and honestly in order to help you avoid their pitfalls as you begin your workout and eating plan for getting in shape God's way. Begin to declare the promises of God and your vision statement to counteract the effect your answers could otherwise have on your progress toward your fitness lifestyle.

1. Is food your only comfort? When do you most likely consume comfort foods? What are they?

   _____

   _____

2. Do you abuse food instead of using it for nourishing your health? What kinds of substances do you abuse? Sugar? Sodas? Alcohol?

   _____

   _____

3. Are you afraid of failing?

   _____

4. Are you anxious about starting a new plan and having a relapse?

   _____

5. Is it an integrity issue? Are you honest with yourself and with others?

   _____

6. Do you worry about what others say about you? Do you feel they are against you?

   _____

7. Are you jealous of the success of others?

   _____

8. Do you feel judgmental toward others, condemning them for the same kinds of things you do?

   _____

9. Do you harbor unforgiveness? Are you angry with God?

   _____

10. Do you hate your body?

    _____

11. Will you allow God into your life and let Him reign in the physical component of your body?

    _____

PART 5

**WORKING IT OUT—LIVING YOUR DREAMS!**
*FITNESS PLAN*

TEN

# YOUR PERSONAL WORKOUT
# AND EATING PLANS

ONGRATULATIONS! YOU HAVE MADE a wonderful decision to begin your fitness-training regimen. You are armed with four keys that will assure your success in reaching your health and fitness goals—God's way. Your journey toward health and fitness will cause you to reign in life and fulfill your divine destiny, which alone can give you total fulfillment and satisfaction.

During the process of reaching your goals, it may be necessary at times to review these keys to release their dynamic power more fully into your heart and mind, unlocking your potential for optimal health. And keep your vision and mission statements with you, along with your "vision board" that you should keep developing, to encourage you to reach your goals. Remember, in order to be dynamic, your goals must be specific.

## FUNCTIONAL INTERVAL TRAINING

Remember, functional interval training involves movements that correspond to real ways you move in life. It combines intervals of exertion, which speed up your metabolism, followed by short rest periods. As you progress, try to shorten your rest periods. As I mentioned earlier, functional interval training has been proven so effective that ten minutes of exercise is as effective as thirty minutes of other aerobic exercise.

## EXERCISE SCHEDULES

- You should exercise three days a week, using the proper form, as we discussed. I have included a DVD for you to see the correct way to perform each movement.

- Whether you follow the beginner, intermediate, or advanced regimen, using the following charts, all exercise should be completed within thirty minutes to an hour.

- When you discount the rest periods between exercises, beginners and intermediates will actually be doing only seven to twelve minutes of actual exercise; advanced will do thirteen to fifteen minutes of exercise per session.

### EXERCISE EQUIPMENT

For the exercises in this chapter, you will not need a lot of special equipment. I do recommend that you purchase a heart monitor, as I discussed earlier. (See Appendix E for purchasing information.)

Also, you will need an elastic resistance band, which is a portable alternative to weights for strength training. The band is a valuable piece of equipment that allows you to feel resistance from two sides: when you push and when it pulls you! I am making available my God's Way Resistance Band to you for use in your workout plan. (See Appendix E for purchasing information.)

For some exercises, you may find it necessary to wrap the resistance band around your wrist once or twice in order to obtain adequate resistance. These photos demonstrate the proper way to wrap the excess band around your wrist until it is comfortable and provides enough resistance to feel the exercise working.

224

## EXERCISE CHARTS

The charts in Appendix D are a simple guide for you to use after you have followed the instructions in this chapter and viewed the DVD to learn your functional fitness regimen. Make copies of each chart and use them as quick reminders of the order of exercises included in your workout as you progress from beginner to advanced.

## BEGINNER WORKOUT

### Ab lift

Lie facedown, flat on floor. Hold in belly button as tight as possible for 30 seconds.

### Ab clap

Lie flat on back with knees bent, feet on floor. Do a sit-up, swinging arms from overhead to under legs, and clap forcefully.

### Ab walk

Lie flat on back with feet in air, hands under hips. Move legs back and forth as if walking in air.

### Hyperextensions

Lie facedown, flat on floor. Reach one arm up in air and lift opposite leg. Keep focus on back and keep your abs tight. (Switch sides and repeat.)

### Plank

Lie on stomach with elbows and balls of feet on the floor. Lift torso and hold it in straight line, flexing torso and focusing on stomach and lower back.

### Reach and throw

Stand with band to the side of your body. Reach across body to grab band, then pull across body, simulating a throw over the shoulder. (Caution: Do not go too fast too soon. Be sensitive to your shoulder.) (Switch sides and repeat.)

**Pick and push**

Cross body snatch. Act as if picking something up from off floor; move to standing position, pushing it up and across your body. End with arm over head. (Switch sides and repeat.)

**Balance with row**

Slightly lift one leg about 6–8 inches. Say to yourself, "I am balanced. I am balanced." While balancing on either leg, try to imitate rowing a boat. Keep stomach tight and squeeze your back as you pull your arms in that rowing motion.

**Side-to-side jumps**

Jump side to side, back and forth.

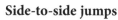

**Single-leg RK Lifelift**

Stand on one leg. Reach both hands down to floor and then stand back up, balancing on one leg the entire time. Focus on the back of the leg (hamstring), lower back, and middle back.

**RK Lifelift**

Using only your lower back, bend over, keeping knees slightly bent and head in line with spine. Grab onto band in front of you and lift band as you straighten to upright position. Focus on lower back and shoulders.

228

**Biceps curls—double arm**

With band anchored, keeping elbows locked into waist, bend as far as elbow can curl up. Keep wrists straight.

**Single-arm reverse curls**

Reverse your grip with fingernails facing ground. Curl upward, keeping elbows locked into waist.

**Overhead triceps extension**

With band anchored behind you, hold it with one hand and extend that arm straight up into air. Keep abs and core tight and elbow locked into head. And extend from elbow, using triceps to flex.

## Bent-over triceps extension

With torso bent forward, extend arm straight out in back of you, keeping elbow tight to body. Keeping back straight and head up, squeeze arm, isolating the triceps muscle you are using.

## Two-minute cooldown

Walk around the room or the gym for two minutes, bringing your heart rate down.

## INTERMEDIATE/ADVANCED WORKOUT

## Ab lift

Lie facedown, flat on floor. Hold in belly button as tight as possible for 30 seconds.

## Ab clap

Lie flat on back with knees bent, feet on floor. Do a sit-up, swinging arms from overhead to under legs, and clap forcefully.

### V-sits

Seated on floor, balance body and extend legs in front of you without touching floor. Hold this position for 30 seconds.

### V-sits with kicks (advanced only)

Seated on floor, balance body and extend legs in front of you without touching floor. Keeping legs together, move them in and out, bending at the knees.

### Hyperextensions

While lying on your stomach, tighten the stomach with the arms stretched out in front of you and your legs straight, keeping your head up. Lift your arms and legs at the same time

and breathe out. If it's too difficult, try lifting one arm in conjunction with the opposite leg. Make sure to lift the entire leg.

**Hyperextensions—with swim (advanced only)**

Perform hyperextension as directed above. While lifting both arms and legs, try simulating a criss-cross motion back and forth, crossing the arms and legs simultaneously.

**Plank**

Lie on stomach with elbows and balls of feet on the floor. Lift torso and hold it in straight line, flexing torso and focusing on stomach and lower back.

**Plank—one leg holds (advanced only)**

With the body in a solid plank position, with your legs, the core of your body, and your arms straight and tight, lift one leg and hold for a period of time. Then switch legs.

**Push-up on knees (advanced only)**

Make sure head and spine are aligned and push up with arms from your knees.

**Band press (advanced only)**

Place the band behind your back just under your arms, wrapping the excess band around your hands to make up the slack. With your elbows lifted and parallel to the ground, press and breathe out. Come back down slowly.

**Reach and throw**

Stand with band to the side of your body. Reach across body to grab band, then pull across body simulating a throw over the shoulder. (Caution: Do not go too fast too soon. Be sensitive to your shoulder.)

**ADVANCED:** While coming to the top of the throw, simultaneously "explode" with a

slight jump, using your coordination to match the jump at the end of the throw and at the same time land feet on the ground.

**Pick and push**

Cross body snatch. Act as if picking something up from off floor; move to standing position, pushing it up and across your body. End with arm over head.

**ADVANCED:** While coming to the top of the push, simultaneously "explode" with a slight jump, using your coordination to match the jump at the end of the throw and at the same time land feet on the ground.

**Balance one leg**

Slightly lift one leg about 6–8 inches. Say to yourself, "I am balanced. I am balanced."

**VARIATION:** Keep stomach tight and squeeze your back as you pull your arms back in a rowing motion, lifting your knee 4–6 inches.

**Balance with row—high knee**

Keep stomach tight and squeeze your back as you pull your arms in a rowing motion. Lift your knee as high as possible while balancing. A variation for your grip: try an underhand grip as well as an overhand one.

**Band jumps**

Use band to add resistance to jumping. Hold band with good tension and jump. Control coming down. Add side-to-side and tiny jumps as variations.

### Jumps with knees to chest (advanced only)

Jump into air, raising the knees up to the chest. Breathe accordingly.

### Single-leg RK Lifelift

Stand on one leg. Reach both hands down to floor and then stand back up, extending one leg straight out behind you as you reach the floor. Focus on the back of the leg (hamstring), lower back, and middle back.

### RK Lifelift with shoulder raise

This is a variation of the RK Lifelift. As you're standing up, keep your arms slightly bent, thinking on your frontal shoulders. Raise your hands to your current neck level, breathing out.

**ADVANCED:** Continue raising your hands overhead, simulating a throwing motion. Breathe out forcefully at the very top, and control your speed coming back down.

### Knee-ups

Raise knees up as high as you can, alternating as fast as you can. Keep your abs tight and core tight!

### Knee-ups with split kicks (advanced only)

Jump into air and part legs, keeping knees straight only in air. Bend knees as you get near the floor to absorb shock.

**Bicep curls**

With band anchored, keeping elbows locked into waist, bend as far as elbow can curl up. Keep wrists straight. VARIATION: Stand on one leg.

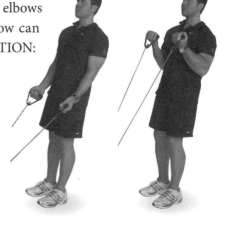

**Single-arm reverse curl**

Reverse your grip with fingernails facing ground. Curl upward, keeping elbows locked into waist.

**Overhead triceps extension**

With band anchored behind you, hold it with one hand and extend that arm straight up into air. Keep abs and core tight and elbow locked into head. And extend from elbow, using triceps to flex.

**Bent-over triceps extension**

With torso bent forward, extend arm straight out in back of you, keeping elbow tight to body. Keeping back straight and head up, squeeze arm, isolating the triceps muscle you are using.

**Triceps freeze**

Seated upright on floor, place hands on floor behind you. Push up on hands, flexing triceps and keeping elbow locked out. Lift one leg and return. Alternate legs.

**Ab rotators**

With band attached, grab band with tight resistance. While seated in upright position, twist side to side. (Switch sides and repeat.)

### Hip lifts

Lying flat on back, lift hips straight up in air until back is in a straight line. (Be cautious of pressure on neck.) Squeeze glutes and core.

**ADVANCED:** Prior to beginning of the lift, point the toe and lift the leg straight in the air, keeping the leg tight and lifting the hips off the floor. Squeeze your gluteus and tighten your stomach, breathing out.

### Forward lunge—band behind

Hold attached band behind you and relax arms. Lunging forward, take a big step away from where band is attached and return to neutral position. Repeat with alternate leg.

**ADVANCED:** Hold the band anchored behind you. As you come to the top standing up, do a slight jump in the air. Come together with the feet. Squeeze the gluteus again and go back into the lunge, alternating legs.

**Reverse lunge with band (advanced only)**

Hold band in front of you with both hands. Take big step backward with one leg, keeping front knee aligned with toe. Bend back knee while keeping torso straight, head up. Return to neutral position. Repeat with alternate leg.

**Squats with hip reducers**

Squat down, keeping back straight and head up. As you stand, lift one leg to side of body.

**Directional lunges (advanced only)**

Keep band attached and use in front of you for support. Hold on to band as you take a big step to the side and than back to other side. Take big steps, keeping back straight and breathing out as you come up.

**Two-minute cooldown**

Walk around the room or the gym for two minutes, bringing your heart rate down.

## WHAT IN THE WORLD TO EAT—OR NOT?

Now that you are beginning your physical workout regimen, you will also want to consider changes to your eating patterns. I have included here a simple list of the "Best Foods" in the world to eat, along with a "Do Not Eat" list to help you make necessary changes.

As you progress in embracing the law of movement, you will find that your taste buds will actually change. Your body will crave the pure water that it needs to flush toxins and bathe every cell with its cleansing properties. Fruits and vegetables will become more appealing to you, and sugary, starchy foods will actually lose their appeal. Sound impossible? With a little self-control on your part—or a lot—you will discover the freedom of nourishing your body with what it needs to meet your fitness goals—and enjoying it.

**FITNESS PLAN** You can conquer only what you confront.

If you feel like your palms are sweaty and there is a knot in the pit of your stomach as you read this, please remember that you are not trying this on your own. You have embraced the keys to getting in shape God's way, which are empowering you to become the person you long to become. Take a deep breath, and pause a moment to consciously embrace again these powerful, divine keys to your success:

EATING PLAN

- **Revelation.** You understand through your *fitness beliefs*, as you continue to receive God's love through revelation, that your body is not yours; it belongs to God. You are His temple, and He desires to dwell in a healthy temple. Your past has lost its power, and you are new creation.

- **Declaration.** Your *fitness words* are empowering you to live your fitness beliefs. By faith you can declare, "I have my appetite under control, and I am getting in shape God's way."

- **Application.** As you begin to walk in your new *fitness function*, you will apply exercise and healthy eating habits to your daily life. You are breaking long-standing habits of the "couch potato syndrome" and "junk food junkie" through the empowerment you are receiving through revelation and declaration of the truth of God's Word for your life.

- **Manifestation.** I don't want you to try this as one more way to begin a fitness plan for a while. You must choose to make this godly approach to living your new lifestyle—for life. For some, this means changing forty years of doing it the wrong way. So be patient, but ruthlessly persistent. Remember, now you are on God's team, and He never loses. He has promised you His abundant health.

## DIFFERENT STROKES FOR DIFFERENT FOLKS

I have kept the eating plan here very simple to encourage each of you to choose what works best for you. Everyone's metabolism is different. Some people adjust better to a high-carbs and low-fat approach than to low carbs and high fat. Others adapt better to high protein and low carbs; still others prefer high carbs and low protein. I have found generally that balancing a combination of carbs, protein, and fat is essential to optimal health. Of course, eating organically grown foods is the optimal choice for wholesome nutrients for your body. If cost is a factor, do your best. Try to buy organic foods when possible.

When it comes to what *not* to eat, however, there are some things that simply cause problems for everyone, such as too much sugar. And a lack of vegetables and vitamin-rich nutrients always results in health problems. "Dead" foods, which include packaged junk foods of all kinds, simply do not give the body the nutrients it needs to maintain health.

To begin your healthy eating regimen, I recommend that you simply cut back on the amount of food you eat each day and add in more fruits and vegetables to help cleanse your body of toxins. In his best-selling book *Toxic Relief,* Dr. Don Colbert, nationally acclaimed physician and author, confirms the need to reduce your food intake to relieve your body gently of toxic buildup:

> When treating patients with degenerative diseases, I began to notice a pattern. Most of these individuals weren't underfed. In fact, most of them were big overeaters.... This was particularly true of people with obesity, cardiovascular diseases, arthritis, type 2 diabetes, migraine headaches, a host of different allergic conditions, psoriasis, rheumatoid arthritis, and lupus....I began to realize that one of the main causes of these degenerative diseases is overconsumption of sugary, fatty, starchy, and high-protein foods—foods that have been processed, fried, and further devitalized.... This kind of burden creates enormous stress for your entire digestive tract.[1]

Dr. Colbert refers to fiber as nature's detoxifier. He recommends cleansing the GI tract by including high-fiber foods in your diet, such as raw fruits, raw vegetables, whole grains, beans, legumes, and seeds. He also recommends adding 1 tablespoon of freshly ground flaxseed, which can be sprinkled on oatmeal or placed in a smoothie or other foods, two or three times a day to increase your fiber intake.[2]

**Your first week**

During your first week that you are cutting back on your food intake, I recommend that you begin with a partial fast. Because fruit is high in fiber, it not only gives the body needed nutrients in a natural form, but it also cleanses the GI tract of toxins at the same time.

For the first day, I recommend that you eat at least five servings of only one type of fruit, while also drinking plenty of water. Then, for the next three days, eat a mixture of fruits or freshly juiced fruits (avoiding bananas). Please refer to the World's Best Foods list for fruits to use during your first week.

On days five through seven of your first week, you can add an organic mixed-greens' salad with a light dressing, along with some raw nuts and seeds. Eat your mixed fruits in the morning and at midday, then add your salad for dinner with a portion of fresh fish of your choice. You can add to your green salad some fresh fruit, pumpkin seeds and/or sunflower seeds, a small amount of goat cheese, and 1 to 2 tablespoons of an all-natural dressing, such as oil and vinegar or fresh, squeezed lemon. A small amount of raw cheese sprinkled on your salad would be fine to add as well.

I recommend that you drink more water than you normally do during your first week of the plan. Instead of drinking one-half ounce per pound of body weight, drink three quarters of an ounce per pound of body weight each day.

Never forget the source of your empowerment for your fasting regimen; give thanks for the revelation that you are receiving, and declare your faith in God to help you maintain your goals for a healthy lifestyle—daily.

**Colon cleanse**

I also recommend that you take time to cleanse your colon of its inevitable toxicity. My good friend and Bible coach Jordan Rubin, author of *The Maker's Diet,* suffered from life-threatening Crohn's disease and other debilitating complications of the digestive system. He knows what he is talking about regarding the need to cleanse the colon. He explains that you have twenty-five to thirty-five feet of digestive tract, from end to end. During your lifetime, sixty tons of food will pass through the gastrointestinal tract. He describes the health problems caused by not caring for this vital organ:

If the digestive system is not given a chance to restore itself—through body therapies known as cleansing and fasting—then digestive-related disorders and disease can and will occur, affecting the very core of how the body grows, repairs itself, gains energy, and reaches its perfect weight.[3]

Jordan Rubin has developed a wonderful product for the purpose of cleansing your colon. (See Appendix E.) I recommend that you use this powerfully effective product to give your colon a chance to restore itself to health as you proceed toward your fitness goals.

## Your second week—and beyond

After you have given your body a head start on cleansing through your partial fast of the first week, you can begin to eat every three or four hours, choosing from the list of the World's Best Foods. Of course, you need to keep your portions small. And remember to thank God for the motivation He is giving you and His promise of abundant health. You might pray this way:

*Lord, I give You thanks for this food. You said in Your Word that if we obey Your commands, You would remove sickness and disease far from us (Deut. 7:15). I want to become a healthy temple for Your presence. I bless this food in Jesus's name and thank You that I am eating to glorify You in my body. I declare to my metabolism, "Speed up! Body fat, decrease!"*

Remember to eat slowly and chew your food well. Try to eat in a relaxed environment, and avoid eating when you are overly stressed. I suggest that you restrict your liquids with your meals. Drink fluids if you must, but food digests better with no added liquids.

## THE WORLD'S BEST FOODS LIST

(Please refer to Appendix C, "Quick Online Food Resources Guide" for ordering many of the following foods.)

### Water

And lots of it! Sixty-four ounces per day is required.

| | |
|---|---|
| Penta Water (For more information about Penta Water, visit their Web site at www.pentawater.com) | Voss water, bottled in glass |
| Coconut water (especially to replenish after workout) | Spring water |
| Mineral sparkling water | |

### Fats and oils

| | |
|---|---|
| Extra-virgin coconut oil | Olive oil |
| Ghee butter | Raw cow's milk butter (use sparingly if you trying to reduce your body fat) |

### Fruits

Days 1 through 3 of the first week, only the following fruits are recommended. Choose organically grown fruits only. Make sure you are eating some type of fruit (or juicing fresh fruits) every three hours.

| | |
|---|---|
| Apples | Lemon |
| Acai berries | Lime |
| Blackberries | Oranges (limit quantity because they are high in sugar) |
| Blueberries | Raspberries |
| Cherries | Strawberries |

Days 4 through 7 of the first week, add in any of the following. Keep frequency of eating to every three or four hours.

| | |
|---|---|
| Apricots | Melon |
| Cantaloupe | Passion fruit |
| Coconut | Plums |
| Cranberries | Pineapple |

## THE WORLD'S BEST FOODS LIST

| | |
|---|---|
| Dates | Pomegranates |
| Figs | Prunes (limit quantity because they are high in sugar) |
| Grapefruit | Raisins (Limit quantity because they are high in sugar) |
| Grapes (red and dark purple are best) | Peaches |
| Guava | Pears |
| Kiwi | Watermelon |

### Fish and seafood

(If you are vegetarian or vegan, consider other options from the food list.)

| | |
|---|---|
| Halibut | Sole |
| Salmon | Tuna |
| Sardines | Trout |
| Sea bass | Yellowtail |
| Snapper | |

### Meats

| | |
|---|---|
| Beef (grass-fed organic) | Lamb |
| Buffalo | Turkey (Diestel brand or organic) |
| Chicken | |

### Dairy

(If you are prone to allergies, check with your physician or nutritionist to create alternatives.)

| | |
|---|---|
| Coconut milk | Kefir |
| Goat yogurt | Low-fat milk in small amounts |
| Goat's and/or sheep's mild cheese (no rennant) | Whole milk and cream (organic) |

### Eggs

(No Egg Beaters)

| | |
|---|---|
| Egg whites | Omega 3 DHA organic eggs |

### Vegetables

## THE WORLD'S BEST FOODS LIST

Other veggies may be added; these are the top choices.

| | |
|---|---|
| Asparagus | Mustard greens |
| Avocado | Olives |
| Beets | Onions |
| Broccoli | Peas |
| Cabbage | Peppers (bell) |
| Carrots | Peppers (hot) |
| Cauliflower | Pumpkin |
| Celery | Spinach |
| Corn | Sprouts |
| Cucumber | Squash |
| Eggplant | String beans |
| Fennel | Sweet potatoes |
| Garlic | Swiss chard |
| Green beans and peas | Tomatoes |
| Kale | Turnips |
| Leeks | Wheat grass |
| Lettuce (every type) | Yams |
| Mushrooms | |

### Beans and legumes

| | |
|---|---|
| Black beans | Lentils |
| Garbanzo beans | Soybeans |
| Kidney beans | White beans |

### Breads and cereals

| | |
|---|---|
| Bran cereal (low sugar/organic) | Seven- or nine-grain breads |
| Ezekiel 4:9 breads | Steel-cut oatmeal |
| Pita bread | Whole-grain, organic, all natural cereals |

### Sweeteners and desserts

| | |
|---|---|
| Almond butter with fresh strawberries | Raw honey (avoid late at night and use sparingly) |

## THE WORLD'S BEST FOODS LIST

| | |
|---|---|
| Dark chocolate (organic) | Raw sorbet |
| Maple syrup (limit use because it is high in sugar) | Soft-serve original yogurt |
| Raw coconut | Stevia |
| Raw cheesecake, unsweetened (for more information, visit Rawbc.org and raw-creations.com) | Cinnamon (1/4 teaspoon a day helps control blood sugar) |

### Nuts and seeds

Everything in the nut family is very high in fat content, although it is good fat. Eat sparingly if you are trying to lose weight.

| | |
|---|---|
| Almond butter | Raw hazelnuts |
| Barley | Raw macadamia nuts |
| Buckwheat | Raw pecans |
| Pumpkin seeds | Raw sunflower seeds |
| Raw almonds | Raw walnuts |
| Raw flaxseeds | Sesame seeds |

### Seasonings and condiments (organic)

| | |
|---|---|
| All-natural ranch dressing | Natural marinades (preservative free) |
| Ketchup (made with fresh tomatoes and no sugar) | Natural salad dressings (preservative free) |
| Mustard | Omega 3 mayonnaise (only if absolutely must-have) |

### Nutritional food bars

Watch out for high sugar content bars. Choose organic, raw, and natural over other brands. (See Appendix C.)

| | |
|---|---|
| 100% Go Raw Bars (all flavors) | Garden of Life bars |
| Cuff Bars | |

### Protein shakes

Combining protein makes for a great bodybuilder's dream shake. But studies are showing that for overall health, they may not be as good for you as some think. Check the ingredients prior to consuming. Some are very good; others are very bad.

| MEAL IDEAS | |
|---|---|
| **Breakfast (ideal for rapid weight loss)** | |
| Go Raw Bar with 1 teaspoon of almond butter and freshly juiced strawberries | Organic coffee or tea |
| **Morning snack ideal** | |
| Hard-boiled egg with fresh sea salt and a small apple or carrots | |
| **Lunch** | |
| Turkey sandwich with mustard, lettuce, tomatoes, and onions (hold the mayo) on seven- or nine-grain bread or Ezekiel 4:9 bread | Cup of green tea |
| Green salad | |
| **Afternoon snack** | |
| Protein and fiber shake with fresh berries | |
| **Dinner** | |
| Grilled or baked salmon over a bed of mixed organic greens, lightly covered in all-natural raspberry vinaigrette dressing | Sweet potato or ½ cup brown rice |

| DO NOT EAT LIST | |
|---|---|
| CAUTION: Always check ingredients listed on the packaging of any food you buy. Learn to read the ingredients of what your eating or drinking, no matter the category. | |
| The following list includes ingredients, foods, and drinks that should be avoided to promote health and a healthy lifestyle. | |
| **Water** | |
| Tap water (usually chlorinated) | |
| **Ingredients** | |

## DO NOT EAT LIST

| | |
|---|---|
| Artificial sweeteners, including aspartame and sucralose | Lists of "added preservatives" |
| Corn syrup | Monosodium glutamate (MSG) |
| High sugar content, especially refined sugar | Spices with sugar |
| High-fructose corn syrup | Sugar alcohol |
| Hydrogenated oils and fats (contained in most salad dressings) | White and processed flours |
| **Meats** | |
| Bacon | Oysters |
| Clams | Pork or pork sausage |
| Crab | Prosciutto |
| Ham | Salami |
| Mussels | Shellfish |
| **Fats** | |
| Canola oil | Lard |
| Corn oil | Margarine |
| Imitation butter | Shortening |
| **Miscellaneous** | |
| Candy bars | Hard liquor |
| Canned sodas | Honey-roasted nuts or peanuts |
| Fast food | |
| **Fruits** | |
| All fruits canned in syrup | |

## HOW MUCH DO I EAT TO LOSE WEIGHT, MAINTAIN WEIGHT, OR GAIN WEIGHT?

Yes, you do need to eat a certain amount of calories each day. If you are not losing weight, you are eating too much. If you are not gaining muscle, you are not eating enough. To calculate your caloric requirements, fill in the chart below:

Desired body weight _____ x 10 = _____ REE (resting energy expenditure or calories you burn a day no matter what!)

REE _____ x 1.1–1.3 to lose weight = _____ calories per day

REE _____ x 1.5 to maintain weight = _____ calories per day

REE _____ x 1.8–2.4 to gain weight = _____ calories per day

Declare: "I eat _____ (calorie goal) calories a day. There is great order in my life, and my appetites are under control."

## SUGGESTIONS FOR HEALTHY "CHEATING" AND OTHER "NEEDS"

As a professional trainer, I have heard a multitude of exceptions that clients try to use to exempt themselves from responsibility for healthy living. Some are listed below with cautions or suggestions as to how to handle *your* pet "need."

**"But I'm a vegan or vegetarian."**

This lifestyle can be very healthy if you learn how to supplement your eating habits with protein, vitamins, and minerals you need for optimal health to avoid deficiencies of nutrients found in other eating patterns. Learn as much as you can about this lifestyle, basing your knowledge on reputable universities and other professionals.

**"But I am dying for a burger and fries!" (Stop saying "I'm dying.")**

Purchase grass-fed, organic beef and make your burger with good bread and natural condiments. Try sweet potato fries. (They are available in more restaurants now.)

**"What about my coffee?"**

Coffee is best if it is organic and is consumed fresh. According to one dietary expert, Jordan Rubin, in his book *Perfect Weight America*, coffee is best when consumed in its natural state.[4] Decaffeinated coffee is highly processed and removes some of the antioxidant benefits contained in the natural coffee beans.

**"But I want a sandwich for lunch."**

If you are eating out, order your sandwich with an acceptable type of meat. Use cranberry sauce instead of mayo. Wholesome sandwiches are easy to make at home with proper ingredients. Stay away from white-flour products.

**"But I need my soda."**

Try a sparking bottle of water. Pellegrino is wonderful. It is served in a glass bottle (not a metal can) and is delicious with a fresh lime or lemon.

**"But I need a 'cheat' day."**

Then have one. Just make sure you are not giving in to an addiction to your favorite food or drink or bingeing because of emotional eating. Emotional eating will lead to an addiction. When you feel a "cheat" coming on, use your key of declaration and read again your vision and mission statements. Make sure it is worth it to lose sight of your goals for even one day. Begin to declare your destiny, developing from your healthy taproot, and spend some time in prayer and meditation.

**"But we're going to a birthday party—mine!"**

OK. So pray before you go for strength to be true to your goals—you are going to need it. Sometimes when I say this to clients, they laugh at me. But did you know that God's Word declare His strength is made perfect in our weakness? (See 2 Corinthians 12:9.)

Before going to the party, declare to yourself, "God is strong in me. I am not going to eat everything I see. I am going to have a small portion of cake. I will choose the olives and the carrots over the chips and dips." You'll be the one who comes out dancing the night away.

**"But I need a drink."**

Addiction to alcohol consumption is no different than any other addiction. As you embrace the keys to freedom we have discussed, your tastes will change and your "need" for alcohol will diminish. Declare the truth about the harm alcohol does to your life, and declare your destiny in God. Cry out to Him for help, and He will come running to you! In faith, begin to declare, "I will never need a drink again!" You will be empowered by God's divine love to make that declaration a reality in your life. And don't be afraid to get some professional help. God will be with you.

**"But my grandfather smoked for years and lived to be eighty!"**

Smoking has a greater negative effect on health in our world because our general health is more at risk from the air we breathe, the food we eat, the pollution in our environment, and the stress under which we live. It is a fact that smoking causes cancer.

I encourage you to meditate on the reality that your body is the temple of God. Would you put your cigarette out before going into church? Most likely. When the revelation hits you that God lives in your temple, not in the church building, it will strengthen your resolve to respect the presence of God in your body. As you do, smoking will be gone forever. Declare it now, "My body is the temple of the living God! I will never need a cigarette again."

**"But I need my bedtime snack."**

To meet your fitness goals, especially regarding losing weight, you must avoid late-night eating. If you are not going to be up for another three hours, why are you eating a five-course meal? When you eat late at night, the food has nowhere to go, except to a storage compartment in your body to be stored as fat—even if it is fat-free. You may store it in your chin, stomach area, hips, and gluteus. It is simply a fact—it will be stored.

## What to Order When I Eat in Public

There are ways to avoid wrong eating patterns even when you are dining in your favorite restaurant or with friends at their invitation. Adhering to the following guidelines will help you avoid harmful foods and maintain your fitness goals.

**How to order**

These eating tips will help you enjoy dining out without guilt:

1. Stick to chicken, turkey, and fish.

2. Eat vegetables raw or cooked.

3. Enjoy pasta in hand-size portions.

4. Ask for egg whites (no butter).

5. Eat only nonfat items.

6. Dairy items should be chosen carefully, including what you add to your coffee.

**What to avoid or use sparingly**

There are food items that you must avoid in order to maintain your fitness goals. They include:

1. Hash brown potatoes (oily, white potatoes)

2. Butter, mayo, cheeses, dressings, desserts

3. Wild game, local (if not reputable) and overseas street vendor foods

4. Fried, creamy, and crispy foods

5. Sauces (especially pasta)

**How to make your requests**

Most restaurants are catering to the reasonable requests of their customers who ask for special consideration. You can ask them to bring your sauce on the side, for example. You can even request politely that they cook an item dry with no oil. It is also appropriate to ask the server the ingredients used in sauces and other menu items. If the server does not know, he or she will usually try to find out for you. It is important that you consider your health needs, even when eating in public. And when you do it reasonably, you will usually receive satisfaction for your requests.

## My Personal Eating Record

Copy the chart on page 258 and fill it in for three days. That will give you time to purchase a journal in which you can log what you are eating daily. Find a journal you enjoy looking at: leather, plastic, decorative, etc., and make it *yours*. You will not need to journal your food and drink intake forever. But for this crucial period of your life, it will help you become conscious of how much food and drink is going into your body. It will also make you aware of your food choices. If you have to log chips and dip or that candy bar, it will prick your conscience and make you aware that you are violating your goals.

As you learn to exercise self-control, your journal will help you master your appetites when you adopt this measurement system of accountability for your eating habits. Measure what goes in your body, and it won't be long until you will be shouting, "My body is back!"

## MY PERSONAL EATING RECORD:
### This Is What I Ate Today

| Date: |
|---|
| Breakfast: |
| Snack: |
| Lunch: |
| Snack: |
| Dinner: |
| Snack |

How was my mood today?

_____

_____

Did I drink water? ❑ yes  ❑ no

| Date: |
|---|
| Breakfast: |
| Snack: |
| Lunch: |
| Snack: |
| Dinner: |
| Snack |

How was my mood today?

_____

_____

Did I drink water? ❑ yes  ❑ no

## In Conclusion

True education is a continual pursuit. You are growing and learning every day. God, in His intent to develop your character, gave you the power of choice. Your free will is a powerful gift that must be used wisely. What goes into your body should be one of the most important things you consider in life. It is more important to your success than your money, car, clothing, or career. Establishing right priorities for a healthy lifestyle will establish a quality of life based on a healthy taproot, which will make you successful in every area of your life.

I have summarized your top considerations for weight loss in what I call the "Ten Commandments for Weight Loss." These simple guidelines will help you meet your fitness goals—if you stick with them! Finally, I want to invite you to participate in our dynamic conferences scheduled around the globe in order to continue to receive revelation and grow through impartation. To check for a conference near you, as well as to access other helpful information, go to my Web site at www.gettinginshapegodsway.com.

# TAKE ACTION

Ten Nutritional Commandments for Weight Loss

1.  Eat a solid breakfast. Drink a hot cup of water with lemon every other morning.

2.  Reduce your calories by 200 every week if you're not losing weight. The average weight loss that will result is .5 to 1.0 pound of body fat per week.

3.  Watch out for *all* sugars. Studies show that the average American consumes 150 pounds of sugar every year.[5] That's what keeps the belly fat around.

4.  Eat small meals every three to four hours, in what is called learning to graze.

5.  Increase your daily water intake.

6.  Eat raw, whole foods, which are micronutrient-dense food.

7.  Pray every day to reduce your stress levels. Cortisol is increased with higher levels of stress and can keep excess body fat around your belly.

8.  No late-night eating. Cut off food consumption two to three hours before bedtime. Replace bedtime snacks with water or sparkling water.

9.  Monitor all your carbohydrates—breads, rice, cereals, pasta, crackers, chips, and all foods made with white flour and sugar. Avoid them.

10. Absolutely no fast food!

# APPENDIX A

# MOUTH FITNESS SCRIPTURES

Be strong and very courageous. Be careful to obey all the instructions Moses gave you....Study this Book of Instruction continually. Meditate on it day and night so you will be sure to obey everything written in it. Only then will you prosper and succeed in all you do.

—JOSHUA 1:7–8, NLT

The mouth of the righteous utters wisdom, and his tongue speaks justice.

—PSALM 37:30

Set a guard, O LORD, over my mouth; keep watch over the door of my lips.

—PSALM 141:3

For the LORD gives wisdom; from His mouth come knowledge and understanding.

—PROVERBS 2:6

Don't talk out of both sides of your mouth; avoid careless banter, white lies, and gossip.

—PROVERBS 4:24, THE MESSAGE

The mouth of the righteous is a well of life, but violence covers the mouth of the wicked.

—PROVERBS 10:11, NKJV

A man will be satisfied with good by the fruit of his mouth...

—PROVERBS 12:14, NKJV

He who guards his mouth preserves his life, but he who opens wide his lips shall have destruction.

—Proverbs 13:3, nkjv

A man has joy by the answer of his mouth, and a word spoken in due season, how good it is!

—Proverbs 15:23, nkjv

The heart of the righteous studies how to answer, but the mouth of the wicked pours forth evil.

—Proverbs 15:28, nkjv

The heart of the wise teaches his mouth, and adds learning to his lips. Pleasant words are like a honeycomb, sweetness to the soul and health to the bones.

—Proverbs 16:23–24, nkjv

The words of a man's mouth are deep waters; the wellspring of wisdom is a flowing brook.

—Proverbs 18:4, nkjv

A man's stomach shall be satisfied from the fruit of his mouth; from the produce of his lips he shall be filled. Death and life are in the power of the tongue, and those who love it will eat its fruit.

—Proverbs 18:20–21, nkjv

Whoever guards his mouth and tongue keeps his soul from troubles.

—Proverbs 21:23, nkjv

Don't gobble your food, don't talk with your mouth full. And don't stuff yourself; bridle your appetite.

—Proverbs 23:2–3, The Message

She opens her mouth with wisdom, and on her tongue is the law of kindness.

—Proverbs 31:26, nkjv

Do not be rash with your mouth, and let not your heart utter anything hastily before God. For God is in heaven, and you on earth; therefore let your words be few.

—Ecclesiastes 5:2, nkjv

The words of a wise man's mouth are gracious, but the lips of a fool shall swallow him up.

—Ecclesiastes 10:12, nkjv

So shall My word be that goes forth from My mouth; it shall not return to Me void, but it shall accomplish what I please, and it shall prosper in the thing for which I sent it.

—Isaiah 55:11, nkjv

But He answered and said, "It is written, 'Man shall not live by bread alone, but by every word that proceeds from the mouth of God.'"

—Matthew 4:4, nkjv

For out of the abundance of the heart the mouth speaks. A good man out of the good treasure of his heart brings forth good things, and an evil man out of the evil treasure brings forth evil things. But I say to you that for every idle word men may speak, they will give account of it in the day of judgment. For by your words you will be justified, and by your words you will be condemned.

—Matthew 12:34–37, nkjv

Not what goes into the mouth defiles a man; but what comes out of the mouth, this defiles a man.

—Matthew 15:11, nkjv

Do you not yet understand that whatever enters the mouth goes into the stomach and is eliminated? But those things which proceed out of the mouth come from the heart, and they defile a man. For out of the heart proceed evil thoughts, murders, adulteries, fornications, thefts, false witness, blasphemies. These are the things which defile a man, but to eat with unwashed hands does not defile a man.

—Matthew 15:17–20, nkjv

But what does it say? "The word is near you, in your mouth and in your heart" (that is, the word of faith which we preach): that if you confess with your mouth the Lord Jesus and believe in your heart that God has raised Him from the dead, you will be saved. For with the heart one believes unto righteousness, and with the mouth confession is made unto salvation. For the Scripture says, "Whoever believes on Him will not be put to shame." For there is no distinction between Jew and Greek, for the same Lord over all is rich to all who call upon Him. For "whoever calls on the name of the Lord shall be saved."

—Romans 10:8–13, nkjv

Watch the way you talk. Let nothing foul or dirty come out of your mouth. Say only what helps, each word a gift.

—Ephesians 4:29, The Message

But now you yourselves are to put off all these: anger, wrath, malice, blasphemy, filthy language out of your mouth. Do not lie to one another, since you have put off the old man with his deeds.

—Colossians 3:8–9, nkjv

A bit in the mouth of a horse controls the whole horse. A small rudder on a huge ship in the hands of a skilled captain sets a course in the face of the strongest winds. A word out of your mouth may seem of no account, but it can accomplish nearly anything—or destroy it!

—JAMES 3:3–4, THE MESSAGE

Out of the same mouth proceed blessing and cursing. My brethren, these things ought not to be so.

—JAMES 3:10, NKJV

# APPENDIX B

# NATURAL SHAKES AND JUICING COMBINATIONS

## NUTRITIONAL SHAKES

These tasty shakes can be prepared for between-meal snacks or as a meal substitute. They are a great alternative for those who have not been breakfast eaters in the past.

Feel free to add any supplements to your shakes, such as almond butter, protein powder, fiber, etc. All shakes can have ice added for thickness and cool refreshment. Don't be afraid to experiment with your favorite fruits.

- *Tropical:* Papaya, blackberries, apple juice, and ½ orange blended
- *Lime Raspberry Zing:* Raspberries, coconut milk, 1 teaspoon organic vanilla, agave (natural sweetener), and lime juice
- *Strawberry Mojito:* Strawberries, apple juice, mint, agave, and lime.
- *Almond Butter and Jelly:* Almond butter, strawberries, chocolate protein, spring water, small amount of nonfat milk, 1 tablespoon of organic honey
- *Blackberry Crema:* Vanilla goat yogurt, blackberries, agave, spring water
- *Acai Berry:* Acai berries with strawberries, apple juice, mango, and 1 teaspoon of organic vanilla
- *Pure Protein:* Almond butter, protein powder, whole milk, or spring water

## REFRESHING JUICE COMBOS

You can purchase a juicer for a reasonable price that will enable you to enjoy the freshest nutrients from vegetables and fruits. This will help to improve your overall health. I recommend you try these combinations and then experiment to your satisfaction.

- *Quick and Easy:* Carrot juice over ice
- *Morning Health:* Beet, carrot, orange, apple, and lemon
- *Green Juice:* Broccoli, kale, celery, green apple, and ginger
- *Pure Energy:* Carrot, beet, apple, strawberry, and ginger
- *Body Cleanse:* Carrot, celery, parsley, and apple
- *Refreshing:* Rhubarb, celery, carrots, and parsley
- *Big Vitamin C:* Orange, apple, and strawberry
- *Simply Sweet:* Apples and carrots

# QUICK ONLINE FOOD RESOURCES GUIDE

**Breads**

- Food for Life: www.foodforlife.com
- Diamond Organics: www.diamondorganics.com
- Rudi's Organic Bakery: www.rudisbakery.com

**Nutrition Bars**

- Go Raw: www.Goraw.com
- LÄRABAR: www.larabar.com
- Garden of Life: www.gardenoflife.com
- CLIF Bars: www.clifbarstore.com
- Perfect Foods Bar: www.perfectfoodsbar.com

**Cereals**

- Food for Life: www.foodforlife.com
- Nature's Path: www.naturespath.com
- Kashi: www.kashi.com

**Milk, Kefir, Creams, and Yogurt**

- Clover Stornetta Farms: www.cloverstornetta.com
- Redwood Hill Farm: www.redwoodhill.com
- Horizon Organic: www.horizonorganic.com
- Organic Valley: www.organicvalley.com
- Brown Cow Farm: www.browncowfarm.com
- Organic Pastures: www.organicpastures.com

**Eggs/Cheeses**

- Organic Valley: www.organicvalley.com
- Gold Circle Farms: www.goldcirclefarms.com

## Produce

- Earthbound Farm: www.earthboundfarm.com
- Diamond Organics: www.diamondorganics.com
- Whole Foods Market: www.wholefoodsmarket.com

## Water

- Penta: www.pentawater.com
- Voss (in glass): www.vosswater.com

## Meats: Organic Chicken

- Shelton's Poultry: www.sheltons.com
- Applegate Farms: www.applegatefarms.com

## Meats: Organic and Grass-Fed Beef

- Peaceful Pastures: www.peacefulpastures.com

## Whole-Food Supplements

- Garden of Life: www.gardenoflife.com

# EXERCISE CHARTS

AKE COPIES OF EACH chart for a quick reference of your workout routine as you progress from beginner to advanced.

| *BEGINNER WORKOUT CHART WEEKS 1–6 | |
|---|---|
| **Beginners** | |
| Heart rate zone | 65–70 percent |
| Routine should be completed in 30 minutes to 1 hour for weeks 1–6. | |
| If time is an issue, just do the reach and throw and the pick and push three times on each side. | |
| Average number of reps per exercise | 15–25 |
| Rest time between exercises | 30–60 seconds |
| Number of sets per workout | 1–3 |
| **Functional Fitness Routine** | |
| **Abs, core** | |
| Ab lift | 30 seconds |
| Ab clap | 30 seconds |
| Ab walk | 30 seconds |
| **Lower back strengtheners** | |
| Hyperextensions | 30 seconds |
| **Chest** | |
| Plank | 30 seconds |
| **Full body functional with shoulders** | |
| Reach and throw | 30 seconds |
| Pick and push | 30 seconds |

## *BEGINNER WORKOUT CHART
## WEEKS 1–6

| Legs and back | |
| --- | --- |
| Balance one leg (with row, as variation) | 30 seconds |
| **Plyometrics** | |
| Side-to-side jumps | 30 seconds |
| **Back strengtheners** | |
| Single-leg RK Lifelift | 30 seconds |
| RK Lifelift | 30 seconds |
| **Biceps** | |
| Biceps curls | 30 seconds |
| Single-arm reverse curls | 30 seconds |
| **Triceps** | |
| Overhead triceps extension | 30 seconds |
| Bent-over triceps extension | 30 seconds |
| **End of workout: Cooldown** | 2 minutes |

## **INTERMEDIATE WORKOUT CHART
## WEEKS 7–12

| Intermediate | |
| --- | --- |
| Heart rate zone | Maintain 75 percent |
| Routine should be completed in 30 minutes to 1 hour for weeks 7–12. | |
| Average number of reps per exercise | 15–25 |
| Rest time between exercises | 15–30 seconds |
| Number of sets per workout | 1–3 |
| **Functional Fitness Routine** | |
| **Abs, core** | |
| Ab lift | 30 seconds |
| Ab clap | 30 seconds |
| V-sits | 30 seconds |
| **Lower back strengtheners** | |
| Hyperextensions | 30 seconds |
| **Chest** | |
| Plank | 30 seconds |
| **Full body functional with shoulders** | |

| **INTERMEDIATE WORKOUT CHART WEEKS 7–12** | |
|---|---|
| Reach and throw | 30 seconds |
| Pick and push | 30 seconds |
| **Legs and back** | |
| Balance one leg; add row as variation | 30 seconds |
| Balance with row—high knee | 30 seconds |
| **Plyometrics** | |
| Band jumps; add side-to-side and tiny jumps as variations | 30 seconds |
| **Back strengtheners** | |
| Single-leg RK Lifelift | 30 seconds |
| RK Lifelift with shoulder raise | 30 seconds |
| **Plyometrics** | |
| Knee-ups | 30 seconds |
| **Biceps** | |
| Biceps curls; stand on one leg as variation | 30 seconds |
| Single-arm reverse curl | 30 seconds |
| **Triceps** | |
| Overhead triceps extension | 30 seconds |
| Bent-over triceps extension | 30 seconds |
| Triceps freeze | 30 seconds |
| **Abs** | |
| Ab rotators | 30 seconds |
| Hip lifts | 30 seconds |
| **Glutes** | |
| Forward lunge with band | 30 seconds |
| Forward lunge—band behind | 30 seconds |
| **Extra—for extremely thin legs and glutes** | |
| Squat with hip reducers | 30 seconds |
| **End of workout: Cooldown** | 2 minutes |

| \*\*\*ADVANCED WORKOUT CHART WEEK 13 AND BEYOND | |
|---|---|
| **Advanced** | |
| Heart rate zone | 75–85 percent |
| Routine should be completed in 35 minutes to 1 hour for weeks 13 and beyond. | |
| Average number of reps per exercise | 15–30 |
| Rest time between exercises | 15–30 seconds |
| Number of sets per workout | 3 |
| **Functional Fitness Routine** | |
| **Abs, core** | |
| Ab lift | 30 seconds |
| Ab clap | 30 seconds |
| V-sits with kick | 30 seconds |
| **Lower back strengtheners** | |
| Hyperextensions—with swim | 30 seconds |
| **Chest** | |
| Plank—one leg holds | 30 seconds |
| Push-up on knees | 30 seconds |
| Band press | 30 seconds |
| **Full body functional with shoulders** | |
| Reach and throw with explosion | 30 seconds |
| Pick and push with explosion | 30 seconds |
| **Legs and back** | |
| Balance one leg | 30 seconds |
| With row, low and high knee | 30 seconds |
| **Plyometrics** | |
| Band jumps; add side-to-side and tiny jumps as variations | 30 seconds |
| Jumps with knees to chest | 30 seconds |
| **Back strengtheners** | |
| Single-leg RK Lifelift | 30 seconds |
| RK Lifelift with overhead throws | 30 seconds |
| **Plyometrics** | |
| Knee-ups | 30 seconds |
| Knee-ups with split kicks | 30 seconds |

| ***ADVANCED WORKOUT CHART WEEK 13 AND BEYOND** | |
|---|---|
| **Biceps** | |
| Biceps curls; stand on one leg as variation | 30 seconds |
| Single-arm reverse curl | 30 seconds |
| **Triceps** | |
| Overhead triceps extension | 30 seconds |
| Bent-over triceps extension | 30 seconds |
| Triceps freeze | 30 seconds |
| **Abs** | |
| Ab rotators | 30 seconds |
| Hip lifts, with one leg lifted | 30 seconds |
| Sit and reach | 30 seconds |
| **Glutes** | |
| Forward lunge with band | 30 seconds |
| Forward lunge with jump | 30 seconds |
| Forward lunge—band behind, with jump | 30 seconds |
| Reverse lunge with band | 30 seconds |
| **Extra—for extremely thin legs and glutes** | |
| Squat with hip reducers | 30 seconds |
| Directional lunges | 30 seconds |
| **End of workout: Cooldown** | 2 minutes |

# APPENDIX E

# PRODUCT PAGE

THE FOLLOWING PRODUCTS ARE available to order from my Web site at www.gettinginshapegodsway.com.

### Exercise Band

I recommend this Getting in Shape God's Way exercise band for your workout—ONLY $12.95 plus tax and $6.95 shipping and handling. We are currently only taking Web site or phone orders at this time. Visit www.gettinginshapegodsway.com to order.

### Audiobook and Encouraging CDs

Faith comes by hearing and hearing. This is much like working out with weights, where muscles come by training and training. Listening to the book on CD is sure to develop and empower your understanding and faith muscles. Listen to it as you work out and drive in your car. You can even download on your MP3 or iPod player.

### DVD

In addition to the DVD included in your book, additional DVDs may be purchased directly from my Web site. Send one as a gift to a family member or friend.

## FREE MOTIVATIONAL CALLS! FREE SUPPORT!
### Call me directly at (323) 622-8565.

Every week I will be leaving personal motivational and fitness strategies to keep you on track. These are messages delivered personally right through your own phone. In addition, you have access to an instant support group with other people who are getting in shape God's way. Ask questions, leave your testimony, tell me how you are feeling, and much more! Totally FREE! I will even call some of you back and personally consult you for FREE!

I think the number one reason people stop their diet or fitness program is because they need the motivation when nothing seems to be working. That's why I want to be able to call all my fans and those who are reading my book! I want to keep you MOTIVATED!

## Heart Monitor

This heart rate monitor may be purchased for $99.00 plus tax and $6.95 shipping and handling. It is trainer recommend. You can also find new and used ones online from $50.00 and up.

## The Official "Getting in Shape God's Way" T-shirt

Be a witness through fitness. Wear this shirt to keep you accountable and to exercise in.

I'm Getting in Shape God's Way T-shirts are available in white with black lettering or black with white lettering. Others styles and colors may be available. Check Web site periodically.

## Free Monthly Webletter

Sign up for the Getting in Shape God's Way webletter for important updates to your fitness goals and health tips and tools for your life and ministry. Go to www.gettinginshapegodsway.com and SIGN UP for this webletter.

## Web Site

Experience "Ron Live" at the Web site for inspiration and timely coaching.

Booking site. www.ronkardashian.tv

Book Web site: www.gettinginshapegodsway.com

Nonprofit Web site: www.kingdomconditioning.org

## OTHER PRODUCTS

**Colon Cleanse**

Perfect Cleanse, from Jordan Rubin, is available from Garden of Life at www.gardenoflife.com.

# NOTES

## CHAPTER 2
### YOU BECOME WHAT YOU BELIEVE—LET'S GET REAL!

1. The ARTFL Project, Webster's Revised Unabridged Dictionary (1913 + 1828), s.v. "revelation," http://machaut.uchicago.edu/?resource=Webster%27s& word=revelation&use1828=on (accessed June 6, 2008).

2. *Webster's New Collegiate Dictionary*, 11th ed., s.v. "revelation."

3. Ibid., s.v. "insight."

## CHAPTER 4
### REFINING YOUR VISION—WHAT YOU SEE IS WHAT YOU GET!

1. Edythe Draper, *Draper's Book of Quotations for the Christian World* (Wheaton, IL: Tyndale House, 1992), accessed through Quick Verse Software 10.0.1, 2006 version, copyright © 2005 by Findex, Inc., "Stephen Wise."

2. Ibid., "Peter Marshall."

3. Ibid., "Helen Keller."

4. Ibid., "E. Paul Harvey."

5. Laurie Beth Jones, *The Path: Creating Your Mission Statement for Work and for Life* (New York: Hyperion, 1996), 3–5.

6. Ibid.

7. For an example of a mission statement, visit the Web site of Nightingale Conant, where you can find an example of a mission statement: http://www .nightingale.com/tmission_examplestatement.aspx (accessed July 16, 2008).

8. Myles Munroe, *In Pursuit of Purpose* (Shippensburg, PA: Destiny Image Publishers, 1992), 31.

9. Anthony Robbins, "The Power of Setting Goals," Day 5, How to Create a Compelling Future, *Personal Power Classic Edition* audio CD (n.p.: The Anthony Robbins Companies, 1996).

## CHAPTER 5
### "LINGUISTICS" TRAINING—WORDS ARE POWERFUL

1. *Webster's New Collegiate Dictionary*, 11th ed., s.v. "linguistics."

2. Jeff Greenfield, foreword to *Words That Shook the World*, by Richard Green (New York: Prentice Hall, 2001).

3.    Draper, *Draper's Book of Quotations for the Christian World*, "Lucius Annaeus Seneca."

4.    Robert Kotulak, "Mental Workouts and Brain Power," in *Inside the Brain* (Kansas City, MO: Andrews McMeel Publishing, 1996), chapter 2.

5.    Ibid., 34.

6.    Ibid., xiv–xvi.

7.    Ibid., 24–25

8.    Library of Congress, "What is the strongest muscle in the body?" Everyday Mysteries: Fun Science Facts From the Library of Congress, http://www.loc.gov/rr/scitech/mysteries/muscles.html (accessed July 16, 2008).

9.    Emanuella Grinberg, "Anna Nicole Smith's Companion Says She Wanted to Be Buried in the Bahamas," CourtTV.com, http://www.courttv.com/people/anna-nicole-smith/022007_ctv.html (accessed July 18, 2008).

10.    Kotulak, *Inside the Brain*, x.

11.    Ibid.

12.    Ibid.

13.    Ibid., xiv.

## CHAPTER 6

### MOUTH FITNESS—YOUR WORDS SHAPE YOU!

1.    *Webster's New Collegiate Dictionary*, 11th ed., s.v. "integrity."

2.    Draper, *Draper's Book of Quotations for the Christian World*, "John Galsworthy."

3.    Rick Warren, *The Purpose Driven Life* (Grand Rapids, MI: Zondervan, 2002), 232.

4.    Draper, *Draper's Book of Quotations for the Christian World*, "Alfred de Musset."

5.    BoxingScene.com, "Motivation: 3 Powerful Quotes from Golfer Tiger Woods," http://www.boxingscene.com/motivation/55486.php (accessed September 5, 2008).

6.    Ibid.

## CHAPTER 7
### BEHAVIOR MODELS—YOUR BELIEFS MOTIVATE YOUR ACTIONS

1.    Scott Cairns, "Speechless," *Christian Century*, January 15, 2008, http://findarticles.com/p/articles/mi_m1058/is_1_125/ai_n24254614/pg_ 1?tag=artBody;col1 (accessed July 17, 2008).

2.    American College of Sports Medicine, "American College of Sports Medicine Position Stand: The Recommended Quantity and Quality of Exercise for Developing and Maintaining Cardio Respiratory and Muscular Fitness, and Flexibility in Healthy Adults," *Medicine and Science in Sports and Exercise* 30, no. 6 (1998): 975–991, http://www.medscape.com/medline/abstract/ 9624661?src=emed_ckb_ref_0 (accessed July 18, 2008).

3.    As related in Dr. Harold Koenig, *Handbook of Religion and Health* (New York: Oxford University Press, 2000), 231–264.

4.    Bishop T. D. Jakes, *HE-Motions: Even Strong Men Struggle* (New York, NY: Putnam Adult, 2004), 154.

## CHAPTER 8
### PROGRESSING THROUGH MOVEMENT—YOUR HEALTHY LIFESTYLE

1.    Michael Rozien, MD, and Mehmet Oz, MD, *You: Staying Young* (New York: Free Press, 2007), 268.

2.    Ibid.

3.    Jordan Rubin, *The Maker's Diet* (Lake Mary, FL: Siloam, 2004), 53.

4.    Ibid., 50–51.

5.    HealthyAussie.com, "Death Begins in the Colon," http://www.healthy aussie.com/deathbegins.htm (accessed September 5, 2008).

6.    Library of Congress, "Everyday Mysteries: What Is the Strongest Muscle in the Human Body?" http://www.loc.gov/rr/scitech/mysteries/muscles.html (accessed September 5, 2008).

7.    Richard A. Swenson, MD, *More Than Meets the Eye* (Colorado Springs, CO: NavPress, 2000), 23.

8.    Renee Jeffreys, MS, "The Pregnant Exerciser: An Argument for Exercise as a Means to Support Pregnancy," *American College of Sports Medicine's Certified News*, volume 15, issue 3 (2005).

9.    "Essentials of Strength Training and Conditioning," *Essentials of Personal Training Symposium, Section V: Aerobic Exercise Prescription* (NSCA Certification Commission, 1997), 6–7.

10.   Ibid.

11.   Ibid.

## CHAPTER 9

## MAINTAINING YOUR FITNESS LIFESTYLE—DON'T QUIT!

1.   *Webster's New Collegiate Dictionary,* 11th ed., s.v. "manifest."

2.   *Webster's New Collegiate Dictionary,* 9th ed., s.v. "equanimity."

3.   Draper, *Draper's Book of Quotations for the Christian World,* "Samuel Johnson"

## CHAPTER 10

## YOUR PERSONAL WORKOUT AND EATING PLANS

1.   Don Colbert, MD, *Toxic Relief* (Lake Mary Florida, Siloam, 2003), 33–34.

2.   Ibid., 150–52.

3.   Jordan Rubin, *Perfect Weight America* (Lake Mary, FL: Siloam, 2007), 131.

4.   Ibid., 95.

5.   Dana Veracity, "The Politics of Sugar: Why Your Government Lies to You About This Disease-Promoting Ingredient," NaturalNews.com, July 21, 2005, http://www.naturalnews.com/009797.html (accessed July 28, 2008).

# INDEX

# ABOUT THE AUTHOR

Ron Kardashian is contagious with abundant life and great health! As a fitness expert and ordained minister committed to helping humanity, he is a certified strength and conditioning coach and has been nominated as Personal Trainer of the Year two consecutive times. He is the founder and CEO of Kardashian Life Coaching and Personal Training, as well as the nonprofit organization Kingdom Conditioning Ministries, Inc., which helps the local church empower and build their people for lasting health and physical development. Ron has over 11,000 hours of consulting people in the realm of physical fitness and life development/coaching. The amazing results of this integrated, holistic approach have made Ron Kardashian a powerful voice for change among professionals, CEOs of major companies, leaders of diplomacy, clergy, and royalty across the world of every age, religion, and creed. The one word that would best describes this man is impassioned! He is impassioned to help people of all vocations all around the world optimize their development in life. Engaging in national and international speaking engagements and television appearance has given Ron the honor to share the pulpit of many nationally acclaimed voices in health, wellness, and ministry.

As a radio and television personality, Ron is pursuing his television broadcast *Getting in Shape God's Way*, reaching forty-seven nations since its inception date in 2004. *Getting in Shape God's Way*, which Ron characterizes as a "reality fitness show," combines a fitness workout with spiritual conditioning that catapults participants into better levels of health and fitness much faster than traditional workouts that ignore the spiritual component. With the demand of appearances and Ron's passion to help this generation, his nonprofit organization is pursuing collaboration and partnerships with others to help build a multimedia world outreach broadcasting center. This will provide an amazing ability to reach the world through multimedia outlets while proving weekly programs for the local community as well as on an international level, revealing the secrets of physical fitness and its medicinal benefits for individuals worldwide. Ron currently lives in California with his beautiful wife and family. For booking, speaking engagements or private consultations please contact him directly anytime:

Ron Kardashian

Kingdom Conditioning Ministries

info@kingdomconditioning.org

www.ronkardashian.tv

www.gettinginshapegodsway.com

www.kingdomconditioning.org